ZIGZAG STREET

NICK EARLS is described as having 'a formidable talent for black comedy' (*Sydney Morning Herald*), *Zigzag Street* is the first of many adult novels Earls plans to write but he has published a collection of short stories, *Passion* (1992), and a novel for young adults, *After January*. His short fiction has appeared in numerous publications and anthologies and his stage play, *The Drowning Point*, was performed at the Village Theatre, London, in 1994. Nick graduated in medicine from the University of Queensland and lives in Brisbane.

If you would like to write to Nick Earls, his e-mail address is **nickearls@peg.apc.org**

NICK EARLS

ZIGZAG STREET

PAN BOOKS

First published 1996 in Australia and New Zealand by Anchor
an imprint of Transworld Publishers (Aust) Pty Limited
15–25 Helles Ave, Moorebank, NSW 2170

This edition published 1998 by Pan Books
an imprint of Macmillan Publishers Ltd
25 Eccleston Place London SW1W 9NF
and Basingstoke

Associated companies throughout the world

ISBN 0 330 35533 3

1 3 5 7 9 8 6 4 2

A CIP catalogue record for this book is available
from the British Library.

Printed and bound in Great Britain by
Mackays of Chatham plc, Chatham, Kent

*This is for SG, for support
and foolishness, both without limit*

1

I basically blew my university days in the pursuit of one girl.

It's only now, half a dozen years later, that the idea strikes me with some clarity. Despite what people said at the time. Despite the fact that at every moment of those several years it must have been obvious to everyone but me.

It was obvious. They told me. But I couldn't listen to them because I still had hope. Several years of an entirely pointless hope, when I should have been having the time of my life. Not that I had a bad time. In some respects, I had a great time. But it could have been better. If I hadn't blown it in the pursuit of one girl.

Of course, hindsight is no substitute for insight, and this is all pitifully retrospective.

I'm playing the album she gave me for my twenty-first. Sitting here on the bare boards of the verandah of this old house, studiously not renovating, listening to The Smiths' *The Queen is Dead*. Watching paint fail to apply itself to the verandah rails.

She gave me this album and a tie, a tie that even at the time was a bad tie, and is now long gone.

Listening to the album makes me think we had no chance anyway. She gave it to me, I'm sure, simply because she knew I liked it, not because of its abundance of ironies, full as it is of loneliness and stricken unrequited love. She was neither cruel enough, nor ironic enough, for it to have been anything but a gift. It's only now that I realise that she lacked irony absolutely, and we were in fact totally incompatible. Throughout the mid-eighties that eluded me, but I can't imagine how.

Since my enthusiasm for renovation has temporarily slipped and it's approaching seven-thirty, I decide to eat. I decide takeaway, then straight back to work. I call Baan Thai at Milton and the guy recognises my voice and says, *Usual order for Hiller?*

He tells me fifteen minutes.

I stop for petrol on the way.

Usual order for Hiller. I still get the usual order for Hiller. Two things have changed. There is no Hiller, and the price has gone up fifty-five cents, but the usual order for Hiller is still the order of choice. It just lasts two nights now. Chicken satay (four sticks), *panang nua*, large rice. Previously fifteen ninety-five, but still a bargain at sixteen fifty.

I nudge the petrol up to the twenty dollar mark, and even this, even petrol, reeks of old crappy memories. The girl at uni, a month short of my twenty-first, my one and only chance.

The rash

We went to a movie. She asked me. And I thought maybe this isn't just us going as friends. Maybe this is a date. I got excited. I imagine I talked throughout the movie and probably annoyed her by trying to impress her. We had coffee afterwards and she talked about what we were going to do for my twenty-first. *We.* I remember that. I remember the enormous thumping erection triggered off simply by the notion of we. And I could see us together at my twenty-first, her standing next to me. I could see I was going to be a winner after all. And on the way back to her place after coffee, already into the sixth hour of this new phase of our relationship, we stopped for petrol. It

2

was winter, two am, cold. The petrol cap didn't come off easily. Something trivial like that. Something trivial that led her to make the vaguely funny emasculating remark that prompted me to take the pump, having finished filling up the car, and point it into my pocket like a pistol, to make a joke of completing the process of emasculation. Of course, at that very moment, the last gravitational penile dribble from the pump, or a twitch of my cold shaking hand (it matters little which), filled my pants with petrol. Really cold petrol, spreading out black across the front of my favourite faded black jeans and running down both legs. Stinking the car out, all the way back to her place. She laughed more than she needed to, and she didn't invite me in. She told me not to go near any naked flames. And when I got home and threw away the pants and saw my dick shrivelled up like a pale poisoned worm I thought, fine, you're no good to me anyway. Over the next few days I lost quite a bit of skin in that area, and I stayed in my room as much as I could wearing nothing from the waist down. It was only when I thought it wasn't getting better that I asked one of my housemates, a hospital intern, what I should do about it. And the story was out. Fuck confidentiality, when there's a story in it.

I think I was given the birthday present by a friend on her behalf. *The Queen is Dead* and a crappy tie, and there seemed to be some understanding that that was that. My one and only chance had passed, and we were better off as friends. 'Let's still be friends', the card might even have said, as though this offered me something I could live with, some survivable compromise.

So here I am, filling the petrol tank of the same car, the same early-eighties Laser I've had since the mideighties, the car that has carried me through a range of foolhardy misadventures and artless attempts at seduction. Here I am, twenty-eight and trashed again. How does this happen? Sometimes with petrol, but what was it this time?

The guy at Baan Thai says, *So how is your wife? I haven't seen her in here for a while.*

No, she's in Melbourne, I tell him.

Oh, business?

I think I must just nod at this, nod and fix on some grin, because I can't bring myself to lie to him, or tell him the truth, hence limiting me to non-verbal options.

I can't believe how many people you end up having to tell when you've been trashed. There are several thousand more opportunities to revisit the instant of trashing than could possibly be anticipated, and most of the time I'd really rather not talk about it. But it comes up. It comes up and there's nothing that can be done to stop it. Bumping into anyone and going through the blandest of social enquiries seems to end up with me having to choose between spilling my guts again or lying. Melbourne, business, a pitiful half-truth. She trashed me. Melbourne, months ago, she trashed me.

We always ordered in her name out of habit, so the guy has no idea I'm not Hiller. And I just can't tell him now. I can't shout this over the top of the cluster of other people waiting for takeaway orders, because whatever I start shouting I'll inevitably end up shouting the trashing story. Then all their conversations about not much will go quiet, and they'll have me to talk about as soon as I've left. Poor bastard, he's so trashed he shouts about it even when he's picking up takeaway.

I pay for the usual order for Hiller and I go, enduring my own idiot grin all the way to the car.

At home I measure my meal into two almost exact portions, and put one into the fridge. It's great, this *panang nua*. Always great.

And Anna Hiller is the bane, and possibly love, of my life. That's how much this sucks.

2

Renovation is endlessly complex, I realise after dinner as I flick from one channel to another trying to work out which movie to watch. It's endlessly complex, despite my mother's assertion that it's quite straightforward if you have a plan. If you take it one step at a time and prioritise.

I have a plan. I have steps, I have priorities. But so does she. So while I'm planning to start at the front verandah and work back, she's coming round with swatches of fabric to talk about blinds, even when I make it quite clear to her that blinds are too far into the house for me just now.

She almost seems worried about me when she has to come to terms with the fact that I'm just not ready to look at blinds yet. As though there was some period in my life when I was stable and normal and easily entertained by chatting about fabrics. She wants the blinds to make me happy. She doesn't say that, but I can tell. I should tell her that blinds have never made me happy or unhappy, so however great the blinds are they are unlikely to resolve any of the big issues, other than the penetration of sunlight into the house. My long-term happiness will not be influenced by the blinds at all.

I told her my front to back plan. I explained its elegant simplicity. I explained that this way I'll miss nothing, and I guaranteed she would be pleased with the result. So she put away the swatches and we had a dispute about the colour scheme for the verandah railings instead. This lasted several weeks.

During that time I painted an old wardrobe, first in regulation white and then with blue dabbed over it using a loofa I found in the bathroom. And while I was doing it I really thought it seemed artistic. Seemed like a hell of a good idea.

Then my mother apologised for making a big issue of the paint and the next time I looked at the wardrobe it looked like trash, like something my mother would hate, something she would take as a personal affront. So I put it in my room and apologised right back to her about my role in the colour dispute, and I said to her that this was her house, so we should use the colours she wanted.

And that, I suspect, is the basis of the problem. It's her house. Ever since my grandmother died. And the deal is that I live here rent-free if I renovate.

So I sit around in the musty, shut-up, old people's smells, the exaggerated security and cardboard boxes, not yet renovating, while my sinuses play up like buggery.

I talk to myself out loud. I talk to Greg, my grandmother's cat, who was there when she died and doesn't yet trust me. I need to hear voices in the house, even if they're all mine. I am adjusting only slowly to living alone.

I can't get into the movies tonight, not any of them.

I look out at the verandah, at the painting that isn't being done, and I think fuck it. Instead I sit down at the piano. I let my hands loose on some scales and they run up and down with the finesse of a couple of fat pink spiders. For some reason, some reason I shall never know, the sheet music for 'Always on my Mind' was curled up under the lid the first time I opened the piano. I've now flattened it out and it's starting to become playable. This evening I do it first as Elvis, then as Willy Nelson, with appropriate introductions, but I can't do it like the Pet Shop Boys. I try to imagine myself sitting under Michael

Bolton's hair and doing it the way he would, and I try to do it like Nick Cave. And when you do it like Nick Cave it's a no-shit song. You can take it from me, when he says you were always on his mind, he means you were always on his mind.

It's probably only Greg's incessant shouting for dinner that makes me stop. He purrs as he eats and he seems happy, in an unreasonably simple way. I want to take issue with him about this. And I want to explain that I didn't mean to make his dinner two hours late tonight, and that this isn't easy for me. That I'm not used to being responsible for feeding anything other than people, not used to living alone, not used to having a piano in the house, not used to arguing about paint, not used to a hundred and sixty-eight days of celibacy, and I'm not quite sure what happens next.

My previous record was a hundred and two. That was at least six years ago, and I must admit, I thought it would never be broken, that I'd be old and toothless and hopeless before I went without for a hundred and two days again.

Greg licks up his dinner and copes with all this change a little better than I do. It must be very different for him here now. The noises I make. Music, TV, 'Always on my Mind', one crap version after another. Very different to my grandmother and her deaf person's exaggerated human sounds, the loud clatter of pots and pans, the casual slamming of unheard doors, the unmonitored flatulence.

Greg, the big-shouldered, confident orange cat named, my grandmother once told me, after her red-headed doctor of whom she was fond. He used to shout at her and write notes and smile, and receive graciously the biscuits she made for him because he looked too thin for his own good.

How can I renovate these loaded rooms? Where do I begin in this House of Boxes? Whose past do I start to dismantle, rehabilitate, dispose of? Mine or my

7

grandmother's? Everything that is each of us is packaged here, dumped into scavenged boxes with the undue haste of death or forced departure.

Dozens of boxes. Many dozens of boxes, scavenged from bottle shops in August last year, and then November.

I need some boxes because I just got trashed.

I need some boxes because my grandmother just died.

But you can't let yourself hear it in your own voice, so you say something like, I'm moving house and I need some boxes to pack things into. When I was doing it the second time at least one person remembered me and said, with some suspicion, *You move a lot.* As though there could be any reason to be suspicious of a person scavenging old cardboard boxes.

From my mother's point of view, the boxes are all part of any reasonable plan. A plan that she says is easy, all you do is go through one box a night. Incredibly pragmatic. Barely possible.

It's hard to believe I lived successfully for years without my mother's reasoned and gratuitous advice. During the months I stayed with my parents before moving in here, she decided to resume high level nurturing and seems to think me incapable of caring for myself.

I'm still your mother, she says, *and I always will be. Your grandmother gave me gratuitous advice until the day she died, and I'm going to be no different.*

So she has become fiendishly full of help, in a bustling, barging, practical way. At certain times (during a war maybe) this is probably a very useful attribute, but it lacks the subtlety required for a routine, suburban personal crisis. And she can see how helpful it isn't, which only makes things worse.

I respond instinctively with the petty childish defence of deliberately not doing whatever it is she's told me to do, and I end up loofa-ing the wardrobe. And after another weekend of renovating, forty-two and a half of the forty-five verandah railings are still unpainted in a particularly piss-weak act of rebellion against her choice of heritage colours.

Heritage colours, even though the house has never been painted in heritage colours before. My grandparents built it in the 1920s, and as far as I know it's spent all of its seventy years as a white house with a red roof. But, as my mother said, the market demands heritage colours. So the white will become one of the many kinds of cream, a colour my grandmother would have said made the house look as though it could do with a good wash. And she would have thought even less of the Brunswick green planned for the trim.

My mother bought the paint and did the first two and a half railings to show me how good it would look, and a few weeks ago she left it to me.

I put away the unopened can, the unused brush, slip *The Queen is Dead* back into its sad green sleeve.

And I can't believe I pursued that girl for all those years, when it would never have worked.

3

So. Monday.

Five more days of worthy achievement before another wild weekend.

Greg eats dry food in the mornings. He's now used to me leaving after breakfast, but the first time I went to work and stayed away all day he was really shitty when I came home in the evening. I have tried to explain the concept of work to him. I have tried to explain the almost inexplicable rewards that are part of working somewhere like Shelton's (The Shelton Guaranty Company of New York, trading as PJ Shelton Bank, Australia).

Greg, it's like this, I've told him. At work I'm a very powerful man. And is not power an aphrodisiac? Day of Celibacy 169. I can vaguely remember what an erection was. In my life an aphrodisiac would be as useful as the Swiss Army knife option that removes stones from horses' hooves. And what sort of a concept is a Swiss Army knife anyway?

More about the Swiss Army knife

So how does the Swiss Army get to be the arbiter of standards when it comes to the multi-function pocket knife? What great claims can the Swiss Army make? It's ducked every war for a hundred and twenty years and it didn't do that by displaying its knife options. The Swiss Army had carrier pigeons until 1994. A Swiss Army knife should be a complete joke. Like an Austrian aircraft carrier or Nigerian thermal underwear or an Antarctic flower press. Swiss Army and knife should go together like safari and suit.

Buses head into town along Waterworks Road every couple of minutes at this time of day, so when I've eaten some cereal and already bored myself with the concept of work I walk up the hill and catch the next one that comes along.

The rest of the unit is already in the office. Deb, our admin assistant, says, *Hi Ricky, how was your weekend babe?* when I walk out of the lift.

Fine, I tell her. The usual. Bit of renovating. Tennis.

I'm still not used to 'Ricky', even though she's called me Ricky from the moment she decided she liked me. My name seems to be treated as though it has an almost infinite capacity for abbreviation, and this is not something I welcome. It does not help my sense of identity. Particularly 'Ricky', but this goes back to my childhood, when someone else was Ricky, not me.

The Ricky Kid

The Ricky Kid, the only kid I knew who was called Ricky by anyone, was Ricky Balaszwecki (pronounced Bal-uh-shef-ski). He was the tiniest kid at school when I was about nine, and whenever anyone had a birthday party Ricky's parents slicked his hair back (in the years when the wet look was dead) and made him wear a bow tie and blazer. And no-one talked to him because he looked so fragile, like a doll. So we'd play football and cricket and Ricky got into the habit of not being picked for a team and just sitting and watching, looking pale and sad and eating tiny sandwiches and talking to someone's mother. I expect by now Ricky has learned to accept the role of the complete micro-nerd, wearing bow ties to this day and thinking of them as some personality substitute, and telling himself he would be nothing without them. Alternatively, he may have long ago taken to his parents with an axe. I'm sure it's kids like Ricky who either pass through life completely unnoticed, or become mass murderers, and the line is probably finer than we realise.

So I'm still not used to 'Ricky' when it comes my way, even when it seems to be meant with some affection, and seems not to mean, *Hey micro-nerd, love the tie, kill any parents on the weekend?* But maybe I did in fact have the kind of weekend grown-up Rickys have. Maybe Ricky Balaszwecki sat round doing fuck all in the name of renovation, ate half a takeaway meal and talked to a ginger cat. Reminiscing, with the fondness of hindsight, about tiny sandwiches and birthday parties.

Deb's weekend was not like that.

Well, I got really pissed on Friday, she says when I ask what she did, *and Saturday I got a new tat. Look.*

She hooks her index finger into her top and pulls it down, proudly revealing the sun rising from her cleavage.

Did that hurt? I ask her.

Less than most.

It's very nice, I tell her, and the nerdy inadequacy of this remark closes around my neck like a Ricky B bow tie. It's a good piece of work. Nice use of the contours.

Thanks babe, she says and grins. *Knew you'd like it.*

Hey Rick. Hillary's voice, coming from her office. She beckons me in and signals me to shut the door. *Did she show you the new tattoo?*

Yeah.

She laughs and holds her head in her hands in mock exasperation. *And we all thought the sun shone out of you.*

I'm sure.

How was your weekend?

Fine. The usual.

The usual.

Yeah.

Sounds good.

Yeah.

I realise I should be saying more, so I try, How was yours?

Good. Great. Dan's sitting up now. He sat up on Saturday for the first time. Took us all by surprise.

He's a smart kid. Some Saturdays I find it hard to work out how to sit up.

Just wait. One day you'll have kids. Sitting up'll be big.

I bet it will. I bet it'll be huge. Only slightly less big than standing, or walking, or cracking the riddle of cold fusion, or brokering a lasting peace in the Middle East.

So which of those did you do on the weekend?

Some standing, some walking. And last night I talked to Arafat and he was sounding conciliatory, so I'm hopeful.

Good boy, Ricky. But Arafat was already conciliatory.

Maybe, but don't call me that.

She laughs. *How's the power station thing going?*

Fine. Fine. I'll be looking at it today. There was some tension on Friday to do with the slide in the greenback, but I'm trying to make it clear to everyone that that's not our problem. If there's a floor at one-oh-five yen it's okay. Below a hundred and it sinks.

Below a hundred it sinks. When did you get to be such a straight shooter?

Hey, it's how I handle every aspect of my life.

You know you worry me, don't you?

Sure.

Hillary is a great boss. This occurs to me about half an hour later, when I've long forgotten about the power station thing and I'm playing Sammy the Snake on my computer. I only realised what a great boss she was when she took a few months off last year to have Daniel and I filled in for her. She manages to stay in touch with everything, to just the right degree, and manages to stay calm. She makes being in charge look very easy. I managed only to do both our jobs badly.

The day she came back I almost, in the moment she walked out of the lift, told her how important she was. I wanted to stop and say to her, You don't know what you mean to me. You don't know that without you here I couldn't survive. But that would have been too strange for both of us, so I just said, It's good to have you back, with a kind of forced wry smile.

This morning Sammy the Snake has my measure. I have an inclination to make a few personal phone calls, but I resist and I try to look at the power station thing. But today the only observation I feel I can make with any confidence about it is that there are far too many pages. I actually hate joint ventures. They involve too many companies, too many hundreds of millions of dollars, too many governments, too many laws. Too many lawyers, and today I just don't feel like being one of them. And I certainly don't feel like a straight shooter. What does she mean by that?

I make myself coffee and sit drinking it slowly, gazing at the pile of overloaded manila folders in front of me.

Hillary is talking to me now. I miss the first part but I hear the bit where she says, *Rick, things don't seem good.*

Well, they have been better.

I'm worried that you're not looking after yourself.

Did my mother just call you?

Before I had Daniel your shirts looked ironed.

I just haven't organised an ironing person as part of my new arrangements yet.

And this makes my crap situation sound surprisingly special. New arrangements. It sounds as though I've made a lifestyle choice.

You could organise an iron though. I'm sure you've even got one. I mean, it doesn't bother me that your shirts are never ironed. That's not it. It's just that some days you don't even seem aware of it. You don't seem happy at all. I'm worried about you.

Thanks. I'll be okay.

If you aren't, if you ever aren't and there's anything I can do, make sure you let me know.

Yeah. Thanks.

So she leaves me with my half a cup of coffee and my stack of documents. She's great. And she's worried about me. She's confident, she's smart, and she's a babe, really. She's married, she's my manager. I can't understand some of my thought processes. They seem as though they're out to harm me.

She's confident, she's smart and she has a perfectly normal nice-person's interest in my wellbeing. That's it. That's what's happening.

I sit staring through a powerful blankness at the calendar that runs down the edge of my 94/95 financial year desk planner, and I tell myself to put the crap of the last six months out of my head, and to get back to the job I'm here for.

Fin Year 94/95: the first two quarters, a summary

The Dow climbs towards 4000. The AUD struggles along in the mid-seventies against the USD, which cops a hiding from the Deutschmark. Hillary goes on parental leave. The pressures of work increase exponentially. I do not cope well. Anna Hiller, my residential partner of several years, unilaterally decides that the course of my life will differ markedly from that which I expected. She tells me she's leaving. One night, like many other nights, we buy takeaway on the way home. We eat it and I can see she's tense and I ask her what's wrong and she says that she cares for me deeply and that I should understand that, but she's leaving. I beg, plead, cry, etcetera. If it's desperate and seems worth a shot, I do it, all that same evening. But to no avail. She tells me she has a new job in Melbourne, starting in a couple of weeks. She organises the division of property, the termination of our lease. So very soon I live with my parents. I call her in Melbourne, in the end probably far more often than a normal person would. She stops taking my calls. My grandmother, to whom I am very

15

close, dies. I can't stand living with my parents. They eat dinner at five-thirty. When I go out at night they don't sleep at all. They worry that my failed relationship reflects their own inadequacies. My mother moves into crisis mode. I have to leave before I start wearing bow ties to birthday parties and slicking my hair down and we all know what that means.

And it's almost impossible to sleep in a bed alone, when it's not what you're used to any more. Any bed now wakes me with emptiness. Leaves me lying there thinking, if you care for me deeply, why did you leave?

The power station thing. That's what I'm here for. That's what I've got to get to now. I should call New York.

I should call New York but it's Sunday evening in New York.

I turn on my computer and open Sammy the Snake.

4

And so passes another day of minimal accomplishment.

I make limited progress with the power station thing, and I'm secretly hoping someone else will find a reason to trash it before I have to understand it fully. Secretly wishing the US dollar ill.

When I get home there's a message on the answering machine, and I can tell just how well I'm coping when I still have to deal with the fleeting hope that it'll be Anna, telling me she got it wrong.

But it's my mother, telling me she drove past today and *didn't notice much renovating, Richard* (note the use of the full name for disciplinary reasons), *and the garden's beginning to look like a jungle.*

I give Greg his dinner and while he's eating I wonder if he's bored all day, now that he lives with someone who goes out to work. I wonder if I'm being as attentive as I should be, or could be.

So, telling myself it's a small step on the road to renovation, I perform a minor task of tidying with him in mind. I clean out my sock drawer. I take all my old socks and I stuff them into one and I knot the end. I find a fat green Nikko and draw a face on the sock, a smiling, simpleton's face with a lazy snake tongue, and I take it to him and tell him I feel bad about abandoning him so often, so I've made him a sock friend. I tell him that this friend will be non-judgemental and will always be there for him, and that its name is Purvis. Now, where that came from I don't know.

Of course, it concerns me that the creation of Purvis the Sock Friend is the pinnacle of my day's accomplishments, and I only feel worse when I try to tell myself that it's better than nothing.

I introduce Greg to Purvis and they seem to get on. I now notice that Greg was so bored before Purvis came along that he went out and made friends with about a thousand fleas. I'm sure he never had fleas before I lived here.

I re-heat my Baan Thai leftovers a little too aggressively in the microwave and seem to enamel some of the sauce to the plate. I eat every part of it a fork can lift and I decide I can figure out how to get the plate clean later.

Tonight, there is no time for renovation. Tonight there is tennis, Jeff Ross, Freddie Stuart, Gerry Venster and me, and a Queensland Uni tennis court from eight to eleven.

Jeff's there when I arrive, sitting on a bench outside the tennis centre and wearing, as always, his black cap with ACE in blue across the front. Not that this cap should be taken as a sign that the ace is in any way part of his tennis repertoire. Jeff manages to ace someone on an almost annual basis. The cap says more about the impressive hint of cruelty in the humour of its purchaser, his wife Sally Gore, who presented it to him on his twenty-ninth birthday, almost a year ago. While Jeff happily missed the point and wore it proudly throughout dinner, someone asked her if it had been too expensive to get the shop to put GROUND STROKE on it, in order to give due acknowledgement to his finest, dull, relentless weapon.

And the ACE cap cuts deeper than that. Jeff has a very dubious story, set some long time in the past (before we met him), that involves a fleeting appearance at the fringes of serious tennis in some crap capacity in some nowhere tournament where someone thoughtlessly gave him the wild card that will allow him to bore his friends for the rest of his life with the story of his fight through to the semis (or maybe even the final) as he played his best tennis ever, until he dislocated his shoulder hitting a smash. And he blames the subsequent shoulder repair, from which he does at least have a scar, for taking the power right out of his game, and making him the person on court least likely to serve an ace. So the ACE cap in fact mocks the whole unlikely story of his moment in the sun, not just the grim play of the present.

He knows we hate him for all of that grimness, for the grinding, talentless way he almost never loses singles, by off-setting a visibly low level of ability with a very low error rate. He has the mental game of a chess champion, and probably the physical game of a chess champion too. But against flamboyant recklessness he wins almost every time.

But some of this is probably unfair. His tennis is no different to the way he plays the rest of his life. He is not a risk taker. I've challenged him about this, and he didn't seem challenged at all. And my tennis is known for its long periods of complete crap, punctuated by flashes of a very random glory.

G'day Miniature, he says when he sees me.

He says it loud enough to make people look around and to be confused by the person of a very standard height who is coming their way and responding to the name. And I'm not going to tell them that it's one of his jokes. That when your parents call you Richard they leave you open to all kinds of names. Miniature, though, is one of the more obscure, and is a fond abbreviation of Jeff's invention, Miniature Dick.

From him this is no surprise at all, as penis size seems to figure prominently in his thinking, we suspect because his own penis is very small. This was substantiated at a dinner party once when Sal said something like, *Well, how big is average? Three inches?* and, far too late, declared herself to be a child of the metric system, and asked how big inches were. By the time she was saying that her guess was that inches were a very large unit of measurement, perhaps the same as a cubit, she was already looking only at Jeff, her face a mask of horrendous apology, as though a bad secret was out. So now whenever he makes remarks about other people's likely anatomy, we just show him three fingers, and he realises he is not speaking from a position of strength. Or at least length.

Freddie and Gerry arrive while we're hitting up, so Jeff crosses the net and takes the backhand court.

It amazes me that Freddie and Gerry play together, since they already live together and work together. I don't know how people can do that, how their lives can be so overlapped and yet they can still play on the same side of the net at tennis.

They write romance novels, the two of them combining on each manuscript and bringing it out under one female name. They seem so different I can't imagine how this works, how each book looks as though it's written by one person. But I can't understand how any two people can do so much together without driving each other crazy.

My concentration is not good tonight, and the harder I try to concentrate the less I can. I cream enough volleys into the net for Jeff's serve to be broken twice, and I know how much he hates that. I apologise and I tell him I don't know what's going wrong today.

And he says, *Mmmm*, and tries not to glare at me and says, *I'm telling myself this is only a game. That this is fun we're having, okay?*

I hit a screaming winner down the line, I hit a pine tree, I hit a cyclist. We're two sets to one down when we run out of time.

The others buy drinks and I buy an Ice Graffiti Icy Pole. Gerry, a cup of Gatorade in each hand, tells me I should be more responsible with my fluids.

20

After he and Freddie leave, their fluid responsibilities duly discharged, Jeff says to me, *How'd the renovating go on the weekend? Same as usual?*

Yeah.

At least you've always got your tennis. If all else fails you, you've still got your very special gift on court.

One day, just wait, one day it'll all come together. I will understand my gift and the game will be mine.

Yeah.

I can tell I'm at least half forgiven already. That generous allowance has been made for my mental state and in a matter of days he'll partner me again, and again he'll begin with the unfounded hope that things will be different.

When I get home the house still smells of satay and *panang nua*. Still smells like the usual order for Hiller, like our flat did on Baan Thai nights. And I want to tell her she's wrecked my tennis, and I want to say to her, *If you leave me, why don't you leave?*

5

Tuesday seems moderately fucked by ten.

I meant to get up five minutes earlier this morning to iron my shirt, but I only remembered when I was on the bus. I'm sure Hillary noticed, said nothing, looked a little sad for me. And I'm also sure she's worried I'm about to sink anything I'm working on through rampant inattention. At least, if she's half the manager I think she is, she's very worried.

Worried about deals going down the tubes, calls from Sydney, New York, Singapore. All trails leading back, inexorably, to my office. And Hillary up on the next floor, trying to put it all into perspective for the state manager, Barry Greatorex, who is not a man we like to deal with at the best of times. And the best of times came and went a while ago.

I meet Jeff for coffee at twelve-thirty. We meet for coffee, not for lunch, as Jeff makes his lunch every day. He is sufficiently fond of money that he is rarely inclined to spend it, and in fact makes lunch every day for both himself and Sally. Sal, I know, on occasions dumps hers in the bin and goes out with friends, but I'm sworn to secrecy.

I do not make lunch. This means I am left with all the possibilities of the coffee shop, and today I go for a big piece of cheesecake. Jeff looks at this unnecessarily disparagingly and tells me how easy it is to get a roll together.

I eat the first mouthful. What does he think I am? I can't even iron my shirt. A roll takes ingredients. Ingredients take planning. You have to be on top of your whole week before you can get a roll together. What does he expect of me?

Looking cheery today, he says. *Looking as though we dressed in the dark in a very crumpled place again.*

I dress for comfort.

And don't you look comfortable. All the contentment of a man with Steelo underpants.

What, they're showing?

Peeping out under the hair shirt.

What a life. What a fucking life.

A life of quality.

A life that can be appropriately defined by the least attractive of undergarments. This is what I'm destined for?

There's that negative self-talk again. It'll do you no good.

Good? What's good?

Good might be what happens next. Give it a chance. Don't condemn yourself to a life of punishing undergarments. Sometimes it just doesn't work out. It might next time. It might not too. You won't know till it happens and that's the way it goes.

But how do I know?

You don't. It's always a risk. And when you're ready to take the risk, you'll take it.

I can hear what he's saying, but what am I supposed to do? What course of action does this give me? He's sitting there, nonchalantly offering me bagfuls of nothing, like some Zen philosopher. The world's most contented man, telling me about risk, and I've never met anyone less likely to take one.

23

Look, he's saying, *you and Anna. There were things there that worked, but you were also very different, and maybe she just decided that it wasn't right for her.*

What do you mean? What do you mean different?

What? You're going to try to tell me now that you were the same? You and Anna? What about the dry sink thing?

You always mention the dry sink thing.

It's a very good example. I don't have to list a hundred and one differences, I just have to give examples. And the dry sink thing just happens to be a very good example.

The dry sink thing

I should have known it wouldn't work out with Anna from the day we moved in together. We washed a lot of plates that had been wrapped in newspaper for the move and she told me, 'If there's one thing I have to have it's a dry sink'. This is most significant as an example of difference as, until that moment, I was totally unaware of the dry sink concept. I think, if she'd even said, 'If there's one thing I have to have it's an antimacassar on every seat', or a gerbora in the bathroom, or even a gerbil in the bedroom, things would have been okay. But once the importance of a dry sink had been stressed to me, I had no excuses. If the sink wasn't dry, it quickly became apparent whose fault it was. And it was highly unlikely that it would ever be Anna Hiller's, as she was the one with the dry sink thing, and with the little towel on a nearby peg, especially for sink drying. We argued and I called her unreasonable and uncompromising and this didn't go down well. She said, 'Is it such a big deal? Such a big deal that you won't take the trouble to remember to do this little thing for me?' So ultimately I had a choice, and I chose to remember and to dry, and Anna was happy.

Jeff's not talking about dry sinks. He's talking about compromise and surrender and compatibility. He's saying, and I know this because he's said it before, that if you start giving in entirely when it comes to bizarre things like dry sinks, in the end there'll be nothing of you left. And it's true.

We'd go to friends' houses, Jeff and Sal's even, and I'd notice the sink wasn't dry, and I'd want to give it a bit of a going over before there were any problems. Wet sinks, sinks with huge, bulging, ugly globs of tap water sitting on them, came to mean trouble, even though Anna didn't care about other people's sinks. Once she even took me aside and said, *Look, I know we like dry sinks, but in other people's houses it's up to them, okay?* I've never told Jeff this, partly because it was his house, and partly because it would give him a triumphant new dimension to his favourite example of incompatibility, control and the loss of the self.

So now I live in a house with a wet sink, and I'm coming to terms with it.

Later, back at work, I'm still reconstructing the past. Still wondering if I'd done things slightly differently, would we still be together? This direction of thought does not impress Jeff. He sees it as counterproductive. He may be right, but sometimes it's unavoidable. Some days, everywhere I look I see her face. Jeff's a great theorist, life, tennis, whatever. A great theorist, but sometimes I think he hasn't a clue. Sometimes when I'm deep down in the middle of all of this it just isn't possible to use any of his irrefutable logic to dig myself out. I'm probably the greatest frustration in his comfortable life and I think we both have the same sickening feeling that I'm not about to make it easy for him.

Most days I come up with some new idea. Something I need to call Anna about right at that instant and tell her, just in case it makes the difference. There was a time when I even thought it was the sink. For several days I wanted to call her and tell her I'd keep the sink dry forever, even when I was using it, if necessary. I think I'm over that now.

But I keep rebuilding the past in all kinds of different ways, and she's been demonised and deified and re-interpreted so many times that I really have no idea what she was like any more.

Sometimes I have no idea what I'm like any more. Some days it seems I only have a past, and at the end of the past I was set adrift somewhere, on some terrible flat sea that seems to go on and on without interruption.

One day I told Jeff this, or something like it, and he said I would begin to make progress when I stopped constructing my lot in terms of crappy metaphors, and thought about mastering one or two everyday practicalities again.

He doesn't understand that some days practicalities are quite foreign to me, and I'm much more at home in a world described only in terms of the crappiest metaphors possible.

6

She handled it like a scientist, the trashing. Stepped back from it and took out all the emotion. Handled it as though it was the decision of some public authority, quite beyond the powers of the two of us.

She gave me a list, typed on her computer at work, headed Suggested Division of Common Property.

And she hardly made eye contact for several days. We stayed in separate rooms then. This was my choice. It was probably hers too, but I said it first. She said what we needed was a clean break, but I think sometimes even she was disturbed by the cold brutality of it all.

Then I'd get upset and she'd get upset, but it didn't change her mind. She'd taken the big step, pushed past the bewildering moment of trashing when the *panang nua* almost fell from my mouth.

I just have to get away for a while. I just have to do some other things. There's no-one else. No-one else. And then, eventually, not really so long ago, on the phone from Melbourne when I kept pushing, *It's over. Don't you know what over means?*

Some of these sounds may never escape my head. I wake up and they're there, they're real, they're here right now. As though, in Melbourne, there's a mouth I know well making the shape of an O. Telling me *Over*. Red lips, next to a phone. O-ver.

I know what it means.

I know what it means.

I make toast, I give Greg his dry food breakfast right on time, I tell myself routine is good. Healthy. A good sign.

I see red lips trashing me, just at a whisper, like they've done most of the night. And the toast doesn't taste good. Not much tastes good at the moment, particularly toast. But that's a different matter, maybe. When I first moved in the toast tasted very strange indeed, not dreadful, not as dreadful as it should have done, but undeniably strange.

After several days of this, several days of thinking maybe my grandmother toasted rye bread and its influence was somehow lingering, I decided to clean the toaster. And a crispy, multiply-toasted mouse's leg fell out. Just the leg, even when I cleaned the toaster thoroughly, just the leg. I had to sit down for a while, and in the end all I could face for breakfast that day was a couple of mouthfuls of Scotch.

I have a new toaster now and soon, I imagine, this discovery shall be widely regarded as nothing more than an urban myth.

7

Sal calls me to suggest takeaway tonight. *We thought we might pick it up and bring it over to your place*, she says. And before I can say, When's the latest I can let you know, she says, *And don't give me any of that when's the latest I can let you know crap*.

My tail gets munched, and a particularly glamorous Sammy the Snake performance goes the way of all before it. The game dissolves in front of me and a groan comes out before I can stop it.

What was that?

Existential angst. Just the usual.

So we're coming round then?

Tonight?

Yeah, about seven-thirty. We might even bring Tim and Chris. Have you got any particular food preference? It seems they're coming round.

I'm not sure.

So does that mean no, you have no particular preference? Or are you actually unsure as to whether or not you have a particular preference?

I suspect that at present I can neither confirm nor deny whether or not I have a particular preference, and I may not be able to do so for some time.

Does this mean I should pick?

I'm not sure.

I'm sorry, did I call you on a bad day for your brain?

As opposed to other days?

Okay, we'll make this easy. Just make sure you have five clean plates, five glasses, five forks and a couple of spoons for serving and we'll handle everything else.

Five, five, five and two. Got it.

Some days my concentration is quite poor. People catch me when my mind is swimming among ideas and not able to grapple easily with conversation. Today I am endeavouring to make headway with the power station thing, and I am endeavouring not to clutter every moment with thoughts of Anna Hiller. But anything that reminds me of anything in the last three years reminds me of her. I am managing to construct an entire universe in which she is central, but absent.

And I'm well aware that this is a particularly stupid thing to do.

At home, I prepare the seventeen items expected of me and I place them on the red Laminex kitchen table. Sal and Jeff bring wine, so I drink quite a bit of it for them and feel more relaxed than I have for a couple of days. And the conversation moves briskly from one topic to another and I wade slowly after it, lurching in from time to time to offer some remark that is only just no longer relevant.

I have trouble moving on, I tell them. Trouble committing to a new topic.

And I'm watching these four people, these two couples, at least as much as I'm listening to them. And being the only presently trashed person among my friends, I seem to spend a lot of my time in odd-numbered groups. Nights with five plates.

While Jeff and Tim debate first the value of the adversarial talk show as a social document and then whether or not there's a cricket career to be made out of the backspinner, I'm privately focussing on the coupling issue and not saying much.

Jeff said to me once, when I asked him (when I said to him, Tell me exactly why and give me detail), *She's smart and she's strong and I like that. Sure, it's not always straightforward, but straightforward never really worked for me. So it has its challenges but that's okay. We've decided she's forthright. We have a deal where I can refer to her as forthright but not uncompromising. She's generous, more generous than me. She does things for people who matter to her.* And then he shrugged his shoulders and said, *And all that's great, but so what? It sounds like a reference. Really, it just happened. One of those things I guess. The L thing, you know.* And for the L thing he offers no theory, and that's rare.

Naturally I haven't let it rest there. In my own time, in my own head, right now in my own mad, troubled swimming among ideas, I've tested all kinds of hypotheses, trying to work out what goes right, what goes wrong. Comparing Sal to Anna, comparing Jeff to me. Comparing Anna to Jeff and Sal to me and Sal to Jeff. I've learned very little of course, but the processes of comparison are sometimes inexorable. And still the most appropriate comparison is usually me to a pair of Steelo underpants and a hair shirt.

Should I try to pursue a relationship with someone like Sal, or with someone quieter, less powerful? Should I call Anna, just one more time and . . .

And what about Tim and Chris? What about the other relationship in front of me right now? Tim and his PhD (Cantab) in history and his Radical Responses to the Queen Caroline Agitations (J Brit Stud, 1995) and his policy job with the state government. Tim and his fondness for recreational theorising and pulling his socks up when he plays tennis. Tim and the thing Sal refers to as his one big moment of 'wanker fame', his credit in the Oxford English Dictionary for discovering the first reference to the term 'rumpy-pumpy':

**Dr Timothy Dylan Carstairs Murray and the
Oxford English Dictionary**
Rumpy-pumpy: from 'rumpy', a popular rum-based

aphrodisiac in Elizabethan times (the recipe no longer extant); the deliriously protracted intercourse said to follow its use, first noted in the correspondence of Robert Greene (also Green), author of 'Greene's Groat's Worth of Wit' (1592), in a letter to the playwright Thomas Kyd concerning the behaviour of a mutual acquaintance, at that time in the Dutch seaport of Vlissingen (Flushing): ' . . . and then they partook of the rumpy and made proceed to the performance of the famous rumpy-pumpy, surely until the dawn hour was near upon them, stopping only when they had rattled every sword in the garrison and laid shameful cracks upon the town walls, and all, 'tis said, for the price of a Dutch shilling'. TDCM

Chris and her quietness, placid non-meaningful quietness. Chris and her complete ignorance of the part of English history we refer to, somewhat strangely, as 'Tim's period'. Chris and her job at a Flight Centre, where they met when she booked a trip for him once, a trip with his previous girlfriend, though it's now referred to as *My trip to America*.

How do they couple? How do they fit together? How did it even cross their minds, and how is it still going now?

One weekend, when they hadn't been going out long, a group of us went to Jeff's family's house at the coast and Tim and Chris woke us several times each night with the sounds of short bursts of vigorous mattress bouncing and one of them (we still don't know which) braying like a mule. Delirious maybe, intriguing certainly, but, in terms of duration at least, way short of rumpy-pumpy. Each morning they would get up late and look smug, knowing that we had heard it all but would say nothing.

There were six of us that weekend. Six plates, six of everything. Except couples, there were three couples.

Some days I'd really be better with Sammy the Snake. It's not quite the same, but no-one gets hurt and the disappointments are bearable.

After they go I lie on my bed. I have had too much wine. Some nights this conversation goes on all around me. What am I going to do?

8

Small manageable tasks, and no more than one or two at a time. That's what I'm going to do. I shall become the master of the small and manageable. Even if that might be a Jeff Ross idea.

Thursday night I go to Toowong Village. I park in the usual area in the basement carpark and I ride the escalators with my small number of tasks in mind. I buy a Whipper Snipper.

The boy in K Mart who helps with my purchase tells me he has just read an article that called Brisbane the Whipper Snipper capital of the world, and he offers this to me as though he is acknowledging my interest in a piece of the action.

Why? I ask him.

Why what? he says slowly.

Why is Brisbane the Whipper Snipper capital of the world?

Oh, because people buy more Whipper Snippers here, or at least have more. People have more Whipper Snippers.

I can see he is not a very analytical person and I take the bottom of the range $55 plastic model that requires limited assembly and comes with a free Home Improvements cap. On the way to the car I stop for a burger at the food court. This was never one of Anna's preferred options. She viewed the food court with disdain. When I'm halfway through the burger I begin to understand her feelings (at least about the food court), but I decide to use this as a test of my ability to commit and I finish the burger.

We used to live in a rented two-bedroom flat near here. We were saving for a deposit on a house and we were just about there. So I can't help shopping at Toowong. It's what I'm used to, even if it's no longer quite the closest shopping centre to where I live.

I buy the groceries, and I buy a flea killing agent to be added to Greg's food. This seems like a deceptively simple way to deal with the problem.

It is. I get home and he doesn't eat the food. He looks down at it, the meal he eats every night, but now with three drops of flea killer mixed in, and he turns back to me with a look that clearly indicates he is unimpressed. I have insulted his intelligence and he would like his dinner now. It's all too clear I won't win. I throw the food in the bin and give him more, this time without the unwelcome poison. He eats it right away. Ten thousand fleas rustle happily in his fur, unaware that this is only round one.

I go through the mail. Despite the inviting wad of apparent correspondence (and the obvious loser hope that maybe she'll write) there is no actual mail at all. Only limitless junk opportunities for changing my life for the better. Arthritis treatments, carpet cleaning, wedding and engagement rings (thanks a lot), wheel alignment, mattresses (with free mattress protector), pizzas, pizzas, pizzas and the poor man's porn of underwear ads.

Why did my grandmother never get herself a No Junk Mail sticker? Did she like this stuff? I think my life is better than that. I still hate junk mail.

On the other hand, you can never have too many pizza vouchers.

9

Friday the US dollar drops. The joint venture partner bails out.

I manage to restrain myself from jumping up and down punching the air until I close my door.

I whip the computer's butt at Sammy the Snake. I should ask for an upgrade on my games package. I'm ready for something more sophisticated.

On the bus going home people around me are talking about weekends, and I realise we're about to have one and I haven't thought this through. Friday night and nothing to do. And then Saturday.

There's a message on the answering machine. Jeff saying, *We're going to the coast. See you Sunday for tennis.*

How did I ever end up with the answering machine in the Division of Common Property? I hate the answering machine. It gives me only false hope and discontent.

Forty-six hours to kill before tennis. I think through my list of people I'd like to do something with tonight. People I would choose to favour with my company. People who are likely to take me on at short notice. I call Freddie and Gerry.

Oh hi, Gerry says. *Had a big week?*

About the usual. How about you?

Oh, it's been a wild week at the House of Romance, as always. Well, lots of fiction anyway.

Sounds like my life.

Oh, you poor glum boy. And what are you doing tonight? Shouldn't you be out doing the girl thing?

Probably, but maybe I'm not ready for the girl thing again yet. Or any thing.

Yeah, who needs 'em? Well we can't leave you at home lonely. We're just having a barbecue on the deck but you're welcome to join us. If that's not too boring.

It's great. It sounds great. In fact, I can come right over and tell you all about what boring is, and you'll see that that isn't it.

The sun is setting as I walk down the hill, a bottle of red wine in one hand, and a blue haze is settling over the brewery and Toowong and the west. Lights are coming on, and there's traffic blocking Milton Road in the distance and moving slowly along Waterworks Road behind me. But not many cars in these small streets, crazy streets like Zigzag Street, made up of curious angles and unexplained decisions, streets that lose themselves in the contours. That end, and maybe somewhere else, begin again. Finding their way among old cottages in every state imaginable, some confidently renovated, some dealt with cruelly in the fifties and sixties, a few leaning as though they could fall with only a lapse in concentration.

Gerry and Freddie, not unpredictably, live in an 1880s colonial with all the work done, right down to the authentic clawfoot bath.

Freddie says, *Hi, come right through, we're out on the deck*. I give him the bottle of wine and he says, *Oh, nice*, after pretending to read the label. Freddie knows fuck all about wine. We all know that.

Richard brought us wine, he says as he leads me onto the deck.

Gerry turns to me wearing an apron with an eclectic design involving a very matronly bosom and lederhosen.

Oh '88 Rouge Homme. You are being nice to us. You must have been very lonely.

37

Freddie fetches a beer for himself and two glasses for us.

Don't take it personally Richard, Gerry says, *but Freddie won't partake of your gift. He actually knows fuck all about wine, so he's doing the decent thing and not wasting it by drinking it just out of politeness. All the more for us I say.*

Freddie takes this impassively. This is the kind of relationship I've never had. The kind where you can say something like that and it's just fine. Anna knows fuck all about cricket, now that would have been okay to say, but wine and cricket are valued very differently. So even though I'm quite convinced Anna does know fuck all about wine, it could never have been said without significant response.

I hope you don't mind, Gerry says. *I've taken the liberty of marinating the steaks without consulting you first.*

The sky darkens and Gerry proceeds to fill the air with the kind of barbecue smells that in my experience have only come from someone else's barbecue. Tonight I'm on the right side of the fence. I'm not the loser at home next door, opening a little cardboard box and taking out my burger, shuffling the fries out of the paper bag. I'm on the barbecue side, and the food is almost as good as it smells, so I eat like a pig and Gerry takes it as a compliment.

We drink the Rouge Homme, and he finds another bottle of red so we drink that too.

You'll be sorry, Freddie says, waggling his finger at Gerry. *You're forgetting your histamine problem.*

Fuck the histamine problem, Gerry says with a defiant wave of his right arm. *Tonight I'm going to live.*

10

In the morning, I too am visited by the histamine problem. Some mornings red wine is not my friend.

I take a Teldane and drink water. Of course, it's possible that the problem is quantity rather than histamine, but I don't think that's likely. I'm far too uncertain of the quantity I consumed to have any reason to think it's a possibility.

Greg comes in and sits on me, allowing several hundred fleas to transfer onto my clothing.

When I get up I open the Whipper Snipper box and confront the task of limited assembly. I am not good with assembly of any kind. I am the limit when it comes to limited assembly. I am best with things you just plug in and switch on.

The first thing I learn from the sixteen-page instruction booklet is that the words of limited assembly are the words of danger. They make it clear that if I fuck up and lose digits the fault is entirely my own, and nothing to do with the inherent over-complexity of the instructions.

I attend to the limited assembly in only an hour and a half and with only two parts to spare. As I always seem to be able to build machines with fewer parts than the manufacturers suggest are necessary, this does not concern me. I keep all my spares, and one day, who knows what I'll be able to build? I have an abundance of grommets and cams and screws and moulded pieces of plastic left over from numerous acts of limited assembly, and in the Suggested Division of Common Property, they all became mine. Anna was good that way. Fair. I got a lot of the things you'd really want. If I looked across from my column where it said Parts, Spare—Assorted, hers probably said something really useless like Motor Vehicle or 57cm Colour Television. But I imagine that this was done with some feeling that, at the end of the relationship, I had a greater entitlement to the debris.

So I stand in the lounge room and hold my green plastic Whipper Snipper like a bazooka and I blow away various household objects, all to the imagined soundtrack of *Apocalypse Now*.

I am not suited to living alone. I think few people are. I think we need to feel that there is some external monitoring of our behaviour or we regress badly. Our self-care and social skills deteriorate, and our interpretation of the role of objects can become eccentric.

I wonder if I should get in a tenant. Perhaps I should get in a tenant and charge no rent providing the tenant does a certain quota of renovating. This is quite a good plan. It only deteriorates when I think that the tenant might be a babe, a female uni student presently without a partner. I see her up on a ladder painting. I see her on the front verandah attending to the railings. But I care not whether she renovates. And within weeks I'm more fucked up than I'm feeling now and I'm back alone in the house frightening the furniture with my Whipper Snipper bazooka.

So. The grass; the true purpose of this fine green plastic device. I shall take this sixteen perch jungle and make it pleasing to the eye.

Of course, when I reach the back steps I realise I can do nothing without a huge extension cord. Using the most advantageous power point available I can Whipper Snip almost half the kitchen but I can't even get close to the back door. I will have to go back to Toowong.

40

In the interests of planning I decide to go down into the yard to have a close look at the situation and work out if there's anything else I need.

I hear a grunting from next door. An old person's grunting suggesting considerable effort. Kevin Butt, my neighbour, has a crow bar under a tree stump and the look of a man about to do himself harm as he sweats and swears away under a battered Akubra while his arm muscles pull like old ropes and get nowhere.

Hey Kevin, you want a hand? I hear a much younger person's voice say. Regrettably, it's mine. Why am I doing this?

Oh, g'day young Richard, he says between deep, desperate breaths. *I think it's bloody got me beat, mate. Not like I bloody used to be.*

He's clearly depressed by this thought, even though it's taken till his mid-eighties for a tree stump to make him aware of his own mortality.

So I tell him, No worries, and I jump the fence. I wonder who I'm kidding with all this. No worries. Jump the fence.

And the first look at the stump tells me he may be as much as a couple of hours away from uprooting it.

He passes me a spade and I dig. He takes a pick and has a go round the other side, but he doesn't last long. He stops and stands with his hands on his hips, breathing heavily.

I should be doing more, he says angrily. *I'm no bloody good.*

This is great, a neighbourhood of negative self-talk. I should get Jeff over for group therapy.

Come on, why do you have to be good at pulling up stumps? I ask him.

Cause I bloody used to be.

Well, I never have been and it doesn't bother me. I'm sure there are plenty of things you're still good at.

Yeah. Some things maybe. Not much I reckon. Not now.

Slide bloody guitar maybe. You want to hear some slide guitar? Some real bloody old-style country guitar?

Sure.

What am I saying? What is happening here? My back is killing me, I'm knee deep in a hole in Kevin Butt's backyard on maybe the fourth time I've met him in my life and he's running up his back stairs to fetch his guitar in order to inflict some real bloody old-style country on me.

He emerges above me, coming down the steps slowly and in time with his strumming. It's like a 'Mull of Kintyre' nightmare, all this strolling and strumming and gazing off into the distance. Kevin Butt Unplugged. It's not a pretty thought. And boy does he slide. It looks like a totally normal guitar, but in Kevin's hands it slides like he's playing it on ice. Slides way beyond reasonable, way beyond the confines of the tune. I think it may merely be Parkinson's disease dressed up as style, but whatever it is it's all his own.

He tilts the Akubra back and struts around his yard in his sweaty singlet and baggy khaki pants, playing defiantly on. Strumming and plucking and extracting every last bit of wobble he possibly can.

He turns and says, *I'm self-taught, you know. Every bloody bit of this. Self-taught.*

And he tells me he's *partial to the music of the old country*, and just as I'm wondering what old country Butts come from he slips effortlessly into a very long and heartfelt version of 'The Rose of Tralee'.

What do you think of that? he says, stopping to wipe his brow when he's finished.

It's great, I tell him. Unique. You've got a very individual touch.

I like to think so.

And he plays it again, even more flamboyantly individual than before.

These roots go forever. This tree was built to last.

At lunchtime we sit on his steps and he gives me ham and tomato sandwiches.

Went on the road in '26, he says. I was sixteen then and I didn't know too much. Did a lot of country dances. Pride of bloody Erin, that sort of thing. You know? And the Depression nearly bloody did me in. And the Japs of course, in Burma.

Soon I'm back in the hole and Kev's sitting on the bottom step, strumming softly. I wonder if he's doing this deliberately. If it's some perverse sport. Persecuting me with the relentless torture of the strumming. And when the hole is deep enough he'll segue effortlessly into 'Mull of Kintyre' and that'll be the end of me.

I try to distract myself, and I think again of my student lodger. Even though there is probably an ethical problem with this (I suspect the Residential Tenancies Act does not condone the taking in of a lodger about whom the landlord has had previous sexual fantasies), I try to draw encouragement from the fact that I have been able to have any sexual idea about a woman I have yet to meet.

Are those fleas? I hear Kevin saying, from somewhere far beyond this embryonic stirring.

What?

Fleas. It looks like you've got fleas on you. I think they're abandoning ship now though. Now that you're working up a good head of steam.

Yeah, they're probably from my grandmother's cat.

Oh, right. Have you stopped using the Martha Gardener?

What?

Martha Gardener. You know, bloody Wool Mix. It's great for fleas. Gave your grandma that tip a while back.

Oh, right. That explains it.

Country music and helpful household hints. I can see we're going to have a great relationship.

I keep working. Mid-afternoon, the stump starts to move. Kevin gets excited, shouts encouragement. He puts the guitar down, picks up his crow bar and starts fiddling around again. I tell him to go easy, but he says we're nearly there. In another hour, when I think Kevin is about to die, the stump comes up. We drop the crowbars and he sits on the ground with his back to the steps saying, *You bloody beauty*, several times, and I lie on the grass looking up at the clouds gathering, maybe for a storm. It's now intensely humid and still hot and already the grass is making my back itch, but I can't move.

Kevin appears above me with a six pack of Fourex.

A few big drops of rain fall, but the storm happens somewhere else.

I can hear it at night, in bed, where I'm feeling the effects of three beers and the insane physical pain which I am trying to tell myself was the result of 'good hard work', because good hard work never did anyone any harm.

So I lie there, sweating quietly in a night not cooled by rain. Woken on and off by distant thunder and the vague dissociated flicker of lightning and a thousand unkind hands gripping every part of my body in a way that is far from intimate.

11

On Sunday I walk like a man far older than Kevin Butt.

Slowly, painfully, with feet far apart and a difficult stoop.

I sit in the bath till it pickles me and I listen to the hymns drifting down from the church up the hill. Greg comes in and shouts at me about breakfast, so I get out and feed him and put jam on a couple of pieces of bread for myself.

I sit, wrapped in my towel and still feeling slightly pulped, and I watch TV. After 'Rage' finishes the options are not appealing and I flick around among the cartoons. I do not find them helpful. Even Sonic the Hedgehog pashes Roxy and gets a free chilli dog lunch. I guess I scored the free lunch yesterday, but there seemed to be a lot of effort required. And nobody pashed me. However, since Kevin was the only person in the vicinity, that's probably fine.

I do, however, miss the contact of lips. Any kind of contact really.

Usually by this time on a Sunday Anna and I would be fighting over who got which bit of the *Sunday Mail*, as though any bit was worth fighting for. Perhaps it was only the principle that was worth fighting for, even though it was ultimately territorial and pointless. I want to call her and say, If it was the *Sunday Mail* it's yours, and I'll even bring it to you in bed.

But I have to learn that if I even think this might be the answer, I'm asking the wrong question. This is probably originally a Jeff Ross theory, but maybe it's right.

In the afternoon, still afflicted by widespread stiffness, I play tennis very badly. And I get the extensive shitting on I expected about my Home Improvements cap, which I wear at an angle accused of being rakish, but that is determined only by the position of the sun. Not that anyone will accept this. The cap is regarded in its full ironic capacity, bearing in mind my limited achievements as an improver of homes. Jeff tells the others they're being unfair, and says I'm only trying to make my status as a Toolman clear. There is some debate as to whether or not I have the equipment to be a Toolman, and for the next hour or so I am known by the name Toolboy.

I ignore this, I concentrate hard, I play very badly. Sets breeze by, and Jeff pretends they don't.

He tells us afterwards that Tim played Veny Armanno on centre court at Milton on Thursday afternoon. Veny, saying he needed a break from some dilemma in the editing phase of his next novel, saying that his concentration was shot and he probably wasn't up to much, won two sets to love. But this seemed temporarily immaterial to Tim, who raved to Jeff about centre court, about how much better it is out there, how it sounds like the real thing when the ball echoes off the condemned empty stands.

And this, the sound of the real thing, is a hint of the pro tennis circuit, the big company we'd like to think we could almost keep, The Tour. Even though the only tour we're ever likely to qualify for would involve a bus, a camera and singalongs. Despite this, I think it's those centre court moments that keep alive an unspoken fantasy shared by at least some of us, as though, in our time, there will come a Tour where large numbers of people pay money to see tennis played by people over twenty-five who aren't very good.

46

12

On Monday morning Deb has no new tats to show me, and as I tell her about my weekend I'm sure it sounds as bland as always to both of us. I can't believe I begin my week by disappointing someone with my weekend.

I went out Friday night, she says. *I was planning to meet a man.*

A particular man?

Oh, a very particular man. We had arranged to meet, but he bored me, so I ended up just pashing Tyson, my hairdresser.

I thought your hairdresser was gay.

So did I. So did he. Maybe it was just a moment's indiscretion, but maybe it's love. Who knows? He was divine and he was wearing red velvet pants, so . . . She shrugs away the inevitability of it.

How was he in the pashing department?

Oh, quite excellent.

And exactly what quality is it that gives a man excellence?

Oh, the tongue. He has an outrageous tongue.

An outrageous tongue. Tyson the Tongue Machine.

And for the next two days, Tyson the Tongue Machine will be all we talk about. Of course, by mid-week she'll be telling me she doesn't love him any more. She'll have found some act she interprets as betrayal or a culpable lack of interest, or she'll have fallen in love with

47

someone else she's bumped into. She once told me she dropped a boy because he wouldn't have 'Deb' tattooed on the inside of his eyelid. I have always hoped she was kidding.

Hillary comes out of the lift laughing and says, *Barry's stopped smoking again. I think you should know that. On the weekend. And he's looking shaky already.*

Barry stopping smoking is not a good thing from any perspective but his own future health. He has tried before and each time he's become very tense very quickly, and it hasn't worked out well.

And we've got a meeting with him at ten.

A meeting.

Yeah. About the bank in Thailand.

The bank in Thailand.

Yeah, one of those things you're working on. One of the reasons you come here. Other than the now-defunct power station and the computer games.

Is there any possibility of having the meeting about the computer games? I think I could cover that.

Trust me. This is the best time to have it. His concentration's shot to bits, so all you have to do is think of a few short, clear things to say and stick to them. I thought you'd been working on that approach anyway.

She leaves me to go through the file and says we'll talk at nine-thirty. I like her a lot. I think it's in her eyes, the way she delivers the backhanded compliment dead-pan and her eyes let you in on the joke. This is insane. Every time I talk to my boss I spend a long time thinking about how much I like her. She makes some passing remark about my slackness, so I show an interest in developing a pathological attachment. There's Hillary, with her perfect life, her career, her baby, her high-flying husband. Doing nothing more than noticing me and it goes straight to my pants.

I focus hard on the task and the meeting at ten with the smoke-free Barry Greatorex.

Barry the Great and the peripheries of glory
Barry the Great has been called, in sophisticated company,
the smartest man ever to leave New Zealand. He is a man
whose admirable past is constructed of relentless near-glo-
ries, and he hasn't forgotten any of them. He nearly rowed
for New Zealand. He nearly played cricket for New Zealand
as a keeper-batsman (but the selectors unfortunately
'turned conservative', and we think he sweated out a
couple of seasons in fourth grade in Auckland before his
knees gave way). He nearly entered the New Zealand
Parliament at the urgings of the PM of the day, who said
he needed more like Barry in his cabinet. He once took
Hillary into his office to tell her confidentially that he was
being head-hunted. This turned out to be Barry's way of
saying he had applied for a job. When he didn't get it he
told her 'I've thought about it, and I realise my work's not
done here. I've got more to do at Shelton's yet. Not that
it wasn't tempting'.

At nine-thirty Hillary is back, checking that I'm ready.
We talk it through and together we come up with a plan.
　At ten Barry is pacing, trying to distract himself from
the pain of withdrawal by looking out his window. Unlike
my office, Barry's has a real view, but today it's clearly
not enough. He is tense indeed, and his face is puffed
up like a toad. Every time he breathes out it seems to
be with some intent, some undisclosed but heavy purpose, and he keeps slapping his hands together. I wonder
if he might be psyching himself up to clean and jerk his
desk.
　So, he says, his eyes flicking between the two of us.
What's our position?
　Hillary looks at me.
　I think it still has problems, I tell him. I think it
doesn't comply with Thai foreign investment law.
　They don't think that in Sydney.
　They can think what they like.

49

He nods, looks out the window. Looks back. *So, what's our position?*

Repetition always unsettles me. Is this a lapse in concentration? Is it the same words but a new question because of the different context? Do we get stuck in a loop if I give the same answer? Hillary is making her right hand, which only I can see, into the shape of a gun next to her thigh, and discharging it down at the floor. I look back to Barry and reinforce my cool, serious demeanour.

Well, unless there's a change in the numbers, or a change in Thai law, I think there's a problem.

Can you put that to them in Sydney?

Sure.

Is there any way, Hillary suggests, *that you can take the particular problem clauses and come up with alternatives that'll keep everyone happy?*

Good clauses. We could do with a few of those. I'll look at it. Maybe it's possible. Of course, if we try that everyone's legal sections will tell us it doesn't conform to their standard documents.

But can it be done? Barry again, sniffing the hint of some minor glory in brokering a solution that may win him hearts in New York. It's unlikely. They hate him in New York.

Maybe. Maybe it can. I can look at it. This week.

It probably needs to be addressed at an organisational level, Hillary says, *as well as the legalities of this contract. I think we're likely to see this type of issue arising more and more. So maybe we should both go to Sydney to sort it out, when Rick's looked at it.*

Barry approves this course of action. We leave him to the crisis of his biochemistry and go back to the lift.

Nice work with the gun, I say to Hillary when the doors shut. I was just sticking to my short, clear things, like you said, and you bring out the gun on me.

Oh yeah, and you didn't deserve it? Rick the straight shooter? Clint fucking Eastwood more like, she says, and laughs at me. *I might have said short, clear things but I don't recall saying spaghetti western. The only people who shoot straighter ride into town with a black hat on and a mouthful of chewing tobacco.*

She has a bizarre and appealing sense of humour, an obscure preoccupation with western imagery and a range of silly signals, designed to challenge my composure when cool is required. Some days I think it's the only intimate thing in my life. Bad train of thought. In my mind I go the finger pistol and blow it away.

Oh, come on. He was getting all Brando on me, I tell her. So, what's our position? So, what's our position like the room was loaded with bugs and I had to speak back in code. I was fine. My response was entirely appropriate.

They can think what they like? Cowboy. And you used to be so thoughtful, so careful with your responses.

Trust me sheriff. Trust me. At least I wasn't the one playing fairy godmother with the happy clauses.

And I'm thinking, why am I like this? Where did this straight shooter thing come from? Is it just because I really don't care about the bank in Thailand? Or because I don't care if I'm right or wrong any more? Do I think it's impressive? I think I was thoughtful. I think my considered opinion was one of my assets. And I just don't consider the way I used to.

This new approach seemed to work with Barry, and that worries me even more. I think I liked it better when I frustrated him with my caution, when my entire work practice was geared around making no mistakes.

But now that I think about it, that does seem a while ago.

13

At home that night, among all the junk mail, is an envelope with Kevin Butt's address crossed out and 'Richard' written on it somewhat shakily in blue biro. It contains a cassette and a scrap of paper which says simply, 'A token of my appreciation', and underneath, quite unnecessarily, the name Kevin J Butt.

The tape has no indication of its contents, and this does not reassure me.

I go inside, feed Greg, and load it into the stereo. I hear Kevin's voice.

G'day young Richard. As I am very appreciative of your assistance with the stump on the weekend last, he says with the obvious style of a person reading a prepared text, *and understanding something of your musical interests, I have today recorded in my kitchen a few of our favourite songs. Should you happen to look out of your back windows, you will also see that I noticed that your grass was in need of doing and I have attended to that too. I hope this is okay by you.* Then, as an afterthought, *And I hope you enjoy listening to these songs as much as I enjoyed recording them for you. Thank you, and good night.*

There follows a small amount of throat clearing and a few practice notes, then a version of 'Rose of Tralee' that could make the deaf weep. There is so much slide going on with that guitar that I'm surprised he doesn't hurt himself, and at times his interpretation is so individual it's only my guess that I'm still hearing 'Rose of Tralee'. He drags his way through a few more of the classics, evoking fond memories of the stump uprooting and ends with *one for you and me mate*, a lively, up tempo 'Pub With No Beer'.

So in the midst of this life of quality I make a friend in the neighbourhood.

At least the lawn looks good.

For dinner tonight I sit at the red Laminex table and rest my head upon it. I am not inclined to cook, or to eat.

14

So I am the one designated to invent the alternative clauses that will make everyone happy.

Hillary reassures me that I'm *just the boy for the job*, and I tell her I shall take my obvious surfeit of happiness and direct it to this important purpose.

I try hard to focus on the screen, but I keep finding myself thinking of other things, or quietly whining my way through the infectious melody of 'Rose of Tralee'. My Can of Worms screen saver emerges and chews its way through my document. I tell Hillary this will all take careful consideration, as there are several competing interests and I must achieve a delicate balance.

And she says, *Good*, but warily.

I stay till six-thirty, but I'm not sure that I get anywhere. Perhaps all I create is confusion. I go home, as though there's any less confusion there.

Greg's fleas are going crazy, multiplying at a quite unsustainable rate but appearing to sustain it so far. I actually wonder if there's any of Greg left in there at all, or if the fleas have hollowed him out and are now operating his limbs in order to maintain the pretence of a cat. I take him to the vet. The vet is not impressed.

He should probably have come in a while back, she says. *He's not looking good.*

I realise it would be stupid at this point to say I've been busy, as I would only end up getting an oblique lecture about the responsibilities of pet ownership. Then I'd have the choice of taking it on the chin, or explaining myself as a victim of circumstances. That it took a death and a trashing to bring Greg and me together. My theory, that every conceivable interaction has the potential to lead back to the trashing, holds. I choose to say nothing, and I try to look contrite.

He's really quite infested, she's saying, *and he's reacting and he's starting to scratch. Have you noticed the scratching? You must have noticed it. He starting to break skin.*

I nod.

Have you noticed it?

Well, I'm out during the day.

This is clearly more like a confession of neglect than an answer, so I am compelled to go on.

He's my grandmother's cat, actually. And she hasn't been well lately, so I'm helping look after him. It's not ideal, but hopefully things'll be back to normal soon.

The problem with this is that every time I go the lying option, I tell a different lie. And I don't keep track of them. I'm scattering lies all over town to avoid talking about the trashing, and I expect this will backfire soon enough.

The vet, of course, displays compassion when she hears the lie, and this only reinforces the likelihood that I will lie again.

She says we will need to use a strong flea wash and if that fails, or if Greg keeps scratching himself, we may need to cut an ice-cream bucket and fit it around his head while we apply something else.

So now I am turning the cat into a loser too. A month or so ago he was entirely functional and flea-free. In a week's time he could have patchy hair loss, widespread self-inflicted wounds and an ice-cream bucket around his head. And they say people grow to resemble their pets. I think I'm dragging him down.

The vet says, *You might find that even if this works*

he may have a few fleas left. Probably the easiest thing to do if that's the case is wash him with some dilute Martha Gardener's Wool Mix. But give it a few weeks first.

Wash him with what?

Wool Mix. You know the stuff? Just make sure it's mixed in with a lot of warm water, and rinse it all off after you've washed him.

I take him home. I explain to him the importance of the flea bath and how calmness is essential. I tell him this is for his own good.

At first he fools me by crouching down low and giving a long whining growl. This intensifies when I drench him and rub the liquid into his fur. I tell him how good he is, how well this is going. I start to wash it off. He loses it.

Every one of his muscles spasms at once and he rips up my arms like a fearsome wet gremlin and over my shoulder, landing on the floor with an inelegant splat. He runs for the door and out into the backyard. I chase him, but he's gone.

I am standing in the dark, quite alone, with no cat sounds apparent in the relative quiet. When I go back into the light and see the mess, I realise that the sensation I took to be water running down my arms is in fact blood. I have several slashes to each forearm, running from my wrists halfway to my elbows. I rinse my arms under the tap and the bleeding continues.

I sit on the steps for about twenty minutes with each forearm wrapped in an old towel. The moonlight reveals a recently cut lawn but not a hint of cat.

When I check my arms again they are still oozing blood. This is really pissing me off. I realise I can't go to bed like this. I can't do anything until this is properly sorted out.

I find my Medicare card and walk down the hill to the medical centre, the towels wrapped again around my forearms.

I explain my predicament at the counter and I'm taken straight into the treatment room, where I sit for more than half an hour listening to the waiting room TV through the wall and bleeding patiently. Just after the third time that I'm told, *It won't be long now*, a doctor walks in.

He says, *Hi*. He says his name is Greg. He has profoundly orange hair.

He looks at my arms and I tell him a cat did it to me, and I almost tell him more. Greg, the orange cat, the cat I am sure is named after him, my grandmother's cat, etcetera. But that would only lead me back to the trashing. So I just tell him a cat did it to me.

Some cat, he says. *What were you doing to it?*

Flea bath.

He fiddles around, washes my arms with a pink solution, seems not to mind about the on-going bleeding. He talks about sutures and says he thinks we can get away without them. He closes some parts with strips and calls the nurse in to give me a dressing with some pressure. He talks about the possibility of an infection and says I should come back tomorrow or the day after to have the wound checked.

And he's looking at me as though he's trying to work something out. As though his mouth might be saying something mundane and procedural, but his brain is off on a tangent. Just when I'm assuming he's feeling the end of a long day and his mind is merely elsewhere he says, *So how are you? Other than this I mean.*

What?

How are you feeling? How are things? Generally.

Fine.

Good. That's good. So, no other problems then? Nothing else you'd like to discuss while you're here?

No. I don't think so.

You're not . . . you're not depressed at all, he says, as though this can masquerade as casual enquiry, *or anything?*

57

Well . . . no. I'm fine.

But I blew it. I paused and I blew it. If I was fine there would have been no pause. I would have laughed. And now we're both looking at my forearms as though the bandages are hiding wounds far deeper than cat scratches.

Well, look, you really don't seem very happy to me. And I'm a bit concerned.

What do you mean?

I know what he means.

Well, those wounds. If they weren't caused by a cat, if it was something else, that'd be okay. We could talk about it. Things can be sorted out you know, even when they don't look good.

It was a cat. It was a cat, really. You want me to bring it in and show it to you? We can do the forensic thing and get the skin out from under its claws. Except I think it's run away. We could have done that if it hadn't run away.

So there's no cat now?

There's no cat now. Now. But there was a cat earlier this evening.

So these wounds were caused by some kind of temporary cat?

No, no. A cat. A regular cat. A cat who didn't like the flea bath, and I think he's gone now.

Okay. He pauses, *I have to ask you something, and I don't want you to be offended, and I want you to answer honestly. Regardless of the cause of these injuries, okay, regardless, can you tell me that if I let you go home now you'll be okay?*

It was a cat.

Fine. It was a cat. And can you give me an undertaking that if you go home now you'll be okay?

I'll be fine. Fine. I'm a bit worried about the cat though. I hope he hasn't run away.

Yes. Me too. Will you promise me that if you're worried about things, particularly if you're worried you might,

58

you know, harm yourself, or anything, you have to promise
you'll contact me first.

I promise. That's fine. I promise. I'm really quite
okay. Okay? My life might not be at one of its high points
at the moment, but I'm fine. I'm getting through this.
I'm going quite well. I'm working and renovating, and
it's all going fine.

Good. I'm glad. I'm very glad. And I'm glad that
we've had this chance to talk. Now, I think it would be
good if we could talk again. So what I'd like you to do
is to come back and see me, maybe in a couple of days.
And we can take a look at those wounds, see how they're
going, and we can talk. Okay?

Well, I'm a bit busy.

Cat scratches can be prone to infection. I really need
to look at those wounds again.

Okay.

Okay.

Thanks.

He smiles, but with some gravity, and he walks out
of the treatment room. The nurse reappears and says,
All done in here? as though she wants me to know she
doesn't know what the talk was about. She shows me
back out to the counter, where I sign the Medicare form.

Now, did you have to make a follow-up appointment?
the receptionist asks.

No. No. Everything's fine. All sorted out.

The intercom buzzes. She picks up the phone, says,
Yes, yes, okay, and turns back to me.

Doctor says he would like you to have another appoint-
ment.

Oh, right, I must have misunderstood.

Yes. He said a long appointment in two days time
would be fine.

Oh, good.

Now, he's working during the day on Thursday, eight
to five, and the morning's filling up.

I could be a bit busy on Thursday.

Yes. Let's make it Thursday afternoon. How about four-thirty?

Four-thirty's fine.

She smiles, and only then lets me go.

At home, Greg (the cat) is waiting on the front steps, as though nothing has happened.

15

I wake every time I roll over. My arms are burning, throbbing, like a red neon light saying Dickhead in very large letters.

I turn up to work wearing a T-shirt and looking like crap. I have worn my best T-shirt, since this is work after all, but unfortunately my best T-shirt is a partially luminous Felix the Cat, given to me for my last birthday by everyone on the fifteenth floor. They made me put it on as soon as I'd unwrapped it and Hillary said, *It glows in the dark, look,* and she cupped her hands against my chest and looked through the eye hole made by her thumbs. And I had to stand quite still while seven or eight people stood around me, looking through their cupped hands at Felix the Cat and going, *Hey yeah.*

Christ Rick, Hillary says when she sees me, *what's wrong?*

Nothing, really, nothing.

It doesn't look like nothing. What have you done to yourself?

Nothing. I have done nothing to myself. I want that to be totally clear. This is not something I've done to myself.

Okay, okay, she says, backing off almost physically. *I just meant it like Hey, what have you done to yourself, you know? What's happened to you? That kind of question.*

Sorry.

Okay, so we'll try it again. This time you answer, like a really calm, normal person. Hey, Rick, what have you done to yourself?

And she's making gestures, as though this is a role play.

I gave the cat a flea bath.

She laughs. I can't help but smile myself.

It's a very tough cat.

That's it? Really? A flea bath?

Yeah. That's all there is to it. Well, the cat did get slightly upset. I have to leave early tomorrow afternoon for the doctor to check things, if that's okay. He said cat scratches get infected easily.

Sure.

After some more reassurance that from the elbows up I'm no better or worse off than yesterday she lets me go to my office to start work. I can see I now have a new dimension to the trashing story, as it has become complicated by the need to deny any suicidal urges. This is not what I was looking for.

And coupled with badly broken sleep it makes today feel less real than usual. I rest my arms in my lap and my chin on my Felix the Cat T-shirt and I lean back in my chair and sleep fitfully for nearly an hour.

I meet Jeff for coffee. He laughs for quite a long time at the chaos that seems to have swept across me overnight, the random hair, the bandages, and he refers to my wounds as a characteristically pitiful gesture of self-harm.

It was Greg, I tell him. I think he was trying to effect a mercy killing.

And I have to tell him the whole story, including the other Greg and his obvious concerns for me.

The Night of Two Gregs, he says. *What an evening of distinction. I think only you could have an evening like that.*

62

Sometimes I surprise even myself. I think I've come up with the gold standard for crap and then, out of the blue, another personal best.

The Bradman of crap.

The Bradman of crap. I always knew there was something Bradmanesque about me. I just had to find my calling.

So does this mean you're out of tennis tonight?

Yeah. Yeah, I think it does. I think I'd burst open and bleed and my friend the GP would probably take me for a breaker of promises and put me away.

My arms begin throbbing again in the hot sun on the way back to work. People watch me as I walk through the mall, watch me as though they are watching one of the mall's resident mad people. They stare as I walk past, as though I'm so mad I won't even know, and I want to stop and say to them, Look, I'm not mad, I'm a legal counsel for a big bank you've never heard of. And then I think, why does this make me any better than the mad people? Why should I want to be separated from them because I'm going to an office now and not staying in the mall, finding my place in the shade and staring intently at passers by?

Back in the toilets at work I look in the mirror, and my hair is like the nest of a confused bird. I want to go into the mall again and explain to everyone that, supportive as I am of the resident mad people, I happen not to be one of them. I happen simply to have a temporary combing problem. But this, like all other stories, works its way back. Combing problem, forearm pain, trivial injury while flea bathing, grandmother's cat, grandmother dead, trashed. So I'll just have to live with it.

My hair has never been easy, but usually its disarray has signalled nothing more than slackness, a windy day, a lost comb, a big night. And I can live with all of those. It's only today that I'd like things to be a little different.

Automatic Hair
Some years ago, Jeff came up with the notion of Automatic Hair to describe the phenomenon occurring on his head. Automatic Hair changes for nothing, for no-one. Automatic Hair is impervious to outside influence. However treated or mistreated, however slept on, sweated through or swum in, his hair automatically assumes the position he thinks is a style. He says it responds well to washing but has no need of combing on a regular basis. And he thinks this is a good thing. He also thinks people as lucky as he is are very rare. He thinks he may be the first white person since Elvis to have Automatic Hair. He thinks Bronwyn Bishop would like us to think she has Automatic Hair, but you don't have to be an expert to know otherwise. And he cares not at all that, perhaps for the rest of his life, he will have the Automatic Hair of the 1980s.

Today I would happily settle for anything styleless, anything automatic, probably any hair other than the madness on my head. Any kind of hair at all that has no association with trashing.

I make myself another cup of coffee and talk to people in various countries about the Thai project, with the aim of achieving the delicate balance I have promised Hillary. And I talk to them like a man in a dark suit, and they have no idea that things are less than perfect. On the other hand, this is the first time it has ever occurred to me that my understanding that they are darkly suited during all our conversations is merely an assumption.

I wonder if I should say to them, I'm wearing a Felix the Cat T-shirt, I have hair like the nest of a confused bird and I'm bandaged from my wrists most of the way to my elbows and I was just wondering how you were looking today. And Harvey, the American expat in Singapore, says, *Well it's funny you should ask me that Richard as today I'm wearing only a cowboy hat and a garter and I think I just lost a grapefruit in my rectum.*

But they all talk like the darkest of dark suits, like men who are very serious about work, garments and fruit. And I can match them in this, every step of the way, as we talk with an unnecessary earnestness about the kind of document that will make us all happy.

16

If you stare at the Can of Worms screen saver long enough, you don't see the worms at all. You see the screen opening up black spaces in front of you, shapes arising with the appearance of order and then metamorphosing into other shapes. Such is the way of the worms.

If I was paying any less attention to my work I would probably be drooling. I expect that by this time next week the ever-considerate Hillary will have fixed a bib to my chin.

I know I'm not doing as well as I used to. I know I'm not kicking out of this just yet. I know that for every little thing I can interpret as an encouraging sign, there are probably several that suggest the exact opposite. And some of the examples of this are obvious and undeniable.

Christmas party, PJ Shelton Bank (Aust), 1993
I drank to moderate excess, as did many others. I sang all the words to 'Khe Sanh', while wearing my tie around my head. I won a prize in the caption competition, though I can't recall the caption. I danced on the pool table. I left at midnight with my caption prize, a collection of Christmas goodies wrapped in green cellophane, and on my way to a cab I tucked it under the arm of a shoeless man sleeping in Albert Park.

Christmas party, PJ Shelton Bank (Aust), 1994
I am unsure how much I drank, and unsure of the consumption of others. I sang 'The Ship Song' with such intensity I made Nick Cave look like he was only kidding. I sang Morrissey's 'The More You Ignore Me' during some strange dance with Hillary, who, fortunately, laughed a lot. I was not placed in the caption competition. Specifically, the picture of a starving toothless refugee was not seen to be fittingly represented by my entry, 'I s'pose a fuck's out of the question'. I vomited in one of the pockets of the pool table (mostly fluid, but it did manage to hold several of the larger chunks). I was put in a cab early, without a prize, and without great awareness of my surroundings. The 1994 Christmas party was for many the first big hint that I was coping quite badly with Anna's departure.

I want things to be better, but they aren't yet. Some days have an inertia about them. And those that move at any speed seem to move also without any control. I have always liked control, and any lack of it does cause me some discomfort.

I have always liked control. It makes me sound like some control freak.

I hope, in my life, for a reasonable level of control. That most days will be manageable, and that most random events that arise should offer me opportunities rather than harm. And I think all that's okay, within the bounds of acceptability in a person, or a partner. That's what I hope.

I am not Jeff Ross, who correctly understands himself to be a creature of routine. A creature for whom change is an enemy. This man's development, as he well knows, was thrown out at the anal stage. He lets nothing go. If sphincters could arm wrestle he'd be a world champion.

I have suggested to him I should change. That maybe I should make myself a nicer person, maybe that would work. But he says nice is dead in the nineties, that this is an age of irony and maybe even cruelty, particularly the cruelties of ambivalence and indifference, and I should run with it. He says that perhaps the only change I should make should be to ease up on the enormous amount of cruelty directed inward. He tells me I dwell too much on the idea that I have been cruel to others, and I now seem to be championing their cause and being very cruel to myself.

He says that the best you can do in the nineties is to be ironic and harmless (that is, to choose to discard the cruelty on offer), to find a small number of people you like and trust, to expect wine of quality and regular tennis and to hold out little hope for the world. I think he is the sort of person who, in the time of fortified cities, would have been quite comfortable during a long siege.

I told him he should write a self-help book, and tour internationally as a guru to the lonely and crapulous. That regardless of his own stated choice to look inward, he had a gift and a duty. He had a special thing to share. And I told him I could see him drawing crappy people from their modest lives into stadiums where they would sing and hug and chant his truisms and learn to love their disease.

A few days after I suggested this, he scared me a little by proving that he'd given it some thought. He said we could do it. He said we should start with bumper stickers. Bumper stickers that said, in very large letters 'CRAP', and then, below, in smaller letters, 'and I'm proud'. He seemed to see this as a very liberating notion.

I am one of his friends. We share tennis and wine and the siege mentality of the age, but that's not to say he doesn't worry me.

He turns thirty tomorrow. I go out at lunchtime to buy him a gift.

I browse, and by the time I absolutely have to go back to work I have nothing. I am standing in front of a shelf of popcorn makers. I tell myself not to dismiss the popcorn makers lightly, and I take myself so seriously

I buy two. My theory is that one will make an excellent gift for Jeff, and the other will facilitate diversity in my diet. Over the last few weeks I have noticed my culinary repertoire constricting, and I don't think this is a good sign. Reading the pack, the popcorn maker looks straight-forward. Add corn. Turn on. And the corn spins in hot air until it pops and pours out into your catcher, then you have all the options in the world.

I leave the store with one under each arm and I go back to work.

Corn will be good. Popcorn will help me. Popcorn and its many possibilities. Maybe I'm better than last Christmas, at least in some ways.

17

At four-thirty I'm back at the medical centre, where I'm told, *Doctor's running a little behind, so please take a seat.*

I sit near the TV and kids with runny noses and palpable fevers clamber across the furniture and tip over a pot plant. At least in the medical centre everyone around me thinks it's fine to have bandages, and probably only the relatively small number of people over the age of ten think I'm wearing them because of some failed suicide attempt.

At five-fifteen my turn comes. Greg's door opens and he calls me in and inspects my wounds in a very business-like way and says he's pleased with the progress. He says we could probably leave them open, but it might be an idea to cover them just so they don't get bumped. Then we sit down for our chat.

So how's it going? he says, in a way that makes it seem very like a standard opening remark.

Fine.

How's the cat? Did it turn up?

Yeah. The cat's fine.

He looks down at my file, as though trying to work out where to take it from here. He clicks his pen a few times, but writes nothing. *Your address,* he says. *I used to look after the woman who lived there.*

Yeah, my grandmother.

This wasn't . . . This may sound a little strange. The cat. It's not an orange cat, is it?

An orange cat called Greg, yes. The cat my grandmother named after you. That's the one. He's very nice normally. Just not a fan of the flea bath.

Who would be?

So you're saying that cutting me to ribbons would be the reasonable response of any orange Greg in the circumstances?

He laughs, though in a slightly unsettled way, as though I might be offering to flea-bathe him. *We miss your grandmother round here. She was certainly a character.*

Yeah.

She always used to bring biscuits. She made them herself. I always looked at her and thought that's what I'd like to be like at ninety.

Yeah, me too. I thought that. There she was, ninety-one and still putting shit on me. You've got to respect that.

So, how do you get to be living in her house?

It's a complicated set of circumstances. Well it's not really. It's actually pretty simple. I was in a relationship. It ended. I had to live somewhere. I stayed with my parents but, you know.

Yeah, I do. I do know. I worked in England for a while and when I came back I stayed with mine for a few months. I hadn't lived with them for maybe ten years. It was very strange. Too strange. They ate dinner really early, and took an intense interest in my day.

Yeah. That's it. That's it, exactly. They're great but they'll drive you crazy. And you want to shake them and say, These things are just habits. They don't matter. You can get over this. People can eat dinner after dark. But you know they wouldn't understand. They think there's something really Bohemian about you because you don't want to eat till seven-thirty.

In the end you have to leave, don't you? You've got to get back to some place that's your own.

Yeah. Or in my case my grandmother's. But it's fine now. I'm settling in.

And the relationship?

It's over. That's been made clear to me. So now I've got to make it clear to me too, and then work out what happens next.

He says these things can be rough. Sometimes they're all you can think about and you can feel them weighing you down, but in the end you pull through, even if there are times when you don't expect to. We talk a bit more, probably until he decides I'm safe, until he believes his feline namesake caused the harm that brought me here two nights ago. And he says that we could talk again, if I wanted. That I can come back if I notice I'm not coming to terms with any of this and I want to talk to someone who's not part of the situation.

And right at this moment I realise that sometimes I still work on the assumption that I'll be fine. That something will happen, or nothing will happen, and this will all lift from me and I'll be fine.

I walk home up the hill. Right now I don't feel bad.

18

On Friday Deb asks me what plans I've got for the weekend and I tell her. I'm going to a thirtieth.

And she says, *Fuck, thirty,* slowly and breathily as though it's almost inconceivable. *You're not thirty are you Ricky?*

No. I've got nearly two years left to do all the 'before I'm thirty' things.

Thirty. I can't even imagine thirty.

You don't have to. It happens anyway. It's like that.

So what are you doing?

Going out to dinner.

No, you've got to do more than that.

I'll give you the guy's number if you want. You can call him and tell him he's fucking up his only shot at a decent thirtieth.

I start working, start looking through this contract again and wading my way with some discomfort to a few things that might become ideas. My phone rings. It's Deb.

You know what I'd do for my thirtieth, Ricky?

What?

I'd get one of those bouncy castles, one of those blow up ones you see at church fetes, and I'd have the party in there.

Good plan, Deb.

Yeah. Thanks babe. You'll be there won't you?

73

Sure.

You'll have to take your shoes off. That okay by you?

Fine. I bounce way better with my shoes off.

Cool.

We all plan to meet at my place for drinks before dinner. Sal decided this a couple of weeks ago because it's near the restaurant and, besides, it would give everyone a chance to see how my renovations are going. Back then there was nothing ironic about it, I fully expected we'd be standing round admiring my handiwork. I wonder if I can keep everyone down at the end of the verandah with the two and a half painted railings long enough to get away with it. I doubt it.

So instead I hide the two and a half painted railings with a table and I try to distract my guests with champagne and the presentation of the gift. And the house is so profoundly unrenovated that the inspection aspect of the visit is entirely forgotten. I extol the many virtues of popcorn. I tell them it's easy, it's healthy and the choices of seasoning are limited only by the imagination. Jeff asks me what seasoning I'm going to try first with mine and I realise I haven't thought this through.

Good imagination, he says.

We go into the kitchen and he loads up both our machines with corn. Within minutes the popcorn is pouring into a large mixing bowl with butter and curry powder and Jeff gets quite excited about the result, but the general consensus is that it might not be quite right with the champagne.

And we do seem to drink quite a lot of champagne before we head off down the hill to Le Chalet.

They seat us at a table for six, with Jeff and Sal on one side, Tim and Chris on the other and me at the end, sitting opposite a distant empty chair that I try to tell myself is not symbolic. Jeff calls one of the staff over and says, *I wonder if you could take that chair away. It's making my friend uncomfortable.*

74

And tonight, Sal says emphatically, as though she has planned to, *no intellectual wanking. No excluding reasonable people with that boy's crap.*

But it's my birthday, Jeff says, *and that's my favourite thing.*

Well that puts me in my place. Your favourite thing is it? Okay, for the birthday boy, for the boy who clearly has an interest in beginning his thirty-first year with a vow of celibacy, wank away. Go on. See if I care.

Excellent.

But nothing about longitude. We've all had enough of fucking longitude.

Debating the Discovery of the Longitude

The on-going debate concerning the Discovery of the Longitude has come to symbolise the pointlessness of all our many on-going pointless point-scoring games. The unspoken ground rules appear to include a necessary lack of any ultimate worth in the topic, and certain minimum and maximum levels of knowledge, so that we each have sufficient material for the game to begin, but none of us ever has enough to bring it to a conclusive end. And this has taken us through all kinds of subjects from sport (obviously), to worm reproduction, to forgotten pop classics of the late seventies, to possible interpretations of the line 'Stuck a feather in his hat and called it macaroni' in its historical context, to the likely effects of Eratosthenes' Error on early cartography and ultimately to the Discovery of the Longitude. This is one of the best because we all know nearly nothing about it, but we each claim to come at it from a valid perspective, Jeff with a Masters in maritime law, Tim with his history PhD, and me, courageously, with no more weaponry than a single quote from the *Notes to Gulliver's Travels* mentioning substantial sums offered by the British Government from 1714 for a means of measuring longitude at sea. And the rest of my position is determined by nothing more than fragments and lies and a loud unreasonable confidence. Despite this, my argument has evolved into something of quite extraordinary detail, and has the respect of all. Of course, when fully sober, none of us is totally sure of his position, and after a few drinks the course of events is dictated solely by a process of flagrant contradiction and one-upmanship. This is usually only brought to a close by Sal shouting, 'You're making it up. You're lying now. That's the lying face. If you don't stop now I'll have to hit Jeff in the balls'.

I drink quickly and the entrees are a while arriving. The others say I'm talking loudly and sounding tense and I tell them, for no known reason, Well of course I'm tense, wouldn't you be?

This only focuses the attention more clearly on me. Everyone seems to be talking at once and I can hear Jeff making remarks about my tension and its probable sexual nature, my hundred and eighty days of celibacy, the likelihood that I am an expert snake-handler by now, which he gleefully workshops into the concept of 'going the Ram Chandra'. I deny this, and he calls me Onan the Barbarian. He appears to be speaking from a list of Famous Masturbatorial Identities.

I take him up on this and we become quite competitive until we reach a point where I seem to decide that my best weapon is to turn the argument on me, and I find myself declaring quite loudly that I am impotent and that my penis is a plumb bob capable of pointing only to the centre of the earth.

And Sal, slightly more controlling than usual when she's drunk, is saying to Jeff, *Little sips, little sips*, and he's giving me a look that suggests I might now be called Bob for the rest of my days. I can see him saying it, *Bob*, and smiling as he's trying to drink, trying to negotiate his mouth to his wine glass as both her hands hold it down.

But things don't go too badly until I declare that I want to make a speech and I headbutt the woman arriving with our mains as I stand. She pirouettes and

76

loses nothing, and the others at the table applaud. I hear my voice shouting quite loudly that Jeffrey is the most handsome of my friends and then I hear myself saying that I need to do a wee now.

The others all start going, *Ssshh*, louder than I think they need to so I say, What do you mean Ssshh? It's only a wee.

They *Ssshh* even louder, I Ssshh back and soon everyone in the restaurant is going *Ssshh* and I'm shouting, You all do wees, don't ya?

Shortly after that things deteriorate.

I know I make several trips to the toilet in the next hour, because making trips to the toilet isn't easy. The number of chairs in the way is quite incredible, and crowds of people I don't know cheer every time I stand. Some of them I think, or perhaps I just fear, whisper, *You all do wees, don't ya?* as I go past.

On one of the trips, perhaps the last, the toilet door is shut. I can hear someone on the other side singing 'That's Amore'. The door opens and Tim lurches out, makes a very rough kind of eye contact, seems surprised that it's someone he knows, says, *Oh, hi. You know that thing? That thing when you've had a few drinks and you look in the mirror and you see Dean Martin? Yeah.* And he gives me a friendly pat on the shoulder, then he does the same to the wall and he makes his way back to the restaurant. I go into the toilet, and of course he's pissed on the floor.

When we leave, someone at the last remaining table shouts, *Make sure you look after Richard* to the others, and they undertake to do so.

I wait till their cab arrives, and then I set off on the climb up to Zigzag Street. This is a much more confusing task than I remember and I can't help thinking of *The Enigma of Kaspar Hauser*, not a film I can say I ever understood, but I have never felt more empathy with the wordless Kaspar than I do at this moment. Almost to the point of being sure I can hear Pachelbel's 'Canon' as my mountain sways in front of me.

I fall several times, mostly onto the pavement and only once into the gutter, but that begins as a fall onto the pavement and ends with a gentle roll to the right dictated by the contours, which in places require vigilance.

But I come to no harm, and in the morning I wake in my own bed.

19

I wake when Jeff phones at around ten and asks if I could go to Le Chalet and pick up the leftover wine. He tells me this is my job as I live nearest.

I tell him I can't believe there could be any leftover wine.

Yeah. We didn't drink much. Not really. We just drank too much champagne at your place. On empty stomachs.

Yeah. Good theory. Do you really think they'll be there now?

After what you did I expect they're still hosing out the toilet.

Now, wait a minute. That wasn't me. That was fucking Dean Martin. That was nothing to do with me.

I think it might have been.

Really?

I put on shorts and a T-shirt and impenetrable sun glasses and I drink about a litre of water, and I go outside. It's hot already and savagely bright. I am almost overwhelmed by an attack of seediness on my way down the hill, but I make it.

It's cool in Le Chalet, and incredibly dark. I stand holding the back of a chair and explaining my situation carefully to a woman who treats me with a cautious and unjustified kindness. She goes through the swing doors and returns with three bottles of wine. During her absence I have mentally constructed an apology, but it falls apart on its way out. One of the bottles of wine is mine, and I give it back to her with a great sense of gesture and I thank her for her very considerate attitude.

I walk outside, back into the hot day, back to the steep, bright, unsteady hill. It seems harder to walk with a bottle in each hand and my thigh muscles become quite tired. When I'm less than halfway home I'm feeling like Burke and Wills and I realise I'm not going to make it.

I get to a bus stop and sit down in the shade. I put the two bottles of wine next to me on the seat and I take some deep breaths. I really need to lie down. I also notice that my bladder is filling and this, of course, presents its own dilemma.

Just when I'm thinking through the consequences, and thinking that I was brought up not to regard highly people who sit in bus shelters with bottles of wine and urinate, Jeff and Sal pull up in their car.

We've just been to Le Chalet, Jeff says. *You didn't sound up to it on the phone.*

I'm not. I can't go any further. I think I'm going to die here. But that's okay.

They drive me home. By car, it takes about a minute. On the way Jeff says, *Hey, how's Bob?*

For perhaps a second I have no idea what he's talking about. And then it all comes back to me.

20

I make a resolution. It comes in three parts. I decide to adopt a low profile, to think before I act and to respond to the trashing in the acceptable, conventional way of throwing myself into my work.

I tell myself Work is good, Work is good.

I open the After Dark files on my computer and I change my screen saver. I trash the Can of Worms and I open the message option and I write Work is good. Then, for emphasis, I change it to Work is GOOD. Then I change tack entirely and end up with the much more cryptic Remember the Three Part Resolution.

While I go to make coffee this chugs across my screen. It occurs to me that if I went missing now the last people would know of me is the compellingly obscure Remember the Three Part Resolution. Who knows what three parts they'd come up with? Three parts that bring down a government. Three parts that sink a currency or a stock exchange, or begin a religion. Three grand acts of terrorism or altruism. And it occurs to me that a lot of the great conspiracy theories might actually have been nothing more than misunderstandings of personal reminder notes.

It should also occur to me that I'm flattering myself that, in the unlikely event of my disappearance, my screen saver will be given a moment's thought.

I decide to lunch alone. Tim has given me his copy

of Veny Armanno's book *Romeo of the Underworld* and I started reading it yesterday, the first of the low profile days. Like work, reading is good. That's what I've told myself. Work and reading. Two of the activities of healthy, normal people. Healthy, normal people whose grasp of consequences probably doesn't lead to them thinking that their screen saver might propel them onto the world stage.

I go to a different coffee shop. I eat a bagel and read. I always wanted to be cool enough to be one of those people who was comfortable sitting alone in a coffee shop and reading. I always thought they had a special allure.

Just as I'm in the process of dismissing allure and deciding 'loser with a book for company' is a better fit, a girl says, *Mind if I sit here?* and indicates the other side of the booth.

I tell her, Go ahead.

She is twentyish. She is a babe. I glance around. There are plenty of free seats. She chose to sit here. And I tell myself this could be the knock of opportunity, and that I should put a lid on my very disabling ambivalence for once. I should say nothing more, go back to the book, pump up the allure.

Her food arrives. I try to stop reading the same line over and over.

Is it a good book? she asks.

Yeah. (And then a judicious pause, the pause of a cool person, the pause of allure.) Yeah it's good. A friend of mine lent it to me. I play tennis sometimes with the guy who wrote it.

Really?

Yeah. He actually inscribed it with a personal remark. Want to see it?

Sure.

I show her the personal remark.

Wow, she says. *That's not the sort of thing you expect someone to write in a book.*

No.

82

I'm doing okay. I can tell I'm doing okay. I just have to stay cool.

So you work in town do you?

Yeah.

I'm sorry. I'm stopping you reading your book. You didn't come here to talk to me.

She smiles. It's a good smile. I'd go some distance not to read a book in the company of this smile, some distance to sit in a booth opposite her confident conversation, her neat, pert, near-perfect body, her hint of impeccable cleavage. I close the book. She smiles again.

So what do you do?

I'm a lawyer. I work for a financial institution. Which is why I'm sitting here reading a novel I guess.

I'm a student, she says. And before I can pick up the baton and ask the obvious question, What are you studying? she says, *Do you like movies?*

Sure.

Good. Cause I want to go and see Pulp Fiction, *but I've got no-one to go with*.

I can't believe this. This girl, this twentyish student babe, appears to be asking me out. And of course I'm going to lie and tell her I haven't seen *Pulp Fiction*.

Do you want to go? she asks.

Sure. Yeah.

I think about possible appropriate timing. I can't look too eager or too blase.

Maybe the weekend, I say, or some night next week.

The weekend might be better. My parents don't like me going out on week nights. Once school's started. She senses concern. *It's okay. I'm nearly seventeen.*

This, of course, is killing me. She is aware of my struggle, and trying to smile me some reassurance. Now the smile, the smile that had such appeal, merely makes her look younger.

I'm not sure it's really such a good idea. I'm not sure how your parents would feel. I'm, well, I'm well into my twenties.

That's fine.

I'm not sure that it's fine.

She's sixteen, and already some bastard's trashing her. And it's me.

Look, don't get me wrong. Don't think that, in a lot of ways, it isn't a great idea. Don't think this is easy. But, I really don't think we should do this.

You think I'm too young.

There's nothing wrong with being young.

You're not taking me seriously because I'm young.

No, that's not it. It's not that I'm not taking you seriously, okay? It's just that, well, my life has been a little confusing lately, and I've decided I should think things through more. Okay? And when I think this through, you, me, *Pulp Fiction*, a lot of it looks great. But then I think, you, me, *Pulp Fiction*, your parents, our very different levels of life experience . . .

Now you're talking down to me. You're treating me like a kid.

No I'm not. I'm not. Throughout this discussion it has not occurred to me to think of you as a kid. Trust me. Look, I think I'd better go. I think it would be better if I went.

You'll regret it.

Yeah, I expect I will. But I think I've got to go. Please, don't take this personally. Don't think it's any reflection on your desirability, okay. But I don't think it would be a good idea for either of us. I'm not in great state of mind at the moment.

She smiles, and continues to smile when I get up. As though she's won some moral victory over me, as though it's not her preferred outcome, but she's ahead on points. And even though I am surely the moral victor in all this, all I feel as I walk out of the coffee shop is some heavy kind of defeat. How can she smile? How can she end such a mutually unsatisfactory exchange by smiling? Perhaps she is still a survivor, an optimist, having not yet endured her twenties. And a significant part of her teenage years. I'm not finding this easy.

I cross the street and keep walking. I am appalled that this involves a struggle against the urge to go back. I tell myself that this must only be because someone was nice to me, made me feel, for a moment, desirable. I tell myself any compulsion to return has nothing to do with the fact that she was a babe, with flagrant disregard for the sixteen problem. I tell myself, you don't do this, you just don't do this, you don't keep thinking of these things, these pert cleavage things, as though they might happen, as though you might go back. And while I'm busy telling myself all of this and reinforcing my weak moral position, I realise that in my haste to leave the coffee shop, my keys must have dropped out of my pocket.

So now I have to go back.

Just for the keys. Just the keys.

This will present its own problems. She will see me approaching, she will think I've changed my mind. And I'll have to be even clearer than before, and this is quite unfair to her. It would be cruel, and I am, after all, endeavouring to diminish my capacity for cruelty. It occurs to me that I should think about the possibility of arranging to see her, maybe once or twice more, just so I get the chance to be clear on all this. Just so she knows it's not her, so it doesn't have any impact on her self-esteem. And then I think, what about her parents? How would they feel about that line of logic? I'm sorry, I had to have sex with your daughter. After I dropped my keys it would have been unfair not to.

I go back to the coffee shop, saying to myself, just the keys, just the keys.

And she's gone. Now I have no dilemma. I look and I see just the keys, but somehow this is not the same concept as a moment ago. It's gone from, Be strong, choose just the keys, to, You have no choice, just the keys. This is morally easy but nowhere near as good. I look out the window to see if she is nearby, and it doesn't matter that I'm telling myself I shouldn't be looking. She isn't there.

I pick up the keys.

I notice a pair of sunglasses on her seat.

The dilemma resumes.

My decision is that I don't actually have to go back to work yet. That, providing there are no interruptions, I can quite reasonably expect to finish the chapter before I go back. I sit down. I look at the page. I read not a word.

Hey, excellent, my sunnies, someone says.

I look up as an incredibly unattractive woman leans her way into the booth. She notices me looking at her.

I left them here an hour ago. I was sure they'd've gone.

I smile through the pain.

Hey, is that a good book?

Yeah, it's fine.

And there's no way she's going to get to see the personal remark. Before she can ask about *Pulp Fiction*, I look at my watch, feign concern (and I care not that this ploy is offensively obvious), say something about being lost in the book and late back to work and I run out.

I run about a block and a half, and I'm not certain why.

Back in the office, after the last snuffing out of this glimmer of unkind hope, I phone Veny Armanno. I tell him what just happened, trying to focus on the babe part, and he says, *It happens to me all the time, sixteen year olds coming up to me while I'm reading and asking me out.*

Really?

Yeah, sure, all the time.

21

The next day I play it safe. I'm too fragile for this.

I only leave the office for lunch when I've arranged to meet Jeff and we can sit back in the usual place at the big window, with most nearby young females safely on the other side of the glass.

I made a decision to adopt a low profile, I tell him, but it didn't go well. A sixteen-year-old babe won onto me.

That's a tough one.

I tell him the story and he says it's very fine and that it probably could only happen to me.

I tell him this bothers me. This notion that crap is my domain. That this is the sort of story that seems to be mine alone. That crap seems to follow me and I can't shake it. That I don't know what to do with my life, in any of its aspects. I don't know if I should be in a relationship or not, and if I should be I don't know what to do about it. I don't know about my job. I don't think I'm very good at it. I used to put a lot of thought into things and now I'm just a straight shooter.

And my hand goes the finger pistol without meaning it to.

I think I need a new job, I tell him. A good job, a job where I do some good. I want to travel the world and have an important job where good things happen.

There are jobs like that? You want to be the next Boutros Boutros-Ghali or something?

Yeah. Richard Richard-Derrington. Yeah. I want to fly in the big plane. I want to talk to the big people. I want a big job. And not with some joke outfit like the UN.

I don't know that there are a lot of those jobs.

I only want one. Just one. And I'd be very good at it. Just watch me. Instead of now, when I'm just good at crap.

Don't be so hard on yourself. There's nothing wrong with being good at crap. And you are very good at crap.

Thank you.

Crap is your best thing.

I have known crap and I am its master.

The master of crap. The Krapmeister.

It's a special gift.

A very attractive gift, and you shouldn't sell it short. People find you very interesting, solely on account of it. Before you discovered crap, you were practically a nobody. You would have had what, a couple of friends, outside your family?

Just a couple.

And now?

Hundreds of friends. Seven hundred at last estimate. I'm very interesting. Very interesting. I'm a very interesting man.

And people talk about you. People take an incredible interest in your glorious failures.

Krapmeister fame.

And you want the big job, the big plane.

That merely shows my insecurity about my shortcomings, I realise that now. All I think I should have now is a small job, a small soft plane that hangs limply and points to the centre of the earth.

Actually, I think there's a way of combining this. Of taking all of your complex ambitions and diverse talents and rolling them into one great high-profile Krapmeister job.

Yeah?

Celebrity partner. It's right up there. World fame, pure fame, fame only for its own sake. A kind of fame as devoid of any association with merit as possible. You could be the next Liz Hurley.

Yeah. Yeah. So I call myself an actor, and I become famous, quite impressively famous, for dating someone famous.

Then people forget why you're famous, and suddenly you're famous in your own right.

Yeah. Yeah. All I've got to do is find the right star. I could be that kind of actor, if I found the right star.

Yeah. So we should make a list, make a plan.

Kylie's available at the moment.

Yeah, and I think she's a lot smarter than they give her credit for.

Really?

Who knows, but if you're going to be dating her soon I'm not going to say anything bad about her, am I? You know me. Even when she trashes you I'm not going to run her into the ground.

You know what would be great?

What?

If I could date Liz Hurley. Now that would be great. If I became famous for dating someone who had become famous for dating someone famous. That would be the ultimate Krapmeister triumph.

Or alternatively, you could make a move on someone who's famous on account of a celebrity relationship that's just ended.

Yeah.

So who have we got?

Helena Christensen? She and Michael are off on account of the Paula Yates thing.

But she's got her own thing going, hasn't she, the supermodel thing? She's not just a celebrity partner.

Yeah, I guess. But being a supermodel is very close to

being famous for nothing. I mean, single supermodels are basically just celebrity partners having some down time.

Okay, so don't strike her off the list or anything, but it does lack purity. She's no Liz Hurley.

Shoshanna Lonstein and Seinfeld are off.

Yeah, yeah. And he's obviously thinking about this one very seriously. *The fabulously-breasted Shoshanna Lonstein trashes the King of Comedy for the King of Crap.*

Hey, she had no choice. It was fame at first sight.

This is good. This could be the one.

I could get my own show. Maybe a talk show. But with credibility. Long ponderous interviews with only personal friends, and always about nothing.

It's good. It's good. But it'd probably be on cable, at least at the start. Until it became recognised as the Seinfeld of talk shows and blew away Oprah and Phil and the rest of them. It's great. They're all talking about transvestites and you've got a panel discussing the importance, or otherwise, of ironing the whole shirt.

This is what I'd been lacking, some sense of career path. I was beginning to stagnate, I think. I realise that now. Suddenly, a future opens up before me. With crap there is hope.

22

But later, when I'm away from the hype, this position starts to look risky. It's possible that the assessment was a little too optimistic, and that crap should not be seen as being quite so versatile.

I determine that I should follow a policy of being more practically oriented. I should take Jeff's other advice of setting small goals and achieving them, and appreciating the validity of limited fulfilment.

I will turn the unwelcoming shapelessness of work into a list of small and accomplishable tasks, and I shall deal with them one at a time. I shall then do the same with my personal life, my diet, the renovations and my living arrangements.

My living arrangements. I am not suited to living alone. I don't need a list to work that out. I think I've already worked it out. I should think seriously about clearing out at least one of the other rooms and renting it to someone. Or I should just live somewhere else, with people. With due consideration a plan emerges. Quite a good plan.

On Thursday I meet Jeff again for coffee.

I know what I need to do, I tell him. I shouldn't live alone.

Good. Probably true.

I should share a house with nineteen-year-old

students. Probably quite a large house and probably three of them.

Nineteen-year-old students?

Yeah.

I'm not sure that nineteen's wise.

It was fine when it was the fabulously-breasted Shoshanna Lonstein.

Yeah, but that's a celebrity thing. It's a specific exemption. Besides, that's more a career move than a relationship.

And this is just a residential arrangement.

Nineteen-year-old students. Three of them.

Yeah.

Yeah, and all of them babes? Correct me if I'm wrong, but is that the plan?

You've got a problem with babes?

Three of them? What are you after? Biodiversity? Three babes and your only dilemma being which one of them to jump at any given time? Maybe the four of you sleeping in one big bed?

Maybe. Maybe, yeah.

This doesn't worry you?

What?

This doesn't suggest any kind of judgement problem to you? You think this is fine?

I think it's very fine.

Okay, three nineteen-year-old students, Friday night, you're in your room, their rugger-bugger boyfriends are all round, the house is filled with the moans of passion and none of them yours? Three bed-heads are rhythmically thumping against walls while yours is marked by the gnashing of lonely teeth? Still fine?

I think about this for a while, and it is a danger. I'm still a bit too fragile for that kind of risk.

Well, twenty-two year-old students then, I suggest to him.

I'm not totally sure that that's the solution. I could be wrong, but I think you might be missing the point. I think

*you're trying to revisit something here. A moment that has
probably passed. I think you're romanticising the notion
of shared student houses.*

But they're great.

*But people can still find themselves being miserable in
them. I think you could be one of those people.*

No.

*I think the moment has passed. I also think you don't
need to pretend that it hasn't. You don't have to explain
your life by trying to convince yourself that you're really
nineteen, or twenty, or twenty-two, or whatever, so it's
okay that you're not in a relationship. I think at the heart
of this notion is some fantasy about recapturing lost youth,
as though this time you could be really good at it.*

I could be much better at being twenty now. Think
about it.

*No, I don't have to. You can't be twenty. And you
don't even really want to be. You're just saying to yourself,
It's all right that I just got trashed cause I'm only twenty
and I can move on. I'm only twenty and relationships
come and go when you're twenty. You're trying to tell
yourself you haven't lost much and you've got some kind
of freedom back in return. And if I believed all that I'd
be happy for you. But I don't think you believe it. I don't
think it would make you happy.*

Yeah, but it wouldn't be bad. Think of it. Students.
Students like we see when we're out playing tennis at
uni.

*Yeah, but you reach a point when you come to terms
with the fact that you won't be bouncing on every babe
you see. That it's just not a game you're in any more.
And it's not a bad thing. The real problem, the way you're
looking at it, is that the students will keep coming through.
Each year a new batch of seventeen year olds, and each
year you're a year older. Okay? Remember that time,
when you were twenty-two, and you had that thing happening with that school captain?*

Yeah.

Okay. Since you were twenty-two it was fairly contro-
versial. Right? Even now, there are people who do not
regard you highly because of it.

They envy me. Some people never score a school
captain.

Whatever. If you managed it again, with the present
captain of the same school . . .

Is she a babe?

Get the babe thing out of your head. If you managed
it now, with the present captain of the same school, you
being twenty-eight, it would be looked on quite badly.
People would not have much respect for you at all. If you
did it in ten years time, which, it occurs to me, is
something you might quite like to do, people would be
completely appalled.

Yeah, just imagine it.

Appalled. They would be appalled.

But if you were single now . . .

If I was single now I'd be looking for the same things
you are. When I was ready again. And those things, when
you really think about it, might not involve cutting a
swathe through the office holders of GPS schools.

She was very mature. She was the captain after all.
She was much more mature than me.

Yeah. And she made the first move, Your Honour.

She did.

So he's not keen on my plan. I can sense that. And
he did work out some aspects of it that I might not have
fully considered. Even though he focussed on seventeen
year olds rather than nineteen year olds, and that's not
an error to dismiss lightly.

Later I recall a guy at uni, a guy who hasn't crossed
my mind for years, who epitomises Jeff's argument
because we all thought he was such a loser.

The day they make me play Sir Toby Belch
He was mid-thirties, in no hurry with his biochem PhD, and
he loved uni. Even though the students he tutored had, as

94

far as we knew, never gone to bed with him. So, failing to score in the biochem department, failing even with the drunk girls at the Rec Club, failing to win the love of all but his own two hands, he joined the drama society. And he worked bloody hard on sets and on committees, so that by the time I got there he was actually appearing in the plays, because they owed it to him. We did *Twelfth Night* and he was Sir Toby Belch. Not Sir Toby Belch because he was one of the great character actors of our time. Not Sir Toby Belch because of his magical gift for comedy. Sir Toby Belch because he was old and fat. And his comedy was ham-fisted and clumsy and forgetful, and he took to his lines with all the grace of a man holding them down and taking punches at them through a pillow. And the cast party was at his place, a place he lived in alone and that looked just like the student hovels we lived in. It's all very sad now. As though he lived in this crap place, well past his time, just to impress us. Grew two small marijuana plants to impress us. Stubbed cigarettes into his landlord's carpet to impress us. And I'm sure if we'd said, 'Hey Trev, why don't you drop a turd on your sofa', he would have done that to impress us too. And of course, he stayed in costume for the whole party, putting on that jolly, rolling laugh as we trashed his house and then went home. And the whole time he looked like the happiest man alive, cause he was still one of the kids. Problem was, he wasn't. And I'm not one of the great character actors of our time, and my gift for comedy is limited. And perhaps one day, in my desire to grasp a moment that may be long gone, they might put on *Twelfth Night* and tell me I'm the one for Toby Belch.

Sal calls and says I'm always welcome at their place, says I can have their spare room whenever I want.

23

On the way up to our Friday meeting with Barry Greatorex, Hillary tells me he's still not smoking, but that he has a bowl of chocolate-coated coffee beans on his desk instead.

And it's not working out well.

She's right. He doesn't look good. He looks very large now, seriously larger than the already excessive largeness of ten days ago, his beady, sleepless eyes set further back in his head, sweat glistening among the grey flaps of his jowls and creeping into broad circles under his arms, despite the air-conditioning. His buttons are straining and a couple are missing, or at least undone, and he is losing his trousers beneath the broad mass of his abdomen, which sits across his thighs like a Stable-table, kept in place by a pair of thick red braces that end somewhere beyond view, as though two mountaineers have just abseiled down his front. He is clearly biology gone wrong, a system without the usual checks and balances, a victim of his own rebellious chemistry.

So, he says, craning up the big sweaty flaps of eyelids, *so*, rocking back at a perilous angle in his chair then cannoning forward again, as threatening as a medieval battering ram. *Fill me in.*

Well, I tell him, feeling really sane, I'm trying to keep everyone involved at all stages, trying to make everyone part of the process, so it's not quite as quick as I'd like it to be. But it's under control and they're with us so far.

Timeframe? he asks, opening his hands into a chubby kind of question.

End of next week probably, before I hear back from everybody and have some kind of response together.

So we think we might go to Sydney the week after, Hillary says. *The timing's not a problem and it gives Rick a chance to shore things up a bit.*

He nods and then looks as though he is distracted by something out the window. He stares at the sky for a while then jerks his attention back to us and nods again. *Hmmm,* he says, and goes through a series of apparently purposeless facial movements. He scoops up a handful of chocolate-coated coffee beans and tips them into his mouth. *Fine, fine,* he says as he crunches, showing us a snarl of brown-stained teeth, and it appears we are free to go.

It's hard to be sure if he trusts our work, or if he's adopting a more hands-off management style, or if he's just losing it.

Good meeting, Hillary says when we're in the lift. *I thought he was a goner when he leaned back in the chair. I thought, if Barry hits the floor he's a dead man. We'll never move him.*

She comes with me into my office.

So, end of next week then.

Yeah.

I've got to organise Sydney, okay?

Yeah. It will be ready. I'm sorry it's taken as long as it has, but I think it's there now. I've done the work, I've liaised appropriately and now it's out there and I've just got to get everyone's views and do whatever I need to to take them into account.

I hate letting her down. This should have been done by now, I know that. And this is the closest she'll get to telling me. Saying the deadline with just a hint of doubt.

I go to Jeff and Sal's for dinner, and as soon as Sal opens the door I smell curry.

It's chicken tikka masala, she tells me. *It's been a big month for chicken* tikka masala.

I had a shopping problem, Jeff says from the kitchen.

As you can see he's slightly defensive about it, as men with his neglected planning skills are prone to be. We have seven cans of tikka masala *sauce and, I have just discovered, no toilet paper.*

I'm really not appreciated, he tells me. *I make the dinner, I make the lunches, I tidy up after breakfast . . .*

Yeah, yeah, we all know. Tidying up after breakfast, the most underrated domestic task.

And your only job is the cleaning and you hire someone. One small misjudgement with the shopping and this is the thanks I get.

Seven cans of tikka masala *sauce and no toilet paper? What is the appropriate way to thank someone for that?*

She turns to me but just at that moment I'm not doing well. And it's not because I've just realised I regularly seek detailed advice from a man who is set up to make a curry for twenty-eight people, but hasn't the foresight to provide toilet facilities. I don't have any theories about appropriate thanks just now. I think seven cans of *tikka masala* sauce and no toilet paper would be just fine. I want to tell them that. I want to say, Sal, don't worry, toilet paper's easy. You can always buy toilet paper. But I can't say a thing. I try to breathe deeply.

We eat the chicken *tikka masala*. We drink wine. I talk and they listen. I spill my guts and it takes who knows how long. I drink more.

Sal says, *You get through these things. They happen and you get through them. And you never know when it's all going to change. When, suddenly, things are different. I didn't think I was ready for anything when Jeff came along. I hadn't gone out with anyone for months. I'd missed exams because of glandular fever. I hadn't worked either, so I had no money. Things could have been better.*

98

And then it all changed. Suddenly, from this diet of potatoes and bread and cheese, there was this boy turning up, with wine. And you know what? I liked him.

It gets late. I stay the night in their spare room.

24

The amount of junk mail astounds me when I get home in the morning. How many pizza deals can one household use? How can junk mail work when there's just so much of it? I'm about to drop the whole pile in the bin when I notice an A-mart Allsports ad.

And I go and pick up a tennis racquet for a *Sensational!!! $100 dollars off.* Maybe I think it'll change my luck. Or maybe this is just emblematic of the change in me. From cautious contemplator to reckless impulse buyer, junk mail sucker, speeding through orange lights with my eighty bucks in my pocket and the flier on the passenger seat.

In the store I weigh the racquet in my hands and it feels very special.

Hey, sensational, I say to the guy.

You obviously know your racquets.

Yeah. What sort of poundage would this be?

Yeah. Yeah, that's the question isn't it? Yeah. You're right you know. With the hi-modulus graphite allowing you to have those non-linear offset strings, you drop five to ten pounds, you get yourself a bigger sweet spot and you lose nothing. So where would that leave you? I'd take you for about a sixty-five to seventy pound man myself.

Yeah. Yeah, about that.

And all this time I'm swishing to impress. I'm on the brink of telling him something about my experiences on the fringe of The Tour, about how I might've made it if my shoulder hadn't given out. Then I realise that's Jeff's bullshit story, not mine, and I'm not sure if there's an intellectual property issue at stake.

I'm swishing backhand after backhand and taking a few slow-motion serves (but still dragging the toe). This racquet is great. This is probably the closest I've been to an erection in months. I want to tell the guy, because my first erection after all this time is going to be quite a moment, but I don't think he'd understand.

At home I toss the cover onto the table and the urge to practise (while in my mind revisiting the great Wimbledon men's singles finals of the early eighties) is irresistible.

So around the house I go. Swish, swish. Swish, swish. And it's particularly fine for backhand volleys. Greg runs past and out, I'm sure thinking, *Who is this dickhead? First the Whipper Snipper, now this. Did no-one tell him about Outside?*

Invigorated by the purchase of the racquet, but thwarted by the lack of opportunity to use it, I decide I should do something. I decide to renovate.

But feeling none too inclined to renovate, I bargain it down to tidy before the decision is binding.

I go into one of the bedrooms but there are far too many boxes.

Before I'm put off entirely I grab a box and take it into the lounge room. Here it is the only box, so it looks manageable.

It's only when I open it that I realise it's one of my grandmother's and not one of mine. On top is one of her treasured possessions, her Scrabble set. Scrabble saw my grandmother at her least compromising. She thought little of losing at Canasta, so if any of her grandchildren were unhappy and needing something grandmotherly she'd usually get the cards out and allow them a thrilling, narrow victory. Scrabble was a different matter. If your cat got run over she'd still shit on you at Scrabble. It was one of those things. She had to. If you were convalescing from the flu and your cat got run over after eating your goldfish and you'd just done badly in something at school and it was someone's birthday and they'd invited everyone but you (or realistically maybe you and Ricky bow tie Balaszwecki), if you were smart you'd say, Do you want to play Canasta, Nan? And soon you'd be feeling slightly better than you were before. If you were stupid you'd say, Want to play Scrabble, Nan? and she'd get that reluctant pained expression on her face, because she knew she'd still have to shit on you. And how was she going to explain that to your mother? The art of being a grandparent is to judge the most important times to engineer a credible loss.

If there were ever any doubts about my grandmother's win-at-all-costs attitude to Scrabble these were dispelled three years ago, when she was eighty-eight. My mother, sensing her first real opportunity since she'd won a narrow victory when my grandmother was distracted by severe gout in 1965, challenged her during a brief hospital admission to stabilise her heart failure. The game, as my mother tells it, had reached some kind of impasse, not seen for almost thirty years, and my grandmother fidgeted and gnashed her edentulous gums before breaking the deadlock by sliding the letters CUN in front of a T and glaring fearsomely at my mother and saying, *Well, it's a word isn't it?*

Beneath the Scrabble set is something I have never seen before. It looks like an old cigarette case, and I'm not sure what it's doing there as neither of my grandparents smoked. It contains a letter, with the envelope postmarked Winton, 21.II.23.

The letter
My Dear Edna,

I know it's been an age since I wrote (last winter I expect), and don't think I'm proud of that. Please don't think for a moment that I haven't been thinking about you. I have. It's just taken me a while to work things out. I won't beat around the bush: I'm coming home. I'm coming home and I know now, more than I ever have, that it won't be home for me unless you're there too, and that's for sure.

This summer hasn't been easy. It's stinking hot and the rains just haven't come. I left the land they gave me and I've kept the sheep moving, but there aren't many left. While I've still got a few I'm going to sell them to someone up here and make my way back to Brisbane.

I want you to know, though, that the drought hasn't affected my thinking. I really do believe that if the land was green and five thousand sheep were mine, I'd still be selling up. I'd just be coming back to you a richer man.

So what am I offering? It's not much. I've only got a few pounds, but I'll work hard all my life. That's my promise. I'll be there, richer or poorer, better or worse. I can make that promise now. I only hope you can accept it. I only hope you're still some fool who's waiting for me and who hasn't done the smart thing and gone and found herself a man. If you have I'll understand.

I haven't been good to you, and you've been very good to me. When you told me to go if I needed to go, and to come back when I was ready, and that you'd be waiting, I knew you were the girl for me.

I'm better now than I was. I'm not perfect, but I'm better. There are still some nights when my eyes sting and I don't breathe too well and I have to tell myself there's none of that stuff out this way. There were still nights last winter when it was cold and I slept with a heavy blanket over my legs and I'm sure I dreamt of wading through the mud at the Somme all night. There are some things, some screams of dying men and some other things, that I'm sure I'll never get out of my head, but I think you know that. I just had to know I could make room for other things, and now I know I can.

I've spent the last few years running and I'm not certain

what I'm running from, but it hasn't caught me yet. Edna, I really want to stop running now.

For the last few weeks I've sat and I've looked up at the stars and I've thought about us. I've thought about us, in Brisbane, buying some land, building ourselves a house, having a family. I can see us all, packing like sardines into a white wooden cottage with a red roof and the garden full of flowers of all colours. I think about this and I want it very much.

I hope you do too.

Please write to me soon, one way or the other. I'll be staying in this area till I sell up, so the Winton PO is as good an address as any.

Truly yours,

Tom

Later that year, the money had come from somewhere to buy a block of land at 34 Zigzag Street, Red Hill. And thirteen years later my mother was born, an only child.

25

This is all new to me, this letter in my grandfather's hand, written when he was maybe six years younger than I am now. I look for others, but it's the only one in the cigarette case, and the only one in the box.

This is like finding one piece of a 3,000-piece jigsaw puzzle and knowing you're a few months too late to find the other 2999. Is the cigarette case part of the same puzzle? It's tempting to say that they mean something together. That maybe Tom came back from France in 1917 and brought the cigarette case, and Edna had it with her while he was away in the north-west. But I'm not entitled to such assumptions.

I knew he'd fought in World War One. He died a while ago, when I was ten, and I can always remember him coughing, particularly early in the mornings, as if he started every day by clearing his lungs. He was tall and stooped and gentle and he had big hands and spoke quietly. He had a pen knife and when he peeled apples with it the peel fell off in one long green ribbon. That much I know.

And my grandmother said once, *You know, until your mother came along we always thought it was just going to be the two of us.*

Maybe these are more pieces, but of course they don't fit. There are too many pieces still missing to think these might sit even close to each other in the finished picture.

Tom sold insurance, I think. Before my mother was born and when she was young he travelled the state selling insurance, and by the time he retired he was state manager. But in 1923 he had nothing to do with insurance. He was a young man wandering with his dying sheep and a head full of war, even though the war had been over for years.

His family came from the Darling Downs where they owned property. He was tall from an early age, and with the body of a farm boy probably, so he enlisted in 1916 when he was fifteen years old. He went to France soon after and was back here the following year. So what I knew was that he had missed Gallipoli and the end of the war, and I always thought of him as just having been away for a while in between. It only occurs to me now that he was at the Somme, that that's what he did in the war.

I wish I'd asked him. I wish he'd told me more. I wish I could know more than this one letter. This is years later, and he's still not even twenty-two. A white house with a red roof and a family. He had done his wandering. He had sat under the stars and worked through what he had to, and now he was ready. And Edna had waited. Had waited in Brisbane, surviving on the occasional letter.

I always looked on them as grandparents. As though they were born grey-haired, met each other grey-haired, as though we came to exist at the same moment, and while I grew up they grew old. It never occurred to me that they were young, or if it did my view of their youth and everything that followed was quite uncomplicated. They knew each other on the Downs. He went away to France. He came back. My mother was born. He worked in insurance. I have telescoped this, without thinking how they might have filled the in-between years.

He went away to France (1916).

He came back (1917).

My mother was born (1936).

With nearly twenty years in there that I didn't seem to use in reaching my understanding of them, as though anyone can go from mid-teens to mid-thirties without incident. As though this whole time was some kind of pause where nothing happened but the house and the selling of insurance. But it was far less simple. It wasn't easy for him, at least not at the start. And why no children? Why no children for years, when it looks like they both wanted them?

We always thought it was just going to be the two of us.

So was my mother an accident, or an unexpected gift? I wonder if she knows.

Jeff calls. Tennis is on for tomorrow.

26

I should talk to my mother about this, the letter, the cigarette case, my questions. But I don't. For the moment it's all just mine.

Sunday morning is busy with phone calls, all to do with tennis. This is the Sunday morning we all dread, when the numbers are wrong, and it happens every second or third week. This is best explained by one of the less acknowledged laws of nature.

The Rule of Three and Five
Tennis is a game to be played by an even number of people, but for which only an odd number of people will ever be available, usually three people or five. (The Rule of One only applies to complete losers.)

Today it's the Rule of Three. We have Jeff, Veny and me. Freddie and Gerry are in Sydney for the weekend for some gathering of romance writers and Tim, a large-familied man, has one of his frequent Sunday barbecues. After a series of unsuccessful phone calls to a mixture of workmates, squash players, confirmed cheats and people we don't really like, we're getting desperate and Veny says he could try his friend Jordan.

He's pretty hopeless but at least there'll be four of us. It's better than cut-throat, maybe.

Maybe. Jordan, like me, is in the state of imposed

freedom that occurs between relationships. The only time he played with us before, Veny agreed to pick him up and found him lying face down on his polished wooden floor, having a bit of a rest after reading Graham Greene's *The End of the Affair*. And he played like someone face down on a polished wooden floor, as though nothing existed beyond his own nose. But just before Veny makes the call, Tim phones Jeff and says his family barbecue's been cancelled.

I arrive early and stand near the tennis centre window, swishing my new racquet but trying to do so unobtrusively.

Alone on the concrete in this ball-free sport of the mind, I am champion and the racquet is the racquet of the gods.

On court, I am not even the champion's bodily wastes. The racquet of the gods hits the ball fearsomely hard, and almost anywhere. Jeff tells me it shows about as much judgement as my previous racquet. People almost fight to be on my side only because it's less dangerous (as long as my serve doesn't take them in the back of the head). After Tim and Veny win two quick sets we all agree it would only be fair to Jeff if we rotated partners.

In the end I go home about as vanquished as is presently usual.

27

I don't feel like dinner. Or really, I don't feel like the hassle of making dinner. It even seems like too much trouble tonight to go down to Baan Thai or to order a pizza. So I prepare myself a straightforward two-course meal. Barbecue chips and flavoured mineral water, followed by Tim Tams and coffee.

I read through the letter again, but they know each other too well for him to need to say much. It won't tell an outsider any more than it has.

At nearly twenty-two he's been through a lot, and he's getting over it. Not getting it completely out of his head, but managing well enough to be ready to commit himself to moving on. This young man, coughing but not yet stooping, wandering the west with his crowded head. And some days make sense to him, some don't. People are kind to him mostly, let his sheep stay alive by giving them a day or two on their dead grass, probably out of some sense of debt. This soldier settler whose land turned dry, who shouldn't be abandoned now.

So how did he get over all this? How did he clear his head? Did he work through it till it made sense to him? Did it just fade slowly further away, allowing him to notice there were other things around? There is no sure sign of the answer here, just a man deciding he must move on. Deciding there is more to him than just the past.

I look for more letters, more of anything. And if my mother came over now she would see me sorting through boxes and she would be happy with me. I don't want to tell her this yet. I don't want to talk to her. She wants to change this place.

I find no letters, just a few things from my own past, when I was twenty and twenty-one.

The Dogs play Wembley Stadium—June 1,2,3, 1987

I still have the poster, the A3, black and white photocopy of a crap photomontage of four boys looking like they're trying really hard to be Velvet Underground. But The Dogs played nowhere. The Dogs were a fantasy that long preceded tennis. They were one of those university bands made up of intense, middle-class young people who got together to thrash instruments under each other's houses. And like the others, The Dogs never got a gig, cause they never played covers. So no-one could say The Dogs sold out. And no-one could say they played Wembley Stadium either. We played nowhere. We told ourselves it was because we never played covers, but it's possible, indeed likely, that we managed to combine this reluctance with an incredible lack of talent. I was on one of the guitars, though I had no gift for it at all. The only thing that held the band together through its three months of hope was the bass player who was a graphic artist and did the poster that made us think we had credibility; that if we stuck with it then, well just maybe, Wembley was ours. I think we also believed that since one of us had something to do with the visual arts we were a bit like the Beatles, at least in our early history, if not in our music. It's probably good it didn't work out for The Dogs. I expect I was destined to be their Pete Best, or, worse still, their Stu Sutcliffe. No, I would have been Pete Best. I wouldn't die young and beautiful of a brain haemorrhage. I'd be dumped cause I was too dumb to notice that haircuts were changing, that I just wasn't part of The Dogs any more. I don't know who played Wembley on June 1,2,3, 1987. It wasn't The Dogs.

Nor was it my subsequent band, The Darrells. Nor the band after that, The Big Pants (planned album title: *Wearing the Big Pants*), though we did play some girl's twenty-first, each with several pairs of football socks down our trousers. We had to stop playing when her father said that if we didn't leave he might have to call the police.

This is not, in any sense, archeological, genealogical or otherwise, a big find. Nor is the video *The Importance of Fruit in Art*, a protracted extemporised exploration of almost nothing, involving a banana, a mandarin, an old brown turtleneck jumper and a beret. Or its sequel (and companion in the archive), *Bedroom Bondage*, a re-make of a Bond movie, almost any Bond movie, shot entirely in one person's bedroom, using only everyday bedroom items as props. In the end, Blofeld is fatally wounded by a Walther PK thong.

I think the theory behind all this is that the more you restrict the range of props, the smarter you have to be to pull it off. And I think we thought we did pull it off. But these are clearly the documents of a far less critical age, and we all look young and hopeful and uncluttered by any sophistication. Each time I watch these videos I feel stranger than the last. Back then it all seemed very satirical.

So I think of my grandfather, the poor, wandering, war-shattered bastard with his starving sheep and I wonder, if he was in his twenties now, would his life still be documented with simple poignant letters, or would he leave a disturbing legacy of video-crap? I can't answer that, of course. Video has now been invented, he isn't here, and none of us fought at the Somme. And it's quite possible that he might have picked up the banana and the beret and talked importantly about fruit. Or played guitar badly in some appalling non-band that didn't quite get to Wembley, but at least they've got the poster to prove it.

Who knows what awful ideas he might have had in the age of irony, how he might have run amok with his risky notions of comedy? How he might have suffered the stresses of purposelessness and trashing, rather than those associated with being face down in mud for a year while a million people die nearby and wondering if you're next.

These are different worlds, and he was always a generous man. He would not compare our experiences. This is what I hope now as I live in his house.

And besides, if Edna had trashed him back in '23, I don't think it would have been easy.

28

On Wednesday evening the *Westside Chronicle* calls.

Kevin Butt has nominated me for their Neighbour of the Month Award.

I'm no sure thing, but this month's Neighbour will be decided on Monday and I'm a definite contender. The journalist asks for a work phone number so I can be contacted to organise a story, if necessary.

And who said living in the late twentieth century was easy?

Thursday it rains. I take the car to work.

I almost tell Hillary about the letter. I want to tell someone, but I also want to keep it to myself. Instead I tell her what she wants to hear. Things are okay for our Sydney meeting next week. And she says this'll be her first night away from Daniel and she even misses him sometimes when she's at work.

So if there are any times when I don't seem the best you have to make allowances. Of course, I'd miss work if I wasn't here, so I can't win really. It is the impossible balancing act people say it is, but what do you do? At least he's onto formula now.

She then moves into a discussion of her early feeding problems, her use of a breast pump. *And, you know, I'd be bringing it into work and milking myself like some bloody cow if it hadn't dried up. How would that be if two or three times a day my door was shut for half an*

*hour while I milked myself and then I ran out to the fridge
with a bottle? Imagine if people started putting it in their
coffee.*

Does it taste the same?

And it seems to be this basic, practical question that
brings us down. That makes us both realise that we're
standing here talking about Hillary's breasts and a pump.
And we've never talked about her breasts before, let
alone milking them, and I think, although it's just biology,
we both fear we have crossed a line.

No, she says. *It doesn't really. But maybe that's just
because I don't have the diet of a cow. I'll get Deb to
sort out our flights. We'll go first thing Tuesday morning.
Okay?*

Yeah.

When I'm back in my room I think of Hillary and
her baby and how good they've looked when I've seen
them together. And I think of Hillary and the breast
pump and I try not to.

She was nauseated most of the pregnancy but she
became quite calm about it. This was fine if you knew
her and you were prepared for vomiting at any moment,
but I think she forgot that other people might not be.
She would regularly interrupt our conversations in her
office with a polite, *Excuse me,* and a lift of the eyebrows
before sticking her head in her bin and bringing up lunch.
At first I found this really stressful and I didn't know
what to do, but after a while we both relaxed. Hillary
learned that if she was talking it was okay to regard such
incidents merely as punctuation, and I worked out that
if I was mid-sentence she expected me to pause for no
longer than the vomiting noise, which echoes loudly in
a bin, and then resume.

We were only reminded that this might not be conventional when the two of us were at a whiteboard giving
a presentation and she did the eyebrow thing. We both
instinctively looked for a bin, but there wasn't one, so
she said her polite, *Excuse me,* and threw up in a large

pot plant. She dabbed her mouth with a tissue, held up her hand to make everyone quiet, and went on with the sentence . . . *and really it gets back to whether this should be thought of as legitimate hedging, or speculation.* And the crowd of men in dark suits, I'm sure, had lost all awareness of the dilemma she was posing as they stared in some kind of fear at this small woman with a giant cue ball under her white dress and the neat glistening pool of vomit in the tan bark.

I must admit I thought it was great. It was one of the most powerful things I've ever seen, and she didn't even know it. And afterwards she said to me, *They had no questions. They sat there like a bunch of fucking stunned mullets and they had no questions at all. I'm the only person today who got no questions. I hate having to bore people by talking about such tedious topics. Was there a problem with what I said?*

All I could do was tell her that her talk was fine, and that her only problem was to find the right collective noun for stunned mullets.

She ate almost all the time, and seemed to vomit for the rest of it, leading her to declare that she was in danger of suffering RSI of the oesophagus. She slept badly and said, *Look at these eyes, I look like a raccoon.* She took her shoes off and then couldn't put them back on again because of swelling. And she worked efficiently until about thirty-seven weeks, when she went home and fitted out the nursery. Then she kept calling me on her cordless phone while she was weeding the garden or building the cot, and she'd ask me to check something and call her back. *It's not that I don't trust you Rick, I just had an idea that's all, and could you . . .*

Then one morning at work I picked up the phone and she said, *Hey Rick, I've had the kid.* And she gave me the stats, the way people with babies always seem to. Boy, seven pounds nine, two-twelve am.

So when was that? I asked her.

Two-twelve am. I just told you.

Yeah, but what day?

Today. This morning.

But it's only eight-thirty now. Shouldn't you be sleeping or something?

Are you kidding? On these beds? I've got him just next to me in a see-through plastic box thing. He's sleeping. He's great. He looks just like a baby.

And she asked me how I was going with the trashing, I think. It was all quite recent then. The only real difference at work was that at that stage it was her job I was handling in a cavalier and arbitrary fashion, rather than just my own.

She seemed so unimaginably happy. She still does. And sometimes I feel very separate from this happiness.

On the way home, driving through rain, I see a woman with a cello, struggling along, getting wet. She's wearing a grey plastic raincoat and it's flapping around, doing nothing.

I turn off Waterworks Road and circle back, but the traffic's not easy and when I get there she's gone. Maybe she caught a bus or a cab, maybe someone else stopped to pick her up, maybe she lives somewhere on this stretch of the road. I drive on home.

I can picture her in my car, wet in the passenger seat, her black cello case wet in the back. Water running from the strands of her dark hair and down her cheeks. She flops back in the seat with the relief of being out of the rain. And we might have had a few minutes of conversation before we reached her house. And she might have said, *Hey, do you want to come in for coffee?* But maybe not.

I should concentrate on the driving, get my head back into the real world. The last thing I need in my day is to go up the rear of the car in front, and to have to say that my mind was on a wet cellist I've never met.

29

Why couldn't she wait until the rain died down?

There was no way she should have been out there with that cello, even if she's sure the case is waterproof. Perhaps it's straightforward. Perhaps I turned up just after the bus had pulled away and she was only a few doors from home. But she looked too wet for that. So why didn't she catch a cab? Didn't she have any money? Why didn't she wait?

Friday on the way home she is not on my bus, she is not walking along Waterworks Road. I've never seen her before, and perhaps I won't see her again.

Around me people talk about weekends, and this weekend I'm actually doing something. Well, Saturday night anyway. Veny is going to live in a studio in Paris for six months, so he's having a party.

Mid-afternoon on Saturday I venture into a room of boxes to select an appropriate bottle of wine. Red I think.

I can't find red.

I find one box full of my winter clothes and another with paperwork, receipts and warranties and old tax returns on top of a folder with phone bills, gas bills, power bills from my time in the flat with Anna. Her neat writing when she's paid them at the bank, my scrawl when I've made a note about the cheque I've mailed, whatever.

How could you make so many calls? I remember

asking her, hassling her, now so needlessly. Why can't you phone people when you're at work like everyone else?

Because I'm working, I think she said.

But I can find no red wine.

The next box is my grandmother's. Cards from her ninetieth birthday, with a rubber band round them. This is unlike her. She didn't keep things, didn't keep cards. She didn't even want to be ninety, the way she told it. *Ninety's just too damn old,* she said to me. *Your knees go and your hearing goes. You start to fall apart and you end up reading these flaming large print books where you spend all your time turning pages. People should be knocked on the head at about eighty.*

She said the last thing she wanted was to live to a hundred and get her telegram from the queen. *I'd send it back and tell her to get herself a blinking job.*

But here are the cards from her ninetieth, bundled and kept, even though she said it was ten years past the last birthday anyone could want. I find the card from me, and then I see it's from Anna too. Anna, writing her own greeting, sending her own love. And it reads like she's part of the family.

Under the cards is the nearly-finished front of the black jumper my grandmother was knitting for me last year. I'd forgotten all about it. It's wrapped around a large ball of wool that has two knitting needles crossed through it, the whole lot rolled up and put away, probably only when she died. I last saw her knitting two days before that, and it's a strange mixture of neat rows and horrendous dropped stitches. I'm sure she'd hate anyone to think it was hers.

I take the box into the lounge room and I put on the radio.

Below the knitting are two Entertainment Centre programmes that I think used to sit on the bottom shelf of the phone stand. Torville and Dean, whose show, she told me, was the best thing she'd seen for at least thirty years, and the World Junior Snooker Championship, from which she was ejected for giving loud and unsolicited advice. She'd been a fan of snooker since at least the days of 'Pot Black', but in snooker, as in anything else, she wouldn't stand for rubbish. So when my mother took her to the World Junior titles for her birthday, she treated it the way she treated snooker on TV. She shouted at it, mainly detailed advice about shot selection. *Go for the blue. Why isn't he going for the blue?* Until the officials spoke to my mother and explained that it would really have to stop. It didn't, and by the middle of the next frame they were out, my grandmother complaining that it didn't look anywhere near over to her.

Beneath these is an assortment of pens and notepads and the several close-typed sheets of airmail paper of her Christmas card list. She sent only the overseas cards last year, early and surface mail, with calendars. But still some cards arrived from people closer to home who didn't know she'd died. My mother told me the Christmas card list must be somewhere, and when she found it she'd write to the people and tell them.

The Christmas before last, my grandmother, working her way down the long list, said to me, *You'd think by ninety you wouldn't have to send so many. Some of these people, I'm sure they're just hanging on to give me more work to do at Christmas. You get nothing back from them. Just a card. And I type every last one of them a blasted letter.*

I should call my mother and tell her I've found the list. I'm counting the names when I realise the sheet is ruled up some way ahead, names and addresses on the left and a grid on the right with columns for the years, with ticks for all living card recipients until 1993, and some for 1994. And enough columns ruled to take her to her hundred and second year. I'm beginning to wonder if she would have complained about the telegram after all.

For now I'll keep the list, and maybe I'll write the letters to these people.

This box must be one of my grandmother's last, packed by my mother in her haste to tidy things when my grandmother died. And we just let her go to it, even though it all looked pointless. This anguished, flurried, unstoppable woman, boxing up her mother's things and moving them aside, achieving nothing.

Then, some time later, leaving the boxes to me. Telling me it's easy, all you have to do is take it one box at a time.

It's eleven o'clock. I realise I've forgotten to go to the party.

30

Jeff calls mid-morning.

So what happened to you last night?

Domestic duties.

The lost art of renovating?

No, that's still a lost art. Just boxes. How was the party?

Good. Really good. That friend of Veny's from Sydney was there, asking after you.

Which friend?

Fiona. The one who thinks you look like Roddy McDowell, remember?

Yeah, great. And that is how I want to be remembered, as a Roddy McDowell impersonator. I wish she'd never said that. What does it mean, that I look like Roddy McDowell? What kind of a taunt is that? Anyway, which Roddy McDowell? Which Roddy McDowell look am I supposed to have? Maybe that's my problem. Maybe I have a crisis of identity, and I'm some incarnation of Roddy McDowell, but I don't know which.

There's always Planet of the Apes.

Thank you.

After I get off the phone I realise that my mother, in telling me I only have to take it one box at a time, never really made it clear what I was to do with the contents. I suppose I'm to throw some things out and do something sensible and tidy with the rest.

But I can't throw any of this out. It looks like junk, but I can't let it go. It's the clearest picture I have of my grandmother, at least of her last few years. I want to tell my mother we need more of this, not less. Older boxes that tell me things I don't know.

Just a few months ago I listened to the rhythm of the knitting in this house, the black jumper beginning. Stood here for measuring and for the nearly-finished front to be sized up against me, held up against my chest by my grandmother's bony hands as the air squeezed noisily in and out of her slowly flooding lungs.

I didn't come here enough then. Every time I visited she'd thank me for coming and I knew I should visit more often. But even in her nineties, even when her heart failure worsened, it didn't occur to me that time would run out.

This is the floor I raced cars on when everyone else watched Neil Armstrong walk on the moon. This is the place where I was looked after when I was sick and couldn't go to school (and my mother got annoyed with my grandmother for peeling grapes for me, saying, *He'll only expect it at home now you know*). This is the place with the best birthday presents, the bottomless lolly jar. The only place I was ever paid five bucks for just being nice.

Sometimes it's still so much her house that I expect I'll walk into another room and find her there and get the chance to ask her any questions I like.

31

On Monday, Renee from the *Westside Chronicle* calls.

I'm the Neighbour of the Month. I have performed the act deemed most neighbourly in the inner-western suburbs in the preceding four weeks. She wants to feature me in the last February edition. She wants to talk to me tonight. I feel powerless to stop her.

Perhaps the 1950s was the age when Neighbour of the Month would have been a good thing. It has Good Old Fashioned Values written all over it. In the nineties it is not a prize to covet. It is not in any way a Late Millenium concept.

Hillary sticks her head round my door. *Things ready for Sydney?*

Sure.

Have you lined up someone to feed your cat?

No.

Don't say I'm not looking after you.

I don't say that I'm Neighbour of the Month either. And how would it make my grandmother feel? The woman who spent, and I do this in my head, about eight hundred and fifty months in the neighbourhood and went unrecognised. I move in, pull up a tree, and in a few weeks I'm a hero. It's a harsh world, our neighbourhood. Fuck it, she's a grandmother. She would have been proud. I'd have said, It was nothing, and she'd be sure

it was false modesty. *But I read about you in the paper.*
And she would have cut it out and shown it to people.

Renee is there with a photographer when I get home.
I apologise and tell her the bus got stuck in traffic.

*So you catch public transport? Is that a decision made
on environmental grounds?*

Sure I tell her, thinking she's kidding.

No. She writes it down. She's going to make me a
greenie as well as a hell of a neighbour. Of course, I
can't go back on it now. I can't say I don't do it on
environmental grounds. It'd seem as though I have some
problem with the environment.

So what exactly did you do for Mister Butt?

I pulled up a tree stump.

And did he ask you to help him with it first?

No. I just went over and did it. With him. He'd
started on it and I saw him and I went over. It probably
seemed like a more manageable task than renovating the
house I'm living in.

All this goes down in shorthand. She must hate doing
these loser stories, surely. She must hate it when her
working day drags on into the evening because a few
weeks ago a guy dug up a tree stump.

Are you a Christian?

What?

Are you a Christian? Was that your motivation?

How do you mean?

Was this an act of Christian charity?

She's getting me again. This is like catching the bus
home. What can I say? I suppose it could at least account
for my hundred and ninety-seven days of celibacy. Renee,
I've decided to wait. No. There must be no hint of
mockery. I must treat this with earnestness and caution,
and declare no affiliations.

It just looked like something that had to be done
Renee, I tell her, and she nods, as though this is very
quotable. Even though it sounds more like John Wayne

talking about something that involved a gun and a lot of bullets.

Now, she says, *we thought we might get a photo with Mister Butt. We've spoken to him on the phone, so if that's okay by you, Richard . . .*

Sure.

As in, sure, why not? Sure, this is already totally beyond my control, so why stop now. Let's go for the cheesy photo too.

And cheesy it is.

Kevin's grinning when we get there, as though he's done me a big favour, or at least repaid a substantial debt in full. And he's wearing his Akubra and a gingery cowboy shirt buttoned right up to the top. I note his guitar is nearby. Kevin is an old pro and never likely to miss a chance for publicity. And he appears to have soaked his dentures in some whitening agent overnight, as they gleam quite incredibly whenever he speaks.

Let's get the photo first, Renee says to all of us. *Jack's got another job to go to.*

The photographer nods, looks around at the light, fits a different lens. *Okay,* he says. *Now I figure we want both of you. And the stump, is it still around?*

No, Kevin says. *I didn't know I should keep it.*

That's okay.

But I've got my guitar.

Kevin insists on the guitar, probably well aware that this is all that gives him the leverage to be described as a Retired Country and Western Performer, rather than just a non-specific old codger. The photographer, accepting that the guitar is not negotiable, says it's good that I've still got my work clothes on. It creates contrast. He suggests I roll up my sleeves to show the muscles that pulled up the stump. I roll up my sleeves. This is going to be awful. I can see this on the front page. This oozes human interest, or at least oozes.

Um, don't worry about it, he says. *Just try rolling them down again.*

I'm not sure how to take this. Renee straightens my tie and Kevin, his guitar swinging around him, is instructed to take one of my hands, which I am to make into a fist, and to hold it up as though I've just won a title fight. And we all know that this pose will be the one. Jack takes about a hundred and ten photos, says, *Great,* with huge sincerity, then goes off to his next job.

Okay, Mister Butt, if we could just have something from you, Renee says. *About Richard and the stump, how it made you feel, that sort of thing.*

Righto. Well, I think the country needs more like this lad, and you can quote me on that. I was struggling away and he was over the fence in a flash. He had his own things to do and his own life to lead, and he gave up a whole day of it to help an old bastard like me. Hang on a tick. You'd better put veteran country and western star, or something like that. He should be given a bloody medal on Australia Day or something, I reckon. He wouldn't have known me from Adam, and he just jumped on over and worked all day like a bloody black. And Renee and I exchange a glance that says that's one remark that's unlikely to find itself in a *Westside Chronicle* feel-good story. *We could do with more like him, that's what I say. You hear a lot of bad things written about the young people of today, but if they're half as decent as young Richard, they won't go far wrong. This sort of lad's our hope for the future.*

And it doesn't stop there.

When I leave with Renee, Kevin tells me that feeding the cat while I'm away is, *The bloody least I could do.*

When we're back at my place she says, *You've got a fan there,* but in a disturbingly genuine way.

She asks me a few questions about the house, and says it's really interesting that my grandparents built it in the twenties and now I'm living here. Maybe the *Westside Chronicle* really is her territory. Maybe she believes in this suburban journalism. I don't mention the letter.

She gives me my prizes and says it's a pity Jack isn't

around to take a few shots. *Anyway, we got some great ones with Mister Butt, didn't we?* And still, no irony at all, or an incredible gift at underplaying it. *There's a medallion too, but it's not engraved yet. We'll give you a call when it's ready, and we'll take a few shots of you wearing it to use as a promo for next month. Drum up a few more entries.*

So, should I ask you how many entries there were this month?

She smiles. *Well, there were several, but Mister Butt was very persuasive. You tipped out a woman with a Neighbourhood Watch story. She'd copied down a number plate when a car with suspicious people in it drove away from a house with most of its appliances. They were actually robbing it. Usually those stories are just people helping friends move house. And there was a guy who intervened to settle a boundary dispute concerning a mango tree.*

What did he do?

Well he basically said that, in an amazing mango season like this one, there are so many mangoes, there's no reason for a dispute at all.

The wisdom of Solomon.

In the very moment I am saying this, I realise its biblical allusions, and that it may not be a good idea.

The wisdom of Solomon, she says, looking at me closely. *Yes.*

Fortunately, she has things to do. She leaves me with my prizes.

My prizes. My selection of prizes from local businesses, interested in supporting neighbourliness. My choice of two bags of tan bark or a hose from a gardening store. My twenty dollar boutique voucher. A free wheel alignment and lube job. And the big one. Dinner for two, Le Chalet.

As if the notion of dinner for two isn't cruel enough by itself.

I call Baan Thai. Usual order for Hiller.

128

There's a storm coming, picking up in the west and pushing in over Mount Coot-tha. Rain starts to fall in big unhurried drops as I park the car. The cicadas go crazy in the gardens near Park Road.

The storm breaks as I leave the restaurant. I stand barefoot in the shelter under the mock Eiffel Tower as ten minutes of astonishing rain thrashes all around me, pounds the bushes and the awnings, overflows gutters, runs warm over my feet.

At home I divide the meal into its two portions and I put Wednesday's into the fridge.

32

As arranged, Hillary turns up in a cab around seven-thirty in the morning.

She's not quite her usual self, not quite as I'd expected her to be. She's not looking great. She's pale and wearing dark glasses and a big leather jacket, as though she's off on some adventure, or maybe flying to face the Red Baron one to one. And she seems to be in a strange mood. She keeps calling me buddy.

I try to recall if she's been like this when we've flown before. Then I realise we haven't flown before. It's usually only one of us who goes, and she usually leaves it to me, telling me it'll be good for me, good exposure.

In the cab I think I notice the smell of bourbon. The cabbie talks on and on and the smell doesn't go away. When we're stuck at lights and he turns around to crap on, as he invariably does, I try to catch the smell of it on his breath. He's starting to slur his speech, I'm sure of it.

I think the cabbie's been drinking, I whisper to Hillary. Bourbon.

Fuck, she says. *Him too?*

There is a strangeness in her eyes and the smell of bourbon as she speaks is overpowering. And I can see a silver hip flask in one of her pockets.

At the airport she says, *I think I should warn you. I get a bit tense when I fly.*

So she paces, and slurps bourbon nervously by holding the pocket up to her lips and tilting it. She probably thinks it's discrete.

It's a very small plane, she says, breaking out in a sweat as I buckle her into her seat.

It's not. It's a 737. It's quite big. It's at least medium-sized. And it's a good plane. The 737 is a good plane. No-one ever got killed on a 737.

How do you know that? You're making it up.

Well, probably very few people have been killed on 737s.

What? People have died in these things? You're taking me up in this thing people have died in?

No. No. This is fine. No-one died. I read it on the weekend. I remember now. Okay? In an aviation magazine somewhere. No-one died.

No-one?

No-one.

Was it a reputable aviation magazine?

The best.

Good. That's good. I feel better now.

And she grips the arms of her seat, squeezes her eyes shut, gnashes her teeth and hyperventilates.

When we take off she goes crazy. Totally crazy. Crazier than a cat in a flea bath.

She bites her pillow and screams into it. She cries. I try to help her and she accidentally lashes out, drawing blood from my left cheek. And she vomits and vomits and vomits, all with her big jacket over her head. She uses her sick bag, and mine, depriving me of its advertised opportunity for cheap photoprocessing (but then, my life isn't exactly filled with photo opportunities). Other passengers seem to form a human chain to deliver sick bags to us, and the flight attendant takes them away in a bucket. Several people in our vicinity decline breakfast. This is something I have never seen on a plane before.

Hillary goes quiet. I pat her on the back. I rub my

131

hand on her back in slow, soothing clockwise semicircles. I don't know why. It seems the thing to do.

Are you okay? I ask her.

I feel her head nodding under the jacket.

She surfaces somewhere well beyond Armidale. She looks very bad now, and she gives me a white-lipped smile. She has a small chunk of vomit on her forehead, just below her hairline. I make her sit still while I remove it with a tissue. She thanks me. Perhaps past events have made us more comfortable with her vomiting, though how she manages to get a chunk of it on her forehead is beyond me.

Was that a problem do you think? Did a lot of people notice, or am I okay?

I'd say you're okay. A couple of people might have worked out that things weren't easy for a while, but no-one made a big deal out of it. And it's probably better to have got rid of that bourbon too.

Yeah. Good point. Hey, your cheek, you're bleeding.

I think it must have happened when I was shaving this morning.

But you were okay in the cab.

Yeah, it must have opened up again with the drop in pressure.

She glances out the window and says, *Fuck it's a long way down.* And she starts to look edgy.

Pretend it's just a picture. It's a lot easier that way.

Is that what you do?

Sure. And I find it's better to distract myself with other things. Could I perhaps interest you in the in-flight mag? It has a fine story on La Paz, the capital of Bolivia, and another on miniature vegetables.

Read me one.

Read you one. Okay. La Paz is at quite a high altitude, so I might read you the one about the little vegetables.

So I read, slowly and quietly and clearly. Slowly and quietly and clearly because I think I have decided to treat her like a mad person and I am striving, above all else, for a sense of calm. She reclines the seat and shuts her eyes.

At the end she says, *You read well.* And then, *Hey, are we descending?*

I think so.

I'm much worse with descents, I have to tell you that. This does not make me feel good. Then she smiles. *Just kidding. Descents are fine.*

So we get through this with nothing more than seat-gripping and teeth-gnashing, and only a small amount of toying with the latest sick bag, rather than loading it with vomit. The combination of bourbon and hyperventilation does make her a little dizzy when we land though.

We stop across the road from the offices of Shelton's for Hillary to eat a breakfast she can hold down, and to have a couple of cups of coffee. She goes to wash her face and comes back wearing new lipstick.

There, she says, *fine.*

And she almost is. She is perhaps a slightly pale ghost of fine, but that's a big improvement.

So we meet and lunch and meet again, and she is competent throughout. Maybe not as enthusiastic as usual, but, as she said, fine. After her pregnancy it's likely that she will never again be fazed by any amount of vomiting, a very useful attribute.

At the end of the day the senior legal counsel asks if we have dinner plans and Hillary says that, to tell the truth, she has a bit of a headache, so she might have to make it an early night. She leaves it open for me, but I'm keen to avoid it too and we take a cab back to the hotel.

I couldn't face any more time with them, she says. *All day today and more of them tomorrow morning. As if we'd want to have dinner with them too.*

Yeah.

I was actually going to suggest that we eat somewhere near the hotel, but I guess there's a remote chance they'd turn up, and it wouldn't look good.

No, it probably wouldn't.

What about just getting room service? Do you want to come round to my room and we could have something there?

Sure.

I might have a shower first. I'm still not feeling the best. So how about seven-thirty?

Fine.

I have a shower, but this creates the dilemma of what to wear. Do I put on tomorrow's shirt? Do I put on today's shirt, when it clearly smells like it's done a good day's work already? Even though I usually sleep naked, I have brought a pair of shorts with me, so in a way that increases my options. Clearly I'd have to wear something with them though.

Why did I bring shorts? I'm only starting to think about that now. I packed them automatically. I think it's a parental thing. Shorts, and sleeping away from home in combustible places. Like clean underwear and being struck by public transport. A habit you get into, despite wanting to resist it because its basis is a pointlessly secondary concern. The man ran naked from the burning hotel, so they sent him back in? The victim was left to die by the roadside when ambulance officers noticed his underpants appeared to have been worn the day before?

So, old shirt, new shirt, shorts, suit?

Why am I standing here in my underpants staring at my clothes on the bed and working out that there are sixteen wearable combinations when Hillary won't be giving it a moment's thought? I think she must be much more normal than I am.

Or possibly at this very moment she could be deciding between ball gown and spurs, or fez, negligee and pumps. But I don't think so. I expect that in her room something very straightforward is happening.

So I go new shirt, today's pants, no shoes or socks.

She opens the door wearing a Gatorade T-shirt and running shorts, and she says, *Hey, semi-formal, nice.*

Unlike you I didn't think to bring a casual wardrobe. *I brought it in case I go for a run in the morning. You mean you aren't going for a run in the morning?*

Not unless there's a fire. However, I did bring shorts with just that possibility in mind.

You don't want to have to bail out in your PJs?

No PJs. I might habitually go to bed early and sleep alone, but I am naked. I take it as a sign that I haven't given up hope entirely.

She offers me her mini-bar and I take a beer. She takes the tiny bottle of bourbon, tips it into her hip flask, and drinks the vodka.

She smells fresh from the shower and her hair is still damp and messy.

We sit down to peruse the menus and we have a minor dispute about the merits of two different wines. *We'll get both then*, she says. *We'll compare. You're being far too casual in your dismissal of the Margaret River.*

I wish I didn't find this appealing. I wish I wasn't sitting here with someone who was married and my manager as well as being very desirable. *You're being far too casual in your dismissal of the Margaret River.* I bet she doesn't know how much I like this sort of game. How, in different circumstances, it could be such a good sign. I wish I wasn't having to sit here trying to persuade my pelvic region that an erection is really very inappropriate at the moment.

There is, of course, an argument that says that even the possibility of an erection should be a thing of joy, since that area has been unresponsive for quite a while. But this is a joy that cannot be shared. Hillary, great news, I think I can have erections again. Not a good idea.

Dinner arrives and a thorough comparison of wines begins. Hillary drinks a glass of each quickly and then pours us both more.

Don't you think mine's livelier? she says, being quite lively to make her point.

Well, maybe, if you're into lively. I'm still a fan of the oak. Call me old-fashioned if you like, but give me some oak. American or French. I can take it either way.

You're a very sophisticated man.

That's what I thought.

I watch her in her detailed study of the wines, a glass in each hand now that dinner is over. She's frowning and sniffing with some gravity and communicating her dilemma with her eyebrows. And even the way the light from the table lamp passes through the wine in the glass and makes a yellow shape on her Gatorade T-shirt really appeals to me. Now that's crap.

I'm not against oak you know, she says. *I'm not against all sorts of things. They just need to be considered appropriately.*

You'd have to be against sparkling burgundy though, wouldn't you?

I think there are some things it's never appropriate to consider, and maybe sparkling burgundy is one of them.

Fashion at its worst. The wine industry equivalent of the safari suit. I expect that in just a few years it'll be regarded as the fruity lexia of the mid-nineties.

So our positions are in fact closer than we realised.

We leave the tray outside the door and we sit on the sofa with our four glasses and two bottles.

I might put some music on, she says. *If that's okay.*

Sure.

I've got a tape that I play in my Walkman when I run. I might just put that on.

Fine. Well, depending on your taste in music I suppose.

She puts her tape on and before she's back at the sofa, the room is full of Nick Cave, 'The Ship Song'. I immediately notice a poorly-focussed feeling of concern.

She's sitting closer to me now. She drinks a mouthful of wine and sits back and leans her head against my shoulder.

136

You sang this at the Christmas party, she says, as though I might not remember. *And, until then, well . . . It was the first time since Daniel was born that anyone did anything that suggested I might be . . . not just a mother. That I might still be desirable. In some way. It was really nice.*

She kisses me, right on the mouth.

This is only half the problem. The other half is I kiss her back.

I put my arms around her and she's breathing quite heavily and this feels very good.

Oh God, she says, but in what way I'm not sure.

I'm feeling very strange myself, as much with the intimacy of it as anything. I can feel her cheek against mine, her body turned against mine, her undried hair under my right hand.

We kiss again, this time till the end of the song and beyond, and she moves so that she is kneeling over the top of me and my head is tilted backwards.

And wine moves through me, slips lightly into my head so I'm drifting, but I'm intensely aware of what every single part of me is feeling, though in a surreal detached way.

My hands are on her skin under her Gatorade T-shirt now and when she moves back the T-shirt lifts up. She pulls it off over her head.

And she looks at me, as though she's still wondering.

She says, *Come on*, and we move to the bed and turn out the main light.

This is a fantasy I should be having in my room, not hers. And even then I wouldn't be impressed with myself.

We lie with our heads on the same pillow, looking at each other, and we seem to take it very slowly. And I'm sure we're both thinking, if you stop this now that's okay. But at the same time we're each thinking we can't stop it.

Whatever, we don't stop it. And I think I abandon

137

any reality outside this room and we keep making achingly slow progress with each other's bodies until we're just so close, holding so close and moving with each other and feeling so good that it just happens. She opens her eyes wide and makes a noise as we both realise and we keep going, faster now, faster. And I'm telling myself, not yet, not yet, despite all these hundreds of days with nothing but a box of tissues and a good imagination, not yet. I can feel her hands on my back, the sweat between us, the frantic movement together, everything sludging in my wine-kicked head, but at the same time incredibly clear. She lets go, lets out a long noisy breath, and then I hold nothing back.

I can't remember it being like this before, I could say that to her honestly.

She sleeps.

My head is full of things. The fear that this was the most awful, foolish act in a life of harmless foolishness. That this was a very bad way to avoid two hundred successive days of celibacy by the narrowest of margins. That I've used her somehow.

But I can't stop touching her, even now. I'm lying watching her, with my arm over her, and I feel really good. Right now, she matters to me incredibly. And those are the boldest terms in which I can face anything I'm feeling. You matter to me incredibly. As though this might be a beginning, and not a disastrous betrayal.

I haven't felt this close to anyone in a long time. Right now, I think I'd put up with anything for this not to end.

33

I am woken by the sound of screaming, distant and strangely distorted.

Hillary has gone.

I find her in the bathroom, screaming with her head down the toilet, the lid and a towel over her to muffle the noise.

I persuade her to come out and we sit on the edge of the bed, both of us naked and staring at the floor, working out how we can begin this.

This isn't good, I say, stating and seriously underplaying the very obvious, but only so some talking starts.

No.

I took it by the toilet thing that you'd realised that.

She nods. *Rick, look, I don't know what to do. You don't know how great that made me feel, just for a moment there.*

I've got some idea.

You don't know how fucked up I feel right now.

Really? Really? I don't know fucked up? I'm breaking new ground in fucked up. The last couple of hours included the greatest thing that's happened to me for a long time and the worst thing I've done in my life. And it's the same thing. And I was already fucked up.

Yeah. Sorry. Look, what I meant was, I was talking about me. I'm sorry. I meant you don't know how I'm feeling right now. I mean, I haven't been honest with you.

Things haven't been great, and I've kept that to myself. And now I'm thinking I've used you in some appalling way. And I really like you. There you are, someone I really like, who's not having the best of luck, and this is what I do.

Are you kidding? You think you did this and I just sat here and had it done to me? I'd really like to say it had never crossed my mind before. I'd really like to say I don't feel like scum. But I can't. I find you incredibly attractive and that kills me. And here we are, you don't travel well, you're away from your baby, you drink far too much, and this is what I do. I can't believe it.

Yeah? Yeah? I play the Nick Cave song. I suggest dinner in my room.

Dinner in your room means nothing.

I suggest two bottles of wine. And I, correct me if I'm wrong, I made the first move.

Hey, I wasn't slow in being second. Any closer and it would have needed electronic timing to pick the winner.

She laughs. Rick, this is so bad. I'm your manager. This is appalling. This is against absolutely everything I stand for. We should be able to work together, just as two people, and this should never even be a possibility. Here I am, a woman in a position of power and this is how I handle it.

That is such bullshit. Thanks very much. So now you're reducing it to some re-run of 'Disclosure'.

No. No, that's not it. What I meant was . . .

I think I know what you meant.

What I meant was, this shouldn't have happened. This shouldn't have become part of our relationship. And I'm really responsible for that.

Why?

I'm the manager. I should do better than this.

Look, sure you're the manager, but it's not that straightforward. It's not like I didn't have some say. It's not like I was against the idea. I've had the chance to get to know you, and sure you're the manager of the unit, but that's only a small part of what I know about you. And tonight that didn't matter at all. And besides, the power theory only works if I think you're holding something over my head. And you just aren't. This didn't happen because of any pressure from you. You didn't abuse any position of power. You don't know . . .

And I don't know how to finish this bit.

. . . you don't know my perspective on this at all.

She stays quiet for a while before saying, *And you don't know mine. Things are different with Peter. He looks on me differently. As though I'm now the mother of his child and maybe that's all. It's made me feel really undesirable. I don't know what's happening with us. I began to wonder if there might be someone else, then hated myself for wondering. It's an awful thing to think, and I really want things to be fine. And this is what I do. This is how I deal with it. This is how I make things fine.*

I thought things were good. I guess I just assumed. You seem so in control.

Yeah, and what a great day this has been for control.

So what do we do now?

What do you mean?

Well, it's three am. We have a meeting at nine. Then we go back to Brisbane. You go back to Peter and Daniel and I go back to, well, I go back to nothing I guess, but I'm still going back. So we've got to work out how to deal with all this.

Yeah. She thinks for a while. *Right now, I don't want to deal with anything outside this room. Right now I want to be a coward just here and curl up and sleep and face none of this.*

Okay. And in the morning, there's no blaming, okay? There's none of us each thinking we took advantage of the other. Guilt about other aspects of it we can sort out later, but tonight, what happened tonight, was mutual.

Okay. Mutual. No power play, no manipulation, no victim.

That's right.

Just, desire, or something.

Desire, some wine and a quite incredible lack of judgement.

We should sleep now.

Yeah.

And we lie there, hardly sleeping at all and careful not to touch.

34

The alarm goes off way too early.

We happen to be facing each other and we make eye contact.

Hi, she says.

Hi.

In case you're wondering, a nine o'clock meeting is out of the question.

Yeah. It'd be funny though. The two of us looking as though we'd both had three hours sleep after telling them at five-thirty that we wouldn't go out to dinner because of your headache.

Yeah. Very funny. I've got an idea. How about you call Shelton's—someone's bound to be there even though it's really early—you call them and tell them my headache was a migraine, and it got worse and I have to sleep now. And can we have the meeting this afternoon. Then call and re-organise our flight home. Later I'll make whatever calls I have to to handle the child-care issue. Dan has to be picked up by five-thirty.

So I sit by the bed, still naked, talking to someone who went in to work early to call New York. I think I can tell from the tone in his voice that he's wearing a dark suit, though he may have taken off the jacket. I hope he can't tell that I am sitting wearing only guilt and bodily fluids (particularly when the bodily fluids are a mixture of mine and my manager's).

Changing the airline booking is easy. They can think what they like.

Then I lie down, and Hillary curls subconsciously back against me and I sleep.

She wakes me late morning.

We should eat.

She orders breakfast.

This is when we realise that we are naked and in the same room. That this is more than simply horribly incongruous, and that it really doesn't matter whether or not it's fine by the person who brings the breakfast.

We should get dressed, she says. *We should have a shower.* There is a pause. *Showers. I should have a shower, and then you should have a shower. That's what I meant.*

She goes into the bathroom and leaves me sitting on the messy bed, facing a chair that has my today clothes thrown over it, looking like yesterday's.

When she comes out she's wearing a towel and the fact that she's covered at all makes my nakedness feel very inappropriate.

I take my clothes into the bathroom and I shower using the one-use-only bottles of hotel shampoo and conditioner, and I shave with the hotel disposable razor. Today, I do cut myself shaving. I'm never good with new razors.

When I go back into the room Hillary is fully dressed and breakfast is on the table. She's looking unsettled.

I just called Peter's parents, she says. *I told them I'd had a migraine. They said they'd love to pick up Dan from child care, so that's all sorted out.*

Good.

So come on, eat.

I sit down and face the unfamiliar choice of fruit, toast and cereal.

Wow, real breakfast.

What do you mean?

I tell her a bit about my diet.

Doesn't that make you incredibly constipated?

Sure. I kind of hoped the popcorn maker would turn it around, but, you know, you've practically got to be in the mood to cook when you make popcorn, if you want it to have any kind of flavour. You've got to have a bowl and a utensil and butter and seasoning. It's not as easy as you think. I tend to like the basics.

Like biscuits and chips and soft drink.

Flavoured mineral water. And you think this is why I've been a bit on the difficult side, down there?

Yeah. You should think about fibre.

So I eat the fruit, and the cereal, and begin my new plan to threaten my sluggish bowel with fibre.

We try to tidy the room, but there are signs of last night that won't go away. The bed will tell no lies for us when we are gone.

You know, I say to her, they'll probably think you had a wild night, and next door I slept so soundly I didn't even crease the sheets.

I doubt it. I can already hear the sound of two and two being put together.

Only in this room, okay? Only hotel staff and only in this room. Whatever else happens is up to us. So stop staring at the wet patch as though your life's about to end.

And the last thing we do before leaving the room is stop so I can take over from her unsteady fumbling hands and fasten her pearls.

She waits in the corridor while I put my shoes and socks on next door, in a room that smells as sterile as when we arrived.

And when we're in the meeting it's as though it never happened. A few polite queries about her migraine, and everything else seems totally normal. I'm watching her perform, effectively, confidently, and my mind's only on last night. People are sitting round the table making notes, thinking up questions, and I have to be ready for them.

Hillary's talking about how we might follow this up, the mechanisms we might set in place, who should be involved. She arranges for a group of business people from Singapore due in Sydney next week to visit us in Brisbane on the way. I'm beginning to realise I have more work to do.

She's tense in the cab on the way to the airport. I tell her she looks tense.

It's just the flying.

By the time we get to the airport she's worse.

You're quite small and about to become very crazy, I tell her. I think I'm going to have to kill you and take you as baggage.

Then I remember some tablets for jet lag left in my toilet bag since I last went overseas with Anna. I think they have some relaxant quality. And I figure my toilet bag might as well be of some use this trip, since I don't think I've opened it yet.

I give Hillary the bottle and she looks at the label.

These things hardly touch me.

She takes three, washed down with a few mouthfuls of bourbon.

Don't do the bourbon thing again, I say to her, detecting an unattractive nagging tone in my voice.

She just glares at me and sits sipping bourbon until we're called to the plane. I have to help her out of the seat, and by the time we're down the walkway, down the aisle and I'm buckling her in, she's forgotten there's a plane involved at all. By take off she seems to have passed out. So this time I have no need to speak of Bolivia and small vegetables.

It still surprises me how much I care for her as she lies unconscious next to me, her head rocking against my shoulder with the slightest of turbulence, saliva dribbling from the corner of her mouth and onto my sleeve.

I take a *Who Weekly* from the flight attendant. Helena's back with Michael. Shoshanna's back with Jerry. Clearly in this business windows of opportunity don't stay open long. And somehow, despite the heroic point-lessness of the notion of Celebrity Partnering, this makes me feel even more crappy. Back when Jeff and I came up with the idea, there was a certain purity to my crappiness. Now I feel an overwhelming sense of seedi-ness. Really crappy, really empty. I can't believe what I've done.

Hillary is still almost unrousable in the cab, so when we get to my place I can see nothing else to do but to lift her out, load her into my car and drive her home. I can't send her off with the cabbie with her address pinned to her jacket like some smashed Paddington Bear.

We drive through the post-peak hour traffic and she sits slumped and with her head to one side, her mouth open and snoring. All the time I'm hoping no-one will be home, and then I'm wondering what to do. Put her to bed and leave a note beside her? Dear Peter, don't be concerned. Nothing of any consequence happened in Sydney. Your wife is only this way due to drug ingestion.

Whether he's home or not, I don't expect this to be easy.

No-one's home.

I drag Hillary and her baggage up the driveway. She manages to tell me, *Purse, purse*, when I shout Key. So I lift her up over my shoulder and I begin going through her purse. Thinking of the contents of women's purses (and wondering why the fuck the keys have to be the last things you find) it occurs to me that last night's sex could hardly be called safe. Not that I think she's a risk, and I'm sure I'm not (unless you really can get it from toilet seats or drinking out of the same glass), but I realise it needs to be addressed. Or rather, should have been at the time. I think we both thought it wasn't really happening.

Just as I'm shaking her up and down on my shoulder and rifling through her bag and shouting various things about safe sex, a car pulls up in the driveway.

A man, a man I have met once before and know to be Peter, gets out and lifts a baby from the back.

Shit, bad migraine, he says.

Yeah. I think it's the medication too. And the flying problem.

She told me she was over that.

Not really.

Is she all right?

Yeah, she's fine.

He notices then that he's standing with his baby over his left shoulder and I'm standing with his wife over mine.

Looks like mine's lighter than yours, he says, and smiles. *Do you mind bringing her in, since I've got Dan already?*

He leads me down a hallway and into their bedroom. This is far too weird.

I put her down on the bed and he kneels beside her, stroking her cheek and saying, *Hill, Hill.*

Safe? Safe? she says. *Of course it was fucking safe.*

She begins to open her eyes, sits up suddenly opening them wide and looking around. She looks like she's about to scream. Her face makes all the right movements but is then overcome by sluggishness. She gives in to the unmanageable weight of her eyelids and her head flops back onto the pillow.

The plane, I say. I think she was very concerned about the safety of the plane.

Oh, always. I've no idea where that comes from.

She's been saying very strange things since she took the flight sickness medication. I don't know who gave it to her. But she's been speaking an amazing amount of rubbish, really.

Well, I'll have to ignore everything she says till she sleeps it off.

While this has all the potential content of a veiled threat, I don't think the notion of threat has occurred to him. He's just giving me a cue to go.

To go and leave them here, this happy, mysterious family. To get back in my car, for the first time in two days responsible for only one person's seat belt. I turn the radio up and I sing along as I drive back across town. To eat, play tennis. Just like normal, but all the way hoping they don't play Nick Cave, 'The Ship Song'.

35

The *Westside Chronicle* is in the mailbox when I get home.

'It was nothing' says our Neighbour of the Month
Young Brisbane corporate lawyer Richard Derrington turned recently to his Christian faith when he saw his neighbour, eighty-four-year-old country music identity Kevin Butt, struggling to uproot a stump in his yard.

Richard, who is living in the home his grandparents built in Zigzag Street, Red Hill and bringing it back to its former glory, spent the best part of a day with pick and shovel as Burma Railway veteran and balladeer Kevin kept him going with 'a few of our old favourites'.

'Our country needs more like this lad', Kevin said when nominating Richard to be our Neighbour of the Month, and at the *Westside Chronicle*, we couldn't agree more . . .

Editorial
. . . It is people like Richard Derrington who give us continuity, who show us Christian concern at a time when values are regarded as 'old-fashioned', who show us that the heart of this city is still beating . . .

And a photo, of course a photo, the photo I had expected, with Kevin and his gleeful menacing teeth and loosely-slung guitar and me looking as though I am straining in some re-enactment of uprooting the stump or fighting against my worsening constipation. I read, and look, as though I'll go through life with short back and sides.

I eat Tim Tams in the car on the way to tennis. And I play the worst tennis seen since at least the 1520s. Tonight, people would rather have a disease than have me as a partner. So Jeff is stuck with me.

Why? he asks. *Why? Why?*

I don't travel well, I tell him.

But you only went to Sydney.

It was a rough trip.

I slow down the game in order to find form. In fact, I slow it down so much that my shots all sound different to everyone else's. My serve becomes almost silent, and is referred to as the Stealth Serve once it is realised that it crosses the net undetected even by radar. I ace Gerry with a serve that actually stops. It sneaks over, plops onto the ground, bounces twice, rolls and stops. He shakes his head, says, *Fuck*, under his breath several times and kicks it back under the net.

And this is the high point. Other than that my serve is so poorly controlled that Jeff tells me I am turning tennis into a game akin to hitting a wet sock with a slack hammock. And that that game never became at all popular, for very good reasons.

Afterwards I am full of apology and the others are quieter than usual. I offer to buy all the drinks but they tell me it doesn't matter. We sit on the benches outside the tennis centre and I eat my Ice Graffiti Icy Pole.

You poor boy, Gerry says. *Love has really done you harm.*

And I can't tell him that right now he can't imagine the harm. For some reason tonight he can't just leave *Love has really done you harm* as a passing remark, and a round table discussion about love evolves over cups of Gatorade. And I'm so out of this I even have a problem with Gatorade now. I'm sitting there beginning to feel incredibly tired, focussing on the Gatorade logo on one of the cups and watching it peel off like a T-shirt. Right now my every muscle feels too heavy to lift, and love seems impossibly elusive.

Of course, Gerry says, *we argue about this all the time. The basis of our relationship may be love but that doesn't mean we think it's the same thing. I think it's something glorious. Freddie's hopelessly pragmatic.*

You make me sound as though I treat it like a transaction. Whenever you get into this stuff.

Hey, if the EFTPOS fits . . . And Freddie just glares. Gerry goes on, *when perhaps it would be smarter not to. Mister Strong Silent Type here always gets shitty with me when I talk about it in public.*

But only because you make me out to be emotionally bankrupt. You've got some quite impractical ideas. They're lovely some of them, but they're complete bloody fantasy. I think it's wonderful that someone like you can survive in the real world.

The real world? Since when have I sought any association with the real world? Haven't I got your big strong arms to protect me from the real world?

Always.

So they're smiling at each other now. They've made it into a joke, maybe even a joke at themselves, and it's as though any glaring never happened. Gerry turns back to me.

Look, I don't know what Anna wanted, and I don't know what you want, but I hope to god you find it soon. You just look so bloody miserable.

At home I microwave my leftover *panang nua*. I can't believe how much has happened since the first half of this meal, how different things feel, and not in a good way.

36

So how do I deal with this?

When I was just a trashed person I at least knew where I stood. I was wallowing maybe, but now I look back on that almost fondly.

Is Hillary telling Peter now? Right now as I'm sitting alone eating the re-heated half meal of a more innocent man is she struggling through the drugs and telling him everything? If she isn't, why isn't she? And if she does, what happens then? And if she doesn't?

This is what I hate most. I'm not letting go of last night. I'm telling myself it was a huge mistake, but I'm not letting it rest at that. I seem to be trying to nurture the tiny possibility that it was only the beginning of something. That she'll call me any time and say, *It's over with Peter*. Etcetera, etcetera. I run through the fantasy that when she tells him he unburdens himself about the affair he's been having, and they agree to part amicably. Beyond this point, the fantasy rages totally out of control, Hillary and me, and Daniel even, this house, my safest place, the white wooden cottage with the red roof and flowers of all colours. My grandfather's dream dreamt somewhere outside Winton in 1923. As though this is some legitimate end, justifying means, even though I'm not at all sure it's what I want. But there were some things about last night that felt great, even though, in any rational mind, it could be seen only to have done harm to all involved.

So maybe this is what I'm telling myself, that last night is okay if I hold some sincere feelings for Hillary. Because if I don't it looks like a pretty awful thing. So I'm telling myself it couldn't have happened if we hadn't both wanted it to. And she wouldn't have wanted it unless there were big problems with Peter. We didn't mean it to happen, we didn't expect it to happen, so it just did. And I'm feeling all the guilt I said I wouldn't.

I don't sleep.

I lie in bed but I don't sleep. I walk around the house. I pace up and down eating biscuits until I run out of them and it's still no clearer.

The phone does not ring.

The sun rises.

I shower and shave and dress for work. I feed Greg and go. I've paced enough. By seven-thirty I'm at my desk. Sitting, waiting. Fiddling around in a document waiting for the sound of lift doors opening.

For an hour it's just me, then Deb arrives.

Hey babe, she says. *How was Sydney? How did the two of you go?*

What do you mean?

Well you weren't sightseeing were you? How were the meetings?

Oh, good, fine. Yeah, good actually. Of course, it only means I've got more work to do.

I try to focus hard on the manufacture of normal conversation, and she can see it's an effort. I tell her I played tennis till eleven when I got back, so I'm tired.

And you're still not doing too well, are you babe? You're still not sleeping well. That Anna, she makes me so mad, you know. What she's done to you.

Hillary's still not in by nine.

I'm sitting, looking out my door, looking for any sign of her. My screen saver keeps telling me, Remember the Three Part Resolution and I have some recollection of

the concept (it was something to do with the government) but not any of its three parts. I make myself
another cup of coffee.

Hillary arrives just after nine-thirty looking really bad,
and she's careful not to glance my way. I watch her talk
to Deb and then go into her office. The door shuts.

I open my vertical blinds a little and see only a back
view of Deb. Nothing seems to be happening on the
whole floor. In bad movies, this is the moment before
ambush when someone says, *It's quiet out there, too
quiet.* Here it stays quiet, and there's enough ambushing
going on in my head.

I sit back at my desk and drink my coffee. I play
Sammy the Snake, but my heart's not in it. I call Deb
on the phone.

Hillary in yet?

Yeah. She's in her office.

Okay.

Did you want her for anything?

No. Nothing specific. I was just wondering if she was
in yet.

This goes nowhere and I can't say anything more.
Soon after, Deb appears at my door.

She's looking really tired, she says. *She was up all
night with Daniel. She said she thought he was unsettled
with her having been away the night before.*

She goes back to her desk. I call Hillary.

Hi.

Rick.

How are you?

Fine.

Fine?

*Well, what do you think? And thanks for the drugs
too, by the way.*

I didn't tell you to take three tablets.

Yeah.

So what's happening?

Nothing's happening. I feel like shit with this hangover,

or whatever it is, and Daniel kept waking up during the night. She pauses, and allows it to become clear to me that some issues are, for the moment, slipping away. *And we've got a lot of work to do for Monday.*

Yeah.

So the conversation ends.

I try to look at the work, starting with the list of questions raised in Sydney. In twenty minutes I've contemplated only the other Sydney issues, then Hillary walks in. I want to tell her things straightaway. Seeing her for the first time since yesterday I want to tell her this meant something to me.

She turns to Deb and says, *We've got to do some work on this thing for Monday, so we shouldn't be disturbed unless it's an emergency, okay?* And she shuts the door, sits down. *About Monday,* she says. Stops and nods, looking past my right shoulder. *About Monday.* Another pause. *Peter said he missed me. That it made him realise he'd been taking me for granted, that having Dan around had meant he'd focussed on him. He said he hadn't been fair to me.*

So what did you say?

Nothing. I didn't know what to say. I don't know what I'm going to say. I think I've hurt all of us.

It's not that simple. But let's not have that conversation again.

Rick, you've got to know, I've got to be honest, I was having a bad time there, and maybe I should have handled it differently, but the way you've treated me has made me feel good. That's not how it's supposed to be, but it's how it is. And I hope I'm not missing the point here, I don't want you to be hurt by this. I don't know what you're thinking at the moment, but I think we both know that what happened shouldn't have.

Yeah.

And that's it. That nothing else will happen.

Yeah.

I think we both know that.

Sure.

I have no idea how to say what I think I'm trying to say here. Two things I suppose. We've got to put it in the past, that's the first thing. And I don't think it's fair if this hurts you in any way. You've been hurt enough. Am I missing the mark here? Is this all stupid? Are you not thinking any of this at all?

No. You're not missing the mark.

I don't want you to think you don't mean a lot to me. You do.

Thanks.

I think it's fair to say we both had feelings for each other.

Yeah.

And that this didn't happen lightly.

Yeah. Hillary, you don't have to say all this stuff. I don't think this could have happened lightly for either of us, okay? But obviously we have to move on, I think we've both worked that out.

Yeah.

So do you think you'll tell Peter?

I don't know. It's really not that easy. I think I should. But even when I try to think what would be the best for him I don't have the answer. Does that sound like I'm rationalising my way out of telling him?

I don't know.

I go out for a walk, since the coffee and the crap in my head and a night spent pacing seem to combine to have me hovering in a very ineffective state between awake and asleep. I don't know where I walk and I don't care. It's a hot day, so I sweat till I stink, and I keep walking till I end up back at work and realise I should be doing some.

I forget to get out of the lift at my floor, and at the next floor Barry Greatorex gets in.

Hi, he says, as though doing so makes him sweat too. As though doing so might reveal something. And he looks nervously around the lift.

157

How are you Barry?
Good. Why?
Just asking.
Right. How are you?
Good.
Good. How's that thing?
Fine. What about you?
Oh, good.
And now we're both looking nervously around the lift. Barry reaches into his pocket for a handful of chocolate-coated coffee beans and crunches on them, his eyes all the time flicking from one thing to another as though there might be danger.

It's only when several people have come and gone that I realise neither of us has pressed a floor button.

Which floor Barry? I ask him.

What? Oh, doesn't matter. Oh, sixteen I suppose.

So I get off at fifteen and leave him in the lift alone.

And Deb tells me Hillary's gone out to lunch, with Peter.

37

Tonight I can't cook. I can't even face ordering takeaway
from Baan Thai and going through the Hiller shit. And
I don't want to walk up to Waterworks Road for Leba-
nese cause it's uphill. I get in my car, thinking I might
drive till I find something that suits me. At West End
maybe, somewhere interesting. Somewhere cheap and
Vietnamese and all by myself.

The car doesn't start. I've flattened the battery by
not shutting the door properly and leaving the inside light
on last night after tennis.

I call the RACQ.

They tell me half an hour at least.

I have almost no food. I wonder how a can of Greg's
Prime Beef and Turkey would be on toast. I've already
eaten all my biscuits. I realise it's Thursday and I should
be at Toowong late night shopping. But I can't. And even
when the car's sorted out I won't.

I sit out on the bonnet with a big pile of toast with
Vegemite on it and I drink tap water. So much for the
idea of driving till I found something that suited me.
Heading off into the night uncertain of my destination,
a pointless non-plan that I think I wanted to romanticise
into something more deliberate: me and my old Laser
and just a hint of road movie. Me and my flat battery
and toast on the bonnet at home. Me and the smells of

other people's cooking and the slow pathos of slide guitar, when the wind blows gently from the west.

It occurs to me that this might be the sort of thing I deserve. That I should suffer in a succession of pathetic ways like this, and all by my own thoughtless hand.

I finish my toast and I find I'm singing along to the slide guitar wafting down from Kevin's kitchen louvres. This is not something I want to do, and I don't find my familiarity with the words at all reassuring.

The RACQ mechanic arrives and jump starts the car. He tells me the battery might survive, and that I should drive around for a while to try to re-charge it. There is no point in explaining to him that I have eaten my fill of toast, and I now have nowhere to go.

I drive. I drive and I sing along to Triple J. This is becoming a habit, and it's not a good one. Even people who sing in cars think people who sing in cars are losers. Jeff and Sally are at some family dinner tonight, so I drive past their house without stopping and out around the uni campus, still singing, past pre-season football training and the tennis courts, past the colleges and back out onto the road, through St Lucia and Toowong and then towards home. And I wonder if I've driven long enough yet. I realise I'm close to Tim's place, so I drive there and leave the car outside with the engine running and sit with him on his front verandah drinking coffee.

When I go to his toilet my constipation still gets the better of me so I do a lot of sitting and not much else. It occurs to me that this may be the price I am to pay. That I will never shit again following the Sydney incident, and that I will grow progressively more uncomfortable until I explode. I wonder if the same will happen to Hillary. I wonder if the same is happening to Barry Greatorex. Maybe he isn't obese at all, just in an advanced stage of faecal retention because of some indiscretion that precedes my own. This might explain why his eyes are beginning to bulge and his concentration is so poor. The idea of Barry Greatorex exploding is very unattractive indeed.

In Tim's toilet, where most people might have an old *Who Weekly* or two, he has a copy of Kyd's *The Spanish Tragedy*. I suppose that shouldn't surprise me. Having nothing else to do but wait I read the first few scenes, then I realise I could all too easily spend the whole evening with my pants around my ankles engrossed in one of the less famous works of Elizabethan theatre, so I skip to nearer the end, and there surely is a lot of tragedy in this play.

A few short notes on *The Spanish Tragedy*
Many's the quiet ten minutes or so I have sat in Dr Murray's smallest room, attending to the necessaries and whiling away any moments of waiting with a scene or two from Mr Kyd's most excellent play, *The Spanish Tragedy*. The room, with its artful consideration of the acoustic, gives pleasing echo to the more declamatory lines, and yet shapes admirably the deceits among the lightest whispers. The play begins . . .

Interesting toilet reading, I tell him when I'm back on the verandah.

It's a great play, he says, as though this makes it reasonable to keep in a toilet. *I read it all the time to my eighteen-month-old nephew and he always asks for more.*

You read it to him in the toilet?

Yeah. Well, when there's no-one else here and you have to go, he has to go too.

You have to take him with you and read *The Spanish Tragedy*?

Well, the play's probably optional, but he is a bit of a fan.

Are you in the habit of taking children to the toilet and reading to them?

Only very young children.

161

I'm not sure that makes it all right.

My car battery, if it will ever be charged again, should surely be charged by now. I drive home and park, and I make sure I shut the door properly tonight. I want to try to start the car, to see if the battery has charged, but I'm not sure if this means I would have to go for another drive. I suppose I could always take in a few more scenes of *The Spanish Tragedy*. Maybe I shouldn't have looked at the end.

I don't sleep. I seem to have stopped sleeping now, and to have replaced the process entirely with angst-ridden, guilt-ridden unproductive thought.

At around two o'clock I walk up to Wee Willie Winkie's on Waterworks Road (Open Twenty-Four Hours a Day, 365 Days a Year) and I buy a packet of Tim Tams. I stand outside the store eating them and watching the occasional cars speed past, heading out of town and down the hill into Ashgrove. An old man wanders up to me muttering something incomprehensible, so I give him a couple of Tim Tams and he wanders on. I watch him go, wobbling off down the hill in a long smelly coat all wrong for this hot night. He veers around things that aren't there and shouts at them in a tangle of sounds that mean nothing to me. Just when I think he must have nowhere to go, he crosses the road to a hostel, and someone lets him in. Before the door shuts I can hear a voice saying quite clearly, *Where have you been?* and the gruff peculiar sounds of the man in reply.

I buy a banana Paddle Pop and eat it on the walk home.

38

I watch TV, a repeat of 'Grizzly Adams' (who would have thought they'd repeat 'Grizzly Adams'?) and a movie called *September Gun* (synopsis: A nun hires an aging gunfighter to help her move a group of unwanted Apache children). I think the three star rating the TV guide gives it borders on the generous. But who'll be watching it anyway? Me and parents feeding infants and maybe some people on night shift. No-one expecting quality. No-one who stayed up just for this movie, or taped it for later. *September Gun* is just what's on.

After 'General Hospital' I change channels for the 'ITN News', 'Daybreak News' and the 'Today Show', which has a story about Liz Hurley scoring a multimillion dollar contract with Estée Lauder. So does this change her status from Celebrity Partner to the Helena Christensen category of Celebrity Partner (Supermodel)? Clearly the whole celebrity partner game moves far too quickly for me. I'm beginning to wonder if I'll ever be a part of it, despite the plan that recently seemed so clever.

At work, Renee from the *Westside Chronicle* calls.

The medallion's ready. Could I drop in to give it to you and maybe take a few photos?

She comes at around eleven with a photographer who takes about a dozen shots of me holding the medallion next to my face, grinning.

Too easy, he says. *That'll do me.*

Renee says she'll catch up with him later, and he goes. She turns back to me, looking not entirely comfortable, and says, *My church group's having a barn dance this Saturday. Are you doing anything?*

I think I might be working.

And for a Saturday night it's hard to find a worse lie than that.

Oh, I'm sorry. Are you involved with someone at the moment?

No. Well, no. I don't know.

Okay, she says, the complexity of my answer only making things less certain. *Well, call me when you know, maybe. If you want to have coffee or something.*

Sure, yeah. Sure. That'd be good.

Only if you want to.

When she's gone I call Jeff. I tell him about my medallion, and he says he should see it as soon as possible. And I tell him about Renee and the Christian barn dance win-on.

She asked you to a barn dance? he says, as though he needs confirmation. *On account of you and the stump?*

My act of Christian charity. She's clearly very confused.

What is it with Christians and barn dances?

I plan never to know.

So you turned her down?

Hey, she's got the Lord. She'll get over me.

At the counter in the coffee shop he makes me open the purple velvet box and take out the medallion, and the girl making our coffee watches it in my hand.

Is that a medal? she says.

Yeah.

What did you get it for? If you don't mind me asking.

I tell her, quite calmly and for no good reason, I pulled a kid out of the surf.

She refuses to charge me for my coffee and says, *It wouldn't be right to take money from a hero, would it?*

You'll have to tell her the details before you go, Jeff says to me when we're sitting down. *I think she has a genuine interest in heroic deeds.*

Yeah. Me too. And some bits of that root were pretty tenacious.

So here I am with my medal, won in perhaps my crappiest year and for a singularly unspectacular act. Jeff sits turning it over in his hands.

So how many Rs would there usually be in Derrington? he says.

Two, usually in the middle.

Not at the Chronicle. And he shows me the single R Derington.

Oh, that Richard Derington. I think he's the one who pulled a kid out of the surf. What a joke. What crap. And do you know what I've read these last couple of days? Shoshanna and Jerry are on. Helena and Michael are on. Liz Hurley's signed a multimillion dollar contract with Estée Lauder. What do these people think they're doing? They get my hopes up, give me some sense of purpose, then they change the rules of the game.

No, no you've got it wrong. That is the game. Don't be fooled. Celebrity partnering is ruled by falsehoods and shadow plays and temporary alliances. If you view anything, anything at all, as permanent, you just aren't a player. Don't be put off by reconciliation. Don't even be put off by marriage. There are reasons for these things, reasons that are much smarter than any plan of lifelong union. When one of the players marries, you don't forget about them. You just drop their name a little further down the list and wait your turn. It's better if they marry. It makes you much bigger news when it's over and your turn comes. You should look on this as just a hiatus.

This is a hiatus? There I was thinking I was sinking and it's just a hiatus. Can you believe they gave me this medal? I dug up a fucking tree.

Sure. And they put your photo in the paper with your neighbour and it is truly gloriously bad.

And the crap goes on, I tell him, because it does.

You're being unfair to your crap again. You just don't understand it do you? Your crap is special. Crap defines you as an individual. Your crap makes you desirable, and right about now you must be one of the most desirable single men in the world. They all want you. You know they all want you. The girl making coffee, Renee from the Chronicle, the sixteen year old with a passing interest in books and a pleasing interest in trousers. Who knows how many more? They're queuing up and you're pushing them all back. Breaking hearts all over town. You and your penis pointing to the centre of the earth. And why do they want you? What is it that gives you this strange, crumpled desirability? Your job isn't special, your law degree isn't special, your soon-to-be-heritage-colours worker's cottage isn't special. It's your crap that's endearing. It's the basis of any relationship, way beyond even the choice of who wins on to whom. It's crap that sustains things. The mutual vulnerability that comes from knowing each other's crap. How shallow would we be if we only felt things for people on account of their successes? How likely would that be to survive? I don't understand why this is making you so uncomfortable right now, why you think you should fight it. This time of glorious failure and perilous achievement is probably your finest hour, but it's not as though it's come out of the blue. I don't know what kind of glamorous past you would like to have had, but you didn't have it. Your life, like mine, is a series of conventional successes that don't count for much, plus good times and crap. And we both know some of my best stuff is crap, and that's why we like me so much.

Some of Jeff Ross' best stuff

Best part-time job: Door-to-door salesperson for McGuigan's Aerated Waters. Presented with a medallion by Lewis McGuigan, the seventy-eight-year-old son of the founder of the company (also Lewis McGuigan), for achieving the Highest Monthly Sales of Pashola on Record

(January 1983) using the sales pitch, 'A bottle of Pashola contains significant amounts of sugar, nature's source of instant energy, and two-thirds of the body's daily requirement of water, essential for life'.

Best inappropriate use of semen story: The story of the student who woke in his own college room, stuck to his pillow with someone else's semen. Apparently he had been out at the Rec Club while two other people had done the deed in his bed and had, according to Jeff, 'Gone the interruptus and the guy let fly onto the pillow'. The student, having rendered himself senseless, returned to his now vacated room and slept peacefully with his head in someone else's intimacy till morning. Jeff was always quite emphatic that this story was not his own, claiming he could have been no part of it as he had never lived in college. It is possible, though, that he visited the rooms there from time to time.

Best failed attempt at a world record: An unsuccessful attempt on the world endurance doubles tennis record (then ninety-one hours and forty-two minutes), when students could use the uni courts free of charge. The attempt failed at six and a half hours on a hot day (the participants having easily endured twelve hours in each of two practice sessions during the preceding month). As they drove home defeated along Sir Fred Schonell Drive, still in the daylight of the first day of the attempt, a news crew drove past them, heading for the uni courts.

And he has not so much outgrown this crap phase as come to terms with it. And I'm sure we could talk him into another tilt at the world record even now, if they'd give us the courts for nothing. I'd have to do no more than suggest it and within minutes he'd be saying, *It's only four days, how hard can that be?* As a kind of mad enthusiasm overcomes him.

39

There is though, I think, one unspoken condition to Jeff's rules concerning crap. I expect the crap should cause no significant harm, particularly to a third party. But I won't be exploring this with him today.

At five I realise I have done no work, but it's too late to change that. So I will have to work on the weekend. I should call Renee and tell her I wasn't lying, even though we both thought I was at the time.

It's Deb's birthday today and she keeps telling me she's years away from the dreaded bouncy castle of thirty, and I shouldn't forget that. A dinner has been organised at a restaurant on the southside, so I hang around the office (and still do nothing) until I've killed enough time.

I catch a cab to Stones Corner. I'm not expecting a great night. I really don't like this sort of thing, but sometimes you have to do it. Deb has booked for fourteen, which means one long table of all the people she has ever liked at Shelton's. And she's far too generous for her own good. She likes far too many losers. I sit between two of them, and some distance from Hillary.

I drink quickly. I drink too much. When I stand up to go across the road to the bottle shop my cutlery falls onto the tiled floor. I move into my new bottle of chardonnay with some speed. And I notice, in one of my furtive glances to the right, that Hillary has gone.

When I go to the toilet, its checkerboard floor disorientates me badly and I have to sit down, even though I only came in with standing-up intentions. I must be there for a while because they send someone in to see if I'm okay and, for no good reason, that really pisses me off and I tell him to tell them that I am reading a play and I am only up to the second act, so I may be some time.

When I go back out and sit down Deb comes up to me and says, *Are you okay babe?* And I hear myself shouting, Are you kidding? Have you ever read *The Spanish Tragedy?* Everybody dies. Everybody dies.

She asks me if I think I should go home and says she could call me a cab, and I tell her I'm just starting to have fun.

Some time after that I am in a cab, but with a few of the others (although I'm not sure who). Then we're at The Underground. I haven't been there for ages and it's packed and smells of smoke and spilt beer. I end up squeezed in a corner, which is fine, and whenever it's my shout someone takes my wallet to the bar and comes back with drinks. My bladder starts to strain and in the confines of the corner this is far from convenient, and I remember it was maybe the old Underground but maybe somewhere else where I saw a prominent Rugby League identity, obviously caught in the same dilemma, flop his dick out and piss very substantially into a pot plant. And I remember thinking, for a prominent Rugby League identity that's a very uninspiring dick.

My bladder becomes the focus of my existence until I realise I can quiet it no more and I climb out and make my way around to the toilets. The toilets by now are busy, with an industrial level turnover and the anticipated copious amounts of floor pissing.

Further observations concerning men and toilets
Why do they bother with any actual facilities in these places? Surely it would be cheaper to have just a gently

sloping floor leading down to a hole. Easier for men involved in the obviously difficult task of urination, easier for hosing out. I've got to admit I've never felt great about urinals. How has the trough concept survived? That's what I want to know. How in the late twentieth century has a Roman notion like communal urination kept going? You stand there, you get it out, you hold it in your hand, you urinate with it, and sometimes you have to maintain a conversation with men on both sides. You, in your work clothes, talking to other men in their work clothes as though you've bumped into them waiting for a lift on the fifteenth floor, with the one exception being that your penises are out of your trousers and urinating. Has no-one thought this is even slightly strange?

A cubicle door slaps open and a man staggers past, his fly at half-mast, and he gives me the thumbs up, but he's looking shaky. And sure enough, he's pissed on the floor. Why can't these guys work it out? Why can't they work out that if you're that far gone you don't just go for the cubicle, you actually sit down? Sure it's the girl thing, but no-one's going to see you. Or is the word out that this is what I like? *No worries Rick*, thumbs up, *pissed on the floor*. As though he's done me a favour. As if I like having to work out where to put my feet, and then trying to go at the bizarre angle this usually imposes. So here I go kind of side saddle, which is quite awkward. And I piss on the floor.

I clean up what I can, and on the way out I tell the next guy, Watch out, the guy before me pissed on the floor.

When I go back to the others, I seem to take a wrong turn and I'm out in the street, then standing for a while in a queue, then sitting in a taxi again, this time by myself. It's only when I get out that I realise I've given the driver Jeff and Sal's address instead of my own.

So I stand in their front garden working out what to do next. It's a nice garden, I realise. They have several grevilleas but their lights are all out, so maybe nobody's home. I sit on their steps and have a rest. It starts to rain, but not heavily.

I decide it might feel good to walk home and soon the rain comes down harder and the roads start to shine and the wheels of the cars spit the warm water up as they drive past. My suit becomes heavy, particularly on my back where most of the rain is landing, and the water runs from my hair down my face. There are puddles now when I'm crossing roads and the water gets into one shoe but I'm not sure why only one. And I go the way I would drive, which is not a fast way but a sure way, and there are more hills than you would be aware of when you usually only come this way driving an automatic car. There are four hills even before you leave Toowong. After that I don't count.

At least I'm not a cellist. But then, you'd be a fool to be a cellist, out on a night like this.

40

In the morning I am quite uncomfortable, in many parts.

In the daylight I see that I am in my own bed, but thrown damply across it with some of my clothes dropped in a pile nearby on the floor. My suit may never be suit-shaped again. It lies amorphously where it landed, with the smells of smoke and wet sheep now oozing out of it as it warms up in the sun.

When I lift the jacket, I notice it is on top of Purvis the Sock Friend, the long-forgotten, dazed-snake-faced companion I made for Greg. Fleas bale out of Purvis in large numbers. I realise while I am watching them that I'm scratching myself, and I think it's more than the power of suggestion. I think the fleas now live in my bed.

I drink water, and as I have no food I drink more water. It sits in my stomach between the constipation and a big gas bubble, as though it's there to stay. I put on loose fitting clothes and sun glasses and I go to Toowong. I have a list of tasks, but first I buy a burger. I drop my suit in to the dry cleaner's, where it is treated with suspicion and they tell me they can make no promises. I return home with an abundance of food and several flea bombs.

I was planning to work at home, but the flea bombs say the house should be evacuated for at least two hours, and evacuated doesn't sound like the sort of word a smart person would disregard. It's also far too hot to work, so maybe I should go in to the office.

Just as I'm feeling that I'm backing myself into a corner and going in to the office is inevitable, Kevin Butt turns up looking very cheery and says, *I've been booked for two gigs since they ran the story on us. Nursing homes. I'm back in the game. We're famous, youngster.*

He insists I go back to his place for lunch and a few beers. So soon I'm sitting in his kitchen and he's talking repertoire and next door at number thirty-four the flea bombs hiss quietly away.

He has a lot of cold beer in his fridge, and all of it Fourex, for which he expresses a great enthusiasm. This obviously stays in his mind, as he whistles a medley of Fourex jingles through his teeth while he's tossing the salad.

And as I take a mouthful of beer, I can't help but wonder who came up with the idea of the Battle of El Alamein Fiftieth Anniversary stubby holder that it's sitting in.

I ask him if he knew my grandfather.

No, before my time I'm afraid. I would have moved here maybe a couple of years after he passed away. I only know what I heard from Edna. Now there was a fine kind of a woman. So if I know only one thing about him I know he was a bloody lucky man. You would have known him though, wouldn't you?

Yeah. I was about ten when he died. So I knew him, but I don't know much about him. He was just my grandfather, you know?

Yeah. I only know what Edna would have told me, and I don't think he told her everything. I think he kept the details of some things to himself. Well, France anyway, she said that. All I know is that the day he copped the gas at Bullecourt, he did something that got him mentioned in despatches as well. Buggered if I know what though. What would it have been?

I don't know.

We drink more beer and we eat, and some time after two I go back to my flea-bombed house to work. I have a lie down instead.

I don't sleep.

In the late afternoon I shower and put on work clothes. I pretend the day is beginning. I drive into town, taking with me a packet of Tim Tams and two bags of Freckles, as I will be too busy to go out for dinner and they go well with coffee.

Some time after eight the air-conditioning turns off and the office becomes progressively more stifling. I keep working, but it just gets worse, and there's no way I can override the timer. So I start taking off my clothes. The shoes and socks and tie go first, but it's not enough. Shortly after eleven I've lowered the pants and the airflow does improve things, but I keep them around my ankles in case anyone turns up and I have to move quickly. By midnight I realise no-one's turning up and the pants are off, and then the shirt. Some time before one I'm totally naked and sitting on my shirt as the upholstery is more scratchy than I would have guessed.

And I'm cruising with this work. It's making sense. I'm going to be okay. Maybe all I ever had to do was let my body breathe. It is strange though, when you've been sitting staring at the word processor and working intently on something and you happen to glance down. The genitalia someone has left in your lap always take you by surprise.

One more cup of coffee. I walk down the corridor and the air moves past my warm clammy body in a very soothing, pleasing way. I see my reflection in plate glass and I feel strangely liberated. Instead of making coffee I turn the Musak on and crank it up as loud as it'll go, and I dance.

And I have just executed a neat leap over an occasional table when the lift door opens and Hillary steps out. I think it's the volume of the Musak that startles her first, but I could be wrong.

It's okay, I tell her, as she starts to lurch back towards the lift. I'm just working but the air-conditioning's off. It got very warm.

Is anyone else here?

No. No-one. It's nothing like that. I'm not like that. It's just hot. I was starting to get some good work done.

You looked like you were dancing.

Yeah. I'd only just started with that though.

Well that's fine then, isn't it? If you'd only just started dancing. She laughs. *It looks like nothing flaccid.*

How big does it need to be for dancing? And what are you doing here anyway?

Dan's got an ear infection. He's not sleeping. It's Peter's night on, but there's no sleep happening in that house. I thought I'd come in and do the work I was planning to come in and do tomorrow. You know, during daytime, outside office nude dancing hours.

I really don't think you should hold this cynical view of office nude dancing unless you've tried it.

Some other time maybe.

This is when we both realise that we're in the foyer at work, having a conversation in which everything's normal except that I'm totally naked. And it all becomes more like the bad dream of an insecure child and a lot less liberating.

How are things with Peter? I ask her.

Okay. But said a little reluctantly.

So what does that mean? What does he know?

Nothing. He knows nothing. I don't know what to do. Am I a bad person if I don't tell him? Am I a fool if I do? I should. I should tell him, get it out in the open. 'Girl from Ipanema' blazes away at maximum volume. *I should be honest with him. Life is just not that easy though. Can I say to myself this is a one-off thing, a once only error of judgement and it'll hurt him more to know?*

It's a good theory, isn't it?

It's a great theory. She pauses. *But anyway, I don't know just yet. I don't know how I sort it out with him.*

175

But how are you after last night? When I left you were standing up at the other end of the table announcing to everyone that you had the cutest arse in the world, but a cock like a pig's tail.

And she's not kidding. As soon as she says the words I recognise them as some part of last night. And it's far too late to wish I'd heard them from someone else's foolish mouth.

Cock like a pig's tail. What does that even mean?

Who knows. You wouldn't say. I don't think anyone thought it was likely to be a good thing.

No. It doesn't sound like a good thing.

But I didn't feel it was my place to either confirm or deny.

The lift door opens again. Barry Greatorex emerges in a dinner suit, stands quite still and stares impassively at both of us, his eyes as lifeless as two currants thumbed into a big bun. 'Girl from Ipanema' slides into another variation. Is that a marimba? Barry reverses his step and the lift doors close and he is gone, like an Alfred Hitchcock effigy in a medieval clock, appearing once to mark the hour, and disappearing in identical retreat.

Some secret we've got, I say to Hillary, but she's still staring at the doors in disbelief, as though she's wondering what's next.

41

After tennis on Sunday I buy a sausage roll and a tube of wine gums.

And you wonder why you don't shit, Jeff says.

I don't wonder. I know why I don't shit.

Beans, eat beans.

Beans, okay.

He insists on taking me home for a meal of beans, and I sit on a stool in the kitchen sucking wine gums while he talks me through the preparation of a kidney bean pilaf.

After we've eaten, and I have to admit that for a bean meal it's really not bad, Sal says, *Shall we give Rick his present now?*

Sure.

So what do I get the present for?

For being such a sad boy. Sal wanted to give you something to symbolise your triumphs.

She comes back in with a T-shirt, a white T-shirt with my fist-in-the-air *Westside Chronicle* photo on it, enlarged. And on the back, in big letters, 'Hero of the 'hood'.

How special, I say. I shall wear it with my medal and they shall call me the mayor of Zigzag Street.

And they can feature you in one of those curious character segments, Jeff says, *when a current affairs show needs lightening up, you know, between the infanticide* story and the pensioner fraud story. And they can edit it and come up with bizarre camera angles to make you look like a complete idiot whatever you do.

Yeah, and I think Kevin would be in that too. We're a double act in the eyes of the media, a sort of Steptoe and Son for the nineties, but very elegant.

I can recall a time before the trashing, perhaps a year ago, when some act of flagrant incorrectness led Sal to buy me a T-shirt with 'Bastard' on it. Perhaps it would be more appropriate if I was wearing that now. But for the moment I'm the 'Hero of the 'hood', and modelling my shirt in their kitchen to some acclaim.

Later Jeff drives me home.

You seem a bit crazy at the moment, he says in the car. *Is it just all that work you did last night? I mean, apart from the usual?*

Yeah. Yeah. No. Well, it's to do with work.

What do you mean? To do with work. Things at work? People at work? Do I get any details?

You want the details?

Sure. Always.

Okay.

But I don't seem to go on.

Okay? There must be more than okay. You realise the longer you spin this out, the better it needs to be.

It's good enough. Okay. Well, last night I went to work. You know that. There's more. They turn off the air-conditioning around eight at night on the weekends and it got very hot. No-one else was there. No-one else had been there the whole time, so some time after midnight, I took my clothes off.

You took your clothes off.

Sure.

All your clothes?

Well, not straightaway. But eventually, yes. All my clothes. And I have to say it felt good. It felt so good that when I saw my reflection in something I just couldn't help myself. This very strange feeling came over me, and I turned up the Musak. And I danced.

You danced naked in the office.

It's not over yet. Anyway, there I was dancing naked in the office, specifically dancing naked in the foyer, in fact, right in front of the lifts. And the lift doors open, and there's Hillary. Of all possible times she picks one o'clock this morning to go in to work.

And you're dancing naked.

Yeah. And this is not just dancing. This is special. I'm putting a lot into this. This is probably some of the best naked dancing the fifteenth floor has ever seen. And it's not over yet. The lift doors open again, and there's Barry Greatorex in a dinner suit.

This is a dream. This must be a dream. You can't tell me this actually happened.

Yes I can. So, he just watches us for a few seconds, and he says nothing, then he backs into the lift—you have to remember he's got a hell of a turning circle, so it's a lot easier to back in—and he goes.

He goes, having seen you and Hillary at work at one am, and you totally naked.

Exactly.

He's likely to get the wrong idea.

Well, here's the twist. I didn't tell you there was a twist, but there is. And the twist is that, well, it mightn't be such a wrong idea. Because, on Tuesday night, in Sydney . . .

And I can't go on now. I can't actually say it.

What? What in Sydney? He's going to make me say it.

On Tuesday night, in Sydney . . . Well, Sydney was tough. Sydney was very strange. It caught us both unawares. And we just, well, we just happened to have sex. It was one of those things.

One of those things? What things?

One of those things where neither of you means it

179

to happen. In fact, you assume it won't happen, so it does.

You didn't mean it to happen? You had sex and you didn't mean it to happen?

Yeah.

How does that work? How do two people not mean sex to happen and then have sex? You were both willing I take it?

Well, sure, but we didn't mean to be.

I'm not getting this yet. You didn't mean it. Neither of you. I think it might have crossed your minds. Otherwise it's a pretty bizarre accident, a real billion to one shot. There you were, the two of you in a meeting, and suddenly, you both realised your penis was inside her. It must have been quite embarrassing. And what did the other people do? Do they think that's a Brisbane thing now? Do they think that up here we find our penises in each other all the time?

It wasn't quite like that. And can I just say all this penis-inside business is a very limited male view of intercourse.

Right at the moment your hold on any high moral ground is at best tenuous.

I'm aware of that.

This is big. This is bad. Did you know this was bad?

I knew it was bad. That's why I assumed it wouldn't happen. I don't do bad things. I do crap things, sometimes insensitive things, but that's usually as far as it goes. I really like Hillary. I think she's great. And I must admit I'd had fantasies, but I thought that was fine, well, not a big deal.

Fantasies are fine.

Good. Well I have plenty of those, and I thought this was just another one.

And then, through one act you go from the crumbly nobility of the Krapmeister to evil Schlong Lord.

I think I still want to be the Krapmeister.

Maybe it's too late.

I can't deal with that. It just happened. We've both agreed it just happened, and that's that. And it wasn't the way you'd think. She's been having a bad time. We both had needs. It was really intimate.

And right now I feel, and I'm sure look, as though I'm going to cry, so he eases up on me. We don't like it when I cry.

This is a very strange time for you, he says.

Very strange.

You must feel quite out of control.

Yes. And I don't like that. I want things to be different. I don't sleep, I can't work, I can't think straight and I feel like fucking Chicken Little, looking everywhere for some kind of affection.

You feel like fucking a chicken now?

Fucking Chicken Little. It was clearly an adjective. It was never a verb. But maybe you've got a point. Maybe not even the chickens are safe. Right now, I just don't know.

I turn down his offer to stay at their place tonight, and he says, *Call if there's a problem. Any time, okay?* And I lie in the dark with my head spinning. I'm not sure any more if Chicken Little was the one who looked everywhere for affection or the one who thought the sky was falling, but either seems applicable.

And tonight I'm angry with Anna Hiller. Tonight it's easier to deal with if it's all her fault.

42

And then it's not her fault, and I don't blame her. I just miss her.

So have I made no progress at all? On nights like this it seems more a descent into madness than any kind of progress. I should be okay now. I really should. I should be okay not in a relationship. I shouldn't fall apart, and this does seem like falling apart.

I have friends, good friends, a job, blah, blah, blah, blah, blah. Not to mention food, shelter, clothing and the consistent and reliable absence of torture. I can make a list that says I'm better off than ninety per cent of the world's population, but that's all meaningless. It doesn't help. It only misunderstands happiness.

So it's dark and still and late and I'm missing Anna. And I thought I'd miss her less by now. I had expected to have moved on, to have swung like a single and not like a plumb bob. To have lived recklessly but harmlessly and without consequences. And my one and only reckless act doesn't fit with this at all. Some people seem to be good at being single. I don't seem to be one of them. I can't work, I can't renovate, I can't remember things, I can't be sure of what's in my own head, and everything just takes such effort.

So does this end? Jeff tells me it ends. Mister Security says things will be okay. He should envy my freedom, and I should piss him off by living wildly, but it's not happening that way. I just make him feel much better about long-term monogamy, a much luckier man. I have days when I want to surround myself with girls, just to make him gnash his teeth, but every part of that's ridiculous.

I think I should go on one of those courses about being a male in the nineties. One of those ones where you get to shout a lot. I think shouting would be good.

And I don't want to change this house. I don't want to talk to my mother, because she will talk to me about changing the house. It should be the way it was. I want to ask her about my grandfather, but from what she's said before I don't know that she knows much more than I do. I think Kevin was right. I think he kept a lot to himself. Maybe my grandmother knew some things, but I missed out on asking her by a matter of months and that pisses me off too.

I'm not sure why I need these answers. Why this has any bearing on the renovations, or on me, but it feels like it does. Maybe I think I've found a family history of periods of despair, and that somewhere in there is an answer. I want to know what my grandfather went through, what he did in the early twenties, what was in his head before he came here and they built this house. There should be other letters, other evidence.

I think I've been attempting to move on through reconstructing some safe platform in my own past, something that includes the answers I need, particularly, I suppose, to the end of things with Anna. I need to be able to put that down to something in the past, so I can believe it won't happen again. Then all this will feel less dangerous. I need to make some sense of it, instead of losing myself in purposeless, painful rumination. But I'm not kicking out of it. Nothing's resolving. Some days there's only more trouble.

And then there's Sydney. I want to sit down with Peter and Hillary and talk, and get whatever I deserve. I also want to run for cover, and pretend it never happened. But it did. And I'm looking at this in a very old-fashioned way, honest retribution, just desserts, as though my life can't possibly be the consequence-free road movie I'd been hoping for the night of the flat battery, because it's already an old western, and I'm now the guy in the black hat, the amoral, straight-shooting gun-slinger with nowhere to call home, pursued by vengeance as long as it takes vengeance to find him. And I hate those films.

And I can't accept that I've made a mess of things with Hillary, that there was something great for a moment there, but I fumbled it. I blew it, and now things can't even be the way they were, and all I'm left with of her is her appalling use of the cowboy movie as metaphor.

Of course I'm thinking, has this been in me all the time? Did Anna know I was like this, and that's why she left? Did she know that there was something bad about me, some unsalvageable flaw that I'm just not brave enough to face?

Why all this guilt? Why this need for punishment?

More questions. More questions. All this thinking and only more questions.

43

It's strange. Giving up sleep should mean I have more time to do things, but I seem to have far less.

I don't even have enough time for bread to toast in the mornings, so I find I'm trying to convince myself that a glass of flavoured mineral water and a handful of Tim Tams is the breakfast of champions.

I have bad feelings about today. Not that this differentiates it from any day in the recent past, but today has the visitors from Singapore, and maybe also some kind of consequences following Barry the Great's brief appearance on Saturday night.

I realise today is a day for an ironed shirt, but I don't have time for that either. So I defer the ironing and I leave home wearing something crumpled and old, and carrying the best shirt I can find in a plastic bag.

I borrow the travelling iron from the executive suite on the sixteenth floor, taking care to go nowhere near Barry's office, and I go back to fifteen and start ironing the shirt on a towel on my desk. As a well-known master of crap, this seems very likely to end in disaster, but for once things go just as they should, and I'm admiring my work, thinking, Hey, maybe I should do this more often, when Hillary comes in. Of course, she catches me in the brief period between shirts and, as I am standing behind my word processor, she thinks I am totally naked again.

Shit, sorry, she says and walks out slamming the door. Before I can do anything the door is open again and she's saying, *What am I acting surprised for? I get to see you naked about every third day.*

Pants on, I tell her. Pants on. I am not naked, merely ironing.

That's good. I could have sworn I heard 'Girl from Ipanema' on the Musak. You had me scared. I was wondering if you were the victim of a cruel hypnotist.

Just don't hum that tune. I can't help myself.

Anyway, I came in with a reason.

Yeah?

Barry. You haven't heard about Barry?

No.

He's gone. He's out of here. Early this morning. The security guard found him in his office. He'd trashed the place. He was hallucinating, seeing naked people, they say. He was climbing the walls and vomiting chocolate and ground coffee. Apparently he was saying all kinds of crazy things. And the last thing he said as he was lifted into the ambulance was, 'You have no idea what I might have been'.

That's good. That's a very good line. Kind of grand and yet enigmatic. I'll have to remember that for my breakdown. So, what's the story with him? I guess he's been weird for a while, but . . .

Yeah. He's been stressed out for a long time. All that bullshitting takes its toll, you know. He thinks they're out to replace him in New York, which is not impossible. But it's people like you who've got him scared. Under thirty and expertise he'll never have.

He only had to ask me. I could have told him I'm no threat to anything at all at the moment.

Well, the man thinks you dance naked here at night. That must mean something mustn't it? It's a pretty bizarre hallucination.

So everyone knows?

Sure. Everyone knows that Barry the Great's gone

mad, and he thought he saw you dancing naked on the fifteenth floor. He even thought I was there too, but dressed. People think it's very funny. It could be worse.

It could. So did he say I managed to be both elegant and hung like a beast?

I don't think so. But he was mad, so who knows?

She leaves me to put on my shirt and to work, and over the next couple of hours a fistful of e-mail messages comes my way from people asking if I do Rick-a-grams at twenty-firsts, questioning the closeness of my relationship with Barry the Great, saying they've cranked the Musak up and when can I be there? So everyone knows about my interest in nude office dancing, and no-one believes it.

Even on my worst days I haven't come close to Barry's last few hours. But maybe that's just a style thing. Maybe the uncompromising scale of his fall gives him the moment of unfettered greatness he has yearned for, and maybe my breakdown will be crap, will creep up on me unnoticed and crumble me down in a much less glamorous way. Or maybe my breakdown is just a worsening inertia, and I'll be able to do less and less, until finally I'll have no idea that I'm doing nothing at all and I'm stuck rigid at my desk drooling down into my keyboard as my sphincters ease lazily open. Some awful oozing kind of breakdown, if such things exist.

Hillary's getting tense. She's pacing up and down, even though everything's ready. Probably because everything's ready and there's nothing for her to do but pace up and down.

Half an hour before they're due to arrive it brings her undone. She snaps a heel on a brisk turn. I hear her swearing in the foyer and she comes into my room hobbling and holding a shoe in one hand and a heel in the other.

What the fuck am I going to do? she says.

We can sort it out, I tell her, though I have no idea how. My voice does sound nice and calm though.

187

How? How? She will not be won by calm. She's rapidly slipping into crazy. *We've only got half an hour. I've checked. They're landing on schedule. The car's there to pick them up. I can't go out and get new shoes. I can't go out in case they get here. Deb's at lunch. What the fuck am I going to do?*

Then I remember the man in Albert Street, the man who always fixed Anna's heels (and she trashed a lot of heels, apparently due to the design of the pavers in the mall).

I think I can get it fixed, I tell her. I think I know a guy who might be able to do it right away. Okay?

Okay? Great. That's great. What do I do?

Leave it to me. You really should be here, just in case. And I know where to go. Just stay calm. Forget the heel. The heel is in my hands.

The lift stops six times on the way to ground and blows at least a couple of my remaining twenty-eight minutes. I run. I run and I sweat any sense of crispness out of my ironed shirt in a second. I run and I manage to dodge everybody except the guy in the wheelchair selling things for the muscular dystrophy Bow Tie Day, but I only wing him, so I keep going. It occurs to me that I might bump into Peter at any moment, and that some innocent circumstance might be my undoing after all; as I collide with him, holding the pieces of his wife's broken shoe, and raise his suspicions a week after the event.

But I don't, and other than nearly spreadeagling the guy with muscular dystrophy, I'm okay. Admittedly my knee is sore from that, and when I look I see I've torn my pants on his chair and I'm bleeding, but the limp doesn't seem to slow me down.

I get to the shoe repairer with twenty minutes to go, and the people waiting step aside as I push through shouting, This is an emergency, and waving the heel like a terrorist with a hand grenade.

The shoe repairer stays calm. He addresses me as Mr Hiller. He asks how Mrs Hiller is. I say she's in Melbourne at the moment, and he makes some lame joke about me coming in with another woman's shoe while she's away.

No it's hers, I tell him.

And then it occurs to him that it might actually be another woman's shoe.

I've seen most of her shoes at some stage, he says. *I've got a very good memory for shoes. But I don't recall a pair like this.*

They're new.

This doesn't look new.

She doesn't wear them much. She might have had them for a while, and she's only started wearing them again lately. They're new to me.

Her feet, and now he's really beginning to doubt me, he's really starting to think I've been fucking the owner of these shoes and it's not my wife, and I just can't get into that now. This is so much more than just the usual attempt to get out of having to face telling the trashing story. *I was sure her feet were bigger than this, by at least a couple of sizes.*

Yeah. They were.

They were?

Sure. She had a fluid problem. It's sorted out now. Some women's thing. This is her natural size. Trust me. And she needs them right away, please. Please.

She's in Melbourne.

Yeah.

But you need the shoes right away. She needs them right away.

Yeah. Yeah. I've got to give them to someone who's just outside in a cab and is about to fly to Melbourne. She and my wife are involved in a business meeting in a couple of hours and my wife says she needs these shoes.

He looks at me, stares at me for what seems like a

189

very long time, as though there is some morality clause involved in shoe repair, and then he says, *Okay*. And he looks at the heel, looks at the shoe, fiddles round for most of the rest of my life and says, *You want a new heel, or you want me to fix the old one back on?*

Whatever's quick. Whatever takes about three minutes.

Okay. Fixing the old one back on is quick, but not as good. And I don't like to compromise. I don't like to think that people are out there walking on work that isn't my best.

Quick is fine. What I need is something that takes about two minutes and forty-five seconds and will last the rest of the day. I promise not to tell anyone it's your work. I'll tell them I did it myself, but that we're planning to bring it to you to get the definitive solution from an expert. Okay?

Okay. The quick fix, and when your wife gets back from Melbourne, she brings it back in and I do the job properly. Okay? And today I won't charge you. Your wife is a good customer and I'm not going to rip her off by charging her for shit that I'm forced to do in two minutes forty-five seconds, okay?

Okay. Great. Thanks.

He takes the shoe and the heel around the corner into his workroom and I hear a single loud whack. He comes back.

I'd say you've got two minutes twenty seconds up your sleeve Mr Hiller. He hands me the shoe.

I thank him profusely for at least the twenty seconds and he stands behind the counter exuding quiet, professional cool. The members of the queue resume their places, confident that their shoes will be safe in his hands.

Who's next? I hear him saying as I run out the door.

I circle round into the mall, watching out for the muscular dystrophy guy, and my shirt is flapping wet against my body with sweat and I feel disgusting. I dodge among shoppers and small children, tourists with ice-creams, crowds around a banjo player, crowds around a fire-eater. Don't these people have anything to do? Can't they at least understand that not everyone is aimlessly browsing? And I get into the inevitable dodging duel with someone walking towards me and at the last second he staggers out of the way, but he does manage to smear his satay stick all over my sleeve.

I decide to cut through a shopping arcade. I run into Broadway but it's packed too, mainly with people just hanging round in the air-conditioning and browsing even more aimlessly than outside. I fight my way up the escalator to the less busy gallery level. Up here I can run. I'm picking up speed. I'm going to make it now. I'll get there on time. I'll get there early and scrape the satay sauce off my sleeve and wear my jacket the whole afternoon. Things will be fine, just fine.

I cover the whole length of Broadway in about ten seconds but it feels like four, and I'm hardly slowing down when I hit the escalator to go back to ground. I'm going to make it now.

And the shoe slips from my sweaty hand and sails out ahead of me off the down escalator and I shout, Look out, just in time for a woman to turn her head and take it in the face.

This is bad, this is one of those horrible moments of slow-motion inevitability. The shoe turning over and over in its downward arc, her turning head. The two of them meeting with an almost mathematical certainty. Her head snapping back, the dark frame of her glasses snapping right in the middle at the point of impact, her knees buckling, her bags dropping, her fumbling, instinctive attempt to catch the shoe as she crumples to the ground between the ornamental figs at the base of the escalator.

And I'm careering down the escalator four steps at a time, vaulting the rubber hand rail, pushing people aside to get to her, and I'm shaking her. I'm shaking her as though that might be useful and I'm shouting, Are you

191

okay? Are you okay? when obviously she isn't. Her eyes open and she fights to see what's going on as she props herself up on one elbow. I put my arm around her to support her and her face is pale, apart from the growing bruise low in the middle of her forehead. And I don't know if that's from the shoe or if she hit her head on a fig pot, but either way it's a bad day for her face, either way it's all my fault.

Um, she says, thinking hard. *I can't see without my glasses.*

This, of course, is a problem, as I have smashed her glasses to buggery. One lens is in pieces about a metre away, with its arm a metre beyond that. I'm trying to work out where the other half is when she pulls it out from beneath her and tries to wear it. She seems unable to understand why it keeps sliding off her bruise.

It's broken, I tell her.

Oh, no, she says. *I just bought them. How am I going to get new ones? I can't afford new ones.*

That's okay. I'll get you new ones.

Really? she says, holding the lens up to her right eye like a monocle. *Why? Why would you get me new ones?*

I broke the old ones.

How?

It was an accident.

I think I'm missing something here. What happened? Am I okay? Hey, I'm sitting down. I'm sitting on the ground in Broadway. Between two little trees. Wait, do I know you?

No, no. Something slipped out of my hand and hit you and you fell over.

Look, take my money. Take my money. I don't have much. It's all in my purse, just, please, don't hurt me. And she starts to cry.

No, no. This is all right. This is an accident. No-one's taking your money. Everything's fine. Everything's fine.

The Mastercard's no good. They cancelled it.

Yeah, fine. That's smart thinking, but just listen to

me. You've had a bump on the head, but things are going to be okay. You're quite safe now.

They cancelled my Mastercard and I was only slightly over my limit.

No-one wants your Mastercard.

By now, we have a ring of people around us, all of them curious to see the woman I have knocked out rediscovering the world, realising she is not being mugged, coming to terms with her credit crisis, looking with her one available eye at the semicircle of knees in front of her. And she seems completely oblivious to the steadily enlarging mass rising from the front of her head.

So, she says, *there was an accident. But I'm okay now.*

Yeah. Basically okay, yeah. But I think we have to get your head looked at. You've got a bit of a bump there.

Yeah. I don't feel very well. I'm a bit thirsty. Are you thirsty?

Well, yeah. It's a hot day. But we can have a drink some other time maybe. I mean you can have something to drink soon, but I think we've got to get your head looked at.

Some problem here? a big male voice says just behind me.

I look around and it's a security guard, a man with shoulders so big they only just leave room for his bullet-shaped head. And a scar on his right cheek, and hands that could crush a watermelon. And I may be stereotyping him, but I don't think he's too clever.

It's just . . . this woman just fell over, I tell him. It's okay. It'll be okay.

He keeps staring at me.

It's really okay. I'm a doctor. I can sort this out. She's just a bit dizzy. A bit dehydrated maybe. It's a hot day.

He kneels down on the ground, and I think my body is about the same size as each of his thighs.

Are you right there? he says to her.

She nods.

Will you be right if I leave you with the doc to sort you out?

Yeah. I'll be fine. Thanks.

Okay then. He stands up again. *Thanks doc. I'll leave her with you if you're happy with that. If there's anything you need, just send someone up to centre management on the first floor and we'll sort it out for you.*

I thank him and he swaggers away (as men with those thighs must), happy that this problem is now successfully delegated.

She'll be right, I tell the people around us. She's just a bit dehydrated.

And they recognise this as the voice of authority, telling them they should leave now.

So am I dehydrated or did I have an accident, or what? she says when she's had time to process this apparent inconsistency. And she peers at me through the lens with big blinks of an attractive grey eye.

An accident. So we're going to get you to a doctor now.

But you're a doctor.

Yeah. I'm not that kind of doctor.

What kind of doctor are you?

That doesn't matter now.

No, what kind?

I'm a dermatologist. Okay?

Wow. You're a very young dermatologist.

I've just looked after my skin well. It's my job. Now, let's try to get you standing, slowly. And I'll help you.

She takes my arm, puts one hand on my shoulder and pulls herself to her feet. She leans heavily against my side for balance. Her face goes pale again, but she tells me she's okay.

Then I remember the shoe.

We're going to get you to sit down for just a second. I've got to get rid of this shoe. Okay? So just sit here and I'll be back in a second.

And I ease her down onto a bench.

I run out to Adelaide Street and I flap my arms till a taxi looks like stopping.

Twenty bucks to take this shoe to an office two blocks away, I say to the driver as he pulls over.

Sure. And who do I ask for mate, Cinderella?

Hillary. I mean, that's very funny, but you ask for Hillary. Hillary Fisher on fifteen.

I write down the address and Hillary's name and ask him to tell her there's an emergency so I can't make it, but everything's okay.

And he takes the shoe and the twenty dollars, says, *No worries*, and sends the car screeching off up the street with a far greater sense of urgency than I ever meant to suggest.

Back in Broadway the woman sits where I left her, still looking dazed. I pick up her shopping bags and lead her outside, and I flag down another cab.

Have you got a doctor? I ask her. A regular doctor? Someone in particular we should take you to?

No.

Okay. Okay, we'll go to mine.

I give the cabbie the address.

I've got this rash, she says. *It keeps breaking out, just on my fingers.*

Yeah, well, we'd better get your head sorted out first. That's probably more important right at the moment.

Sorry, it was rude of me to ask. I just thought, Here I am in a cab with a dermatologist, you know?

Okay, maybe it's the detergent you use. If it's fingers it could be detergent.

Oh, right. So what should I do about it? Is there any cream I should use, or anything?

Cream. Yeah, a cream would be good.

Which cream? Could you give me a name?

She's got me with that one. Just when I'd impressed myself with the detergent theory.

Okay, I've got to be honest with you. I'm not a dermatologist.

195

You're not a dermatologist?

No.

Then why did you say were a dermatologist?

It was a spur of the moment thing. A moment of weakness. It seemed like the thing to say.

So what sort of doctor are you?

A lawyer. I'm a lawyer.

Really? I could have sworn you said doctor back there. That's why I asked you what kind of doctor you were. This is very strange. I guess it's just from being knocked out. I can just hear this conversation, you and some guy, and you're a doctor. Weird.

We turn a corner and the sun comes in her side of the cab, and she shuts her eyes.

It's only now that I look at her properly, without the overlay of horror and fear, and I realise I have KO'd a babe. It concerns me that this has even occurred to me, as though I have some shoe-thrower's ethical duty to offer all victims the same post-injury consideration.

She gets comfortable with her head on the headrest and her eyes still closed and her dark, straggle-ended hair reaching down to her shoulders. And she looks as though she's biting the left end of her lower lip, just slightly, and I think I should look away, but I don't. Here I am, on a work day of some importance, riding out of town in a cab with a babe I've just concussed with footwear.

With a head injury, we're told *Doctor will see you next*, and we're taken into the treatment room. I tell her the story about the flea-bath suicide attempt.

So they're going to think a lot of you now, aren't they? she says. *First you try to kill yourself with a cat, then you try to kill me with a shoe. Not a very competent man.*

Greg comes in and remembers me and says, Oh, hi Richard. *How are things?*

Fine. Good.

So you're bringing your friends here now. That's nice.

Thanks.

196

Now, we don't have a file yet, so you'll have to introduce me.

The woman laughs. *So go on Richard, introduce me to the doctor. Tell him about us.*

I don't know your name, do I?

No.

Greg starts to look confused.

I'm Rachel, she says. *Rachel Vilikovski. And I'm here because Ricky knocked me out with a shoe.*

No-one calls me Ricky.

No-one?

Well, essentially no-one. And the shoe thing was an accident. It slipped out of my hand.

Well, I don't recall it. I was knocked out. He tells me it was an accident.

It was an accident. Just one of those things. I was running for the down escalator. I'd been getting the shoe fixed and I was in a hurry and it slipped out of my hand.

Okay, Greg says, and looks as though he wants to steer this back on track. *So, Rachel, do you have a problem with this, with the shoe, or does it not bother you? I'm just thinking, and you'll have to excuse me for this one Richard, but if you were going to take any action against Richard . . .*

I think he should go to jail for this, she says looking at me.

Piss off. It was an accident. I've got witnesses.

Oh, yeah. Like the security guy? Think about it Ricky. Think about his story.

No, I'm thinking, well, look at Rachel's nose, Greg says, fumbling for control. *The bridge of Rachel's nose. Supposing there's a fracture there that needs cosmetic surgery. I don't think that's likely, but supposing . . .*

I'd pay. It's okay. I'm responsible for this.

I'm just thinking, maybe we should take a couple of photos, document the injury.

Rachel, of course, agrees right away.

So Greg takes down details, checks things out and

thinks she looks okay, and sends her for x-rays, which are fine too. But we take the photos nonetheless, with Rachel grinning like a bulbous-headed babe.

That's a lovely smile, Greg says as he snaps the front-on view. *It'll look great in court.*

He gives her a Head Injury Card to carry with her for twenty-four hours, and a list of things that might suggest she is bleeding inside her skull or that her brain is being crushed by increasing pressure. Good list.

We're about to go when he notices my knee, and I have to tell him I bumped into a wheelchair. He looks at Rachel and she just says it's before her time. So I drop my pants and I cop two stitches and a tetanus needle. Rachel insists it's her right to stay and watch, and every time I wince she laughs.

And Greg says, in the middle of tying the second stitch, *I'm not sure I understand your life.*

I try to think of something useful to say, but in the end I just tell him, It hasn't always been like this.

He gives me a look that suggests considerable doubt, that I think suggests I have just come out with the standard response of a habitually self-destructive person. But I might be reading too much into it. It might just be his suturing face.

Rachel looks round in her purse for her Medicare card and finds someone has put the lensless half of her glasses in there. So the three of us take a roll of surgical tape and fix the glasses together so that they just balance on her face and still manage to make allowances for her altered contours. She looks in a mirror.

Hey, very attractive, she says. *Nice look. I don't know if I'll need new ones. This is very ugly, isn't it.*

She signs the Medicare form and I offer to drive her home and she says, *Okay.* I leave her in the air-conditioning and hobble up the hill to fetch my car. And it occurs to me that maybe I should have thrown my shoe at the cellist in the rain when I drove past her, instead of giving her the chance to get away. Beating a woman over the head and dragging her to your lair is, however, a very paleolithic way to get to know her, and not highly regarded in the late twentieth century.

I bet Sal would be impressed if I began a relationship by knocking a woman out.

Why do I think this? Why, after maybe an hour of female company, do I start imagining myself talking to my friends years later about how our relationship started?

As I'm driving back I begin to wonder if she will still be at the medical centre. If I'll park and they'll say, *It's okay, she caught a cab.* And then I can go back to work.

But she's there.

And in the car all the way to her house at West End I'm thinking, what can I do to see this girl again? And I'm thinking I shouldn't be thinking this, but fuck it, I am, and if I don't think it now there's no point in thinking it at all. I could at least get to know her better. We could maybe have coffee or something. Can I try that? Can I suggest coffee to a girl I've only met through rendering her unconscious? I'm unaware of the etiquette in this situation, but I expect I am not in a position of strength. Besides, she's concussed. Her judgement might be impaired.

But she is terribly attractive. That is, assuming the Elephant Man lump in the middle of her forehead goes down. Assuming it wasn't there before the shoe hit her. And I can't recall now. I can't recall any detail of her, without at least some swelling. I could be sitting here nursing a massive erection through the traffic of South Brisbane, all on account of a girl with a very large additional piece of bone in the front of her head. But I can't get a good look at it now because she's holding an ice-pack over it. Not that it would be right to look.

I think I am a very shallow person. I think it is bad to be put off someone just because of a piece of bone, and bad to be packing an absolute railway sleeper in my pants for someone to whom I feel I owe a duty of care. And there are many other things I can think of that are bad, but I tell myself this is not a time for making lists. This is a time for action.

She wears no rings. I noticed that. Not that that necessarily means too much. She doesn't talk about having a partner. But then, why should she? I don't talk about not having a partner.

How old would she be? Twenty-two? Twenty-three? I think that according to Jeff all babes that age seem to end up in your house at night fucking footballers. I'm not sure what was behind that, but it's likely to have been a bad experience in his early twenties that he's much more comfortable dressing up as a universal truth.

So who do you think'll win the Super Ten series this year? I ask her.

The what?

Doesn't matter.

Excellent. She has no idea about Rugby, and I think, on reflection, it was Rugby Union players who were of concern to Jeff.

So, do you live in Red Hill? she asks me.

Yeah.

Nice area. In a house or a flat?

House. My grandparents' house, or at least, the house they built.

That's nice. Is it just you there or . . .

Yeah. Well, at the moment.

You've got plans?

No, not plans. I just thought I might get some people in to share.

Yeah, I share with a couple of people. A couple of girls. It's good, but they're away a bit. And so are their boyfriends. Which means that when they aren't they keep me awake all night bouncing on their squeaky beds. So when I say it's good, I mean it's good in theory. There are moments when it's good.

We park outside her house, a wooden place with a leadlight porthole window next to the front door and a lawn dominated by tall, slender weed-stalks. The house looks about the same age as mine but it's painted a colour that might be peach. But none of this helps me. I've been working hard to think of a plan, but I'm about to lose my chance. I'm about to blow it, and to have to reconstruct a strike out later on as an honourable choice.

I'll probably get my new glasses in the next few days, she says. *I've got a spare pair I can get by with till then.*

Oh, yeah. Here, I'll give you my card. Send me the bill. Okay? And do let me know if you've got any other problems. I feel very bad about this. This isn't typical of me, you have to believe that.

She takes the card and laughs.

Okay. Maybe I do.

And she puts the card in her purse next to her head injury instructions and gets out of the car. I watch her go past the old rusty gate and up the three concrete steps. She stops and waves to me as I drive away, watching her in the mirror the whole length of the street. And she doesn't go inside yet, doesn't go until I've turned the corner.

I start driving towards town. My knee is really beginning to ache as the local anaesthetic wears off, and I must smell very bad by now. I am sure all I can do with the Singapore visitors in this state is cause offence.

So I go home. I shower and call work, and Deb is clearly worried about me. I tell her I'm okay. Hillary comes on and says, *Thanks for the shoe buddy.*

I'm sorry, I tell her. I'm sorry. You wouldn't believe what happened.

That's probably true.

How's it been?

Fine. Well as fine as you'd expect. I covered it.

I tell her I'll fill her in on the details of the emergency in the morning, so this gives me all night to come up with the right version of the story.

And I don't give it a moment's thought.

44

In the morning I keep it simple and I tell her I was running back from the shoe repairer and I collided with a wheelchair, and that explains my limp (which for the purposes of the story is really quite bad).

And I even had to get stitches in my knee, but the x-rays were okay so that's a relief. The doctor said I should have a couple of days off to rest it, but I knew I was needed here.

Stitches? she says. You got stitches? Show them to me. What?

It seems everyone's interactions with me now start with the assumption that I have no dignity at all.

I won't believe you unless you show them to me.

Fortunately I can roll the leg of my trousers above my knee, so I give her the proof she demands and she makes a face and says, *That's a very unattractive wound Rick.*

So I seem to be forgiven.

I go back to Broadway at lunchtime, completely without meaning to. I just set off walking and it's where I am, soon enough.

And just when I wonder if I might see Rachel Vilikovski there, I see the security guard instead.

Hey doc, he shouts, as though we go way back. *How's that girl?*

I think she'll be fine. Dehydration. I made sure she got some fluids in her.

He looks improbably thoughtful. *Oh, you know doc, I've seen 'em drop like that before, and you know what I reckon it might be? A pituitary tumour.*

A pituitary tumour.

Yeah. When I had my back op there were a couple of fellas in the ward who'd dropped just like that, and they had pituitary tumours.

Yes, I thought about that as a possibility, but when I examined her in my rooms a few specific tests were negative.

Like the old red-tipped pin, eh doc? And he laughs knowingly.

The red-tipped pin. Yes, she failed on the red-tipped pin.

It's a good test that one. Bugger me if the blokes in the neurosurgical ward didn't have markedly constricted visual fields when they were tested with the red-tipped pin.

The ones with the pituitary tumour?

Yeah.

Yeah, she wasn't like that at all.

But you did the CAT scan I suppose. I mean, the pin's good, but these days you don't rely on the pin.

No.

So what did the CAT scan show?

Haven't got it back yet.

He nods, and then says, *Oh, right, ethics, gotcha. Say no more.* And he smiles. *Hey, you don't think it'd be worth my while carrying a red-tipped pin around with me on the job, do you? Just as a quick screening test, you know?*

Sure.

You couldn't write a note to centre management could you? It'd have a lot more clout coming from a bloke like yourself. Rather than me just hitting 'em for a red-tipped pin I mean.

Sure. No problem. I can do it on letterhead paper and send it across.

Beauty, good on you doc. And he sticks both arms out to the side and wobbles his index fingers. *Hey, which finger's wiggling? Just kidding doc. Remember that one? You'd do that one all the time, wouldn't you? The old wiggly finger?*

Sure.

People are looking at us as though the security guard has caught me in the performance of an uncommon sexual practice. Or perhaps is trying to encourage me to engage in one with him.

I tell him I'm late for afternoon surgery, and he gives me a last playful demonstration of the old wiggly finger as I back away, adding Broadway to the growing list of places in my home town to which I can never return.

Mindful of Jeff's dietary advice and my increasingly uncomfortable commitment to constipation, I buy a bean enchilada for lunch, and I ask for double beans. And when you're used to a diet of Tim Tams and barbecue chips, a bean enchilada is a real let down. Still, I must move beyond this focus on immediate gratification, and think of the great comfort it shall bring me soon enough.

I'm annoyed I didn't get her number. There are no Vilikovskis in the phone book, and I don't know where she works. I thought about writing to her or leaving a note in her mailbox, but nobody does that now. She'd think I was stalking her. There must be some acceptable way.

Whether there is or there isn't, I'm now annoyed that I could begin to obsess about a woman who probably has only a patchy recollection of me as the man who decked her. I expect she wants me terribly. I expect she can't live without me. That she's been up all night wanting me, bugging her housemates in the middle of intercourse and saying, *See this lump? See this lump? I want that guy. He knocked me out with a woman's shoe and that makes me so horny.*

What a dickhead. What a dickhead. I'm loading the rest of this therapeutic double bean enchilada into me and thinking, what a dickhead. And why do people eat beans now? How could people possibly eat beans when there are Tim Tams in this world?

I expect that in a few days I'll just get a bill for an exorbitant amount of money, and I'll pay for her glasses. I'll send her the cheque with some faintly foolish note that she will ignore, and that will be that.

I want to call Anna and tell her how well I'm doing. I want to tell her about the opportunities she has opened up for me. In just the last couple of weeks I've turned down a sixteen year old, fucked my boss and knocked out a babe. Had fantasies about all three and more. This is not how I had envisaged my late twenties, but maybe that's just me.

At work there are several messages on my desk. Two from Sydney, one from Jeff. One in Deb's writing that just says, 'Rachel (???) called. Said she'd call back later'.

My outburst of glee is silent and private, and tempered quickly by the realisation that she's probably just bought the glasses and she's telling me how much I'm up for. Stay calm, I tell myself, stay calm.

Twenty minutes later she calls back.

Hi, she says. *I just wanted to thank you for looking after me yesterday.*

Well, it seemed only reasonable.

No, it was more than reasonable. You gave up your afternoon to get things sorted out.

Hey, I knocked you unconscious.

Yeah, I guess. But thanks anyway. I think you did more than a lot of people would.

So how's the head today? I wanted to call you. To find out how you were. But I don't have your number.

Have you got a pen?

And she gives me her work and home numbers, just like that. She impresses me immensely.

I thought I'd come into town tomorrow, she says. *To*

205

get the glasses. I thought, since you were sponsoring them, I should give you the chance to come along and be involved in the choice. I wouldn't want you to buy glasses you hated.

That's very generous of you.

I'm a very considerate person.

Yesterday you wanted me to go to prison.

Yesterday I wasn't myself. I was just some victim of a flying shoe. Far from my best. How about meeting at the place you decked me? You should remember where that is.

Broadway's not so good for me at the moment.

Okay. Eyewear Now, Albert Street, say one-thirty?

Sure. Sure, I'll be there.

Okay. See you then Richard Derrington.

Yeah.

And she goes. Leaves me with my whole name and goes.

45

So I'm thinking, how do I handle this?

I have between now and one-thirty tomorrow to come up with a plan. To have some idea that will be cool, manageable and successful. Whatever successful is. If it's what I want.

I call Jeff.

So, what are you looking for here? he says, treating my ramblings with all the respect due a hare-brained scheme. *I mean, have you thought this through? You sound a bit dangerous to me.*

But she's great. Really.

Okay. Let's just get some perspective on this.

I've got the perspective.

He ignores me. *Okay, this would be at least the third or fourth time in the last few weeks your trousers have had the better of your brain, not that it's a very good brain at the moment. That was okay not long ago when they weren't very good trousers either, but clearly they've made progress. And you worry me with that.*

But she's great.

Sure. I'm sure she's great. This is a town full of great women. They don't all require mugging as a means of seduction. Are you sure you're ready for this? I don't think you're very stable at the moment.

No, I'm not. But . . .

I just want you to be careful, okay. You make whatever

207

decision you want to make, but it would be good if you could be careful. It would be nice if things could just calm down a bit for you, and you could work a few things out.

But what if I want to do things with her?

Well, that depends on the two of you. But, look, less than a week ago you were fucking your boss, and two days ago that was presented to me as something that was intimate and special, but a little misguided. Now you're beating other women to the ground with her shoes as the prelude to some completely different elaborate fantasy.

There's no elaborate fantasy. And if there's any fantasy at all, who's to say it's different? What if I just want there to be a babe in whose company I can do things? A special female babe friend to have coffee with and things.

Rick, never. You couldn't do it. You'd be sitting there at Aroma's and she's calmly sipping a cappuccino, thinking platonic thoughts, thinking isn't it nice to have a male friend who doesn't want to get into my pants. And all you're thinking about is how you do want to get into her pants, and you're wondering if everyone in the place can see the fearsome action going on in yours. And don't pick me up on this. I'm not saying men and women can't have platonic friendships, even if the women are babes and even if the men are single, and vice versa I suppose. What I'm saying is that you can't. That right now, with what appears to be happening in your head, and what appears to be happening in your pants it would be foolish to embark on anything with that kind of notion. And that's because of fantasy, Rick. Because there's always an elaborate fantasy. Nothing is normal for you. You've probably visualised all kinds of relationships with this woman already. You've probably already asked yourself whether or not marrying her is a possibility.

Well, yeah. But you always do that. Just so you can rule out the ones where it isn't a possibility early on.

I don't suppose you realise that's a totally fucked idea.

No.

208

*So, will you just admit to me that when this woman
called and mentioned going shopping for glasses, things
other than coffee and friendship occurred to you?*
Maybe.
So, is this a good time for a relationship for you?
Maybe not.
Okay. And are you over Anna yet?
No.
I try, therefore, to put it out of my head, which of
course I don't. I try not to fantasise. I fantasise.

I go through a complex process of negotiation with
myself that allows me, most of the rest of the day, to
fantasise endlessly about intimacy, but not about sex.

But by the time I'm lounging around on the couch at
home flicking through the Monday night TV with the
remote, I'm totally unaware of how I came to draw that
line. Why the intimacy fantasy is fine, and the sex fantasy
isn't. Maybe I've forgotten the arguments, and it was
meant to be the other way round. Maybe the sex was
fine, and the intimacy was dangerous. Right now that
makes more sense. I'm quite sure that any fantasy involving both sex and intimacy would be incredibly dangerous,
but maybe just sex would be okay.

Then I worry that, much as the sex idea appeals, I'm
also a sucker for the intimacy.

And I think about the things I miss. Sure, until last
week sex was one of them, but there was only a short
period between the resolution of my Post-trashing Impo-
tence Syndrome and the misguided events of Sydney.

I miss the sounds of another person about the house.
I miss the theft of sheets in the middle of the night. I
miss rummaging through tampons in the glove box to
find the video store cards. I miss having tissues appliqued
to my business shirts in the washing machine when I
never use tissues. I miss big stupid arguments over small
stupid things. I miss two smart people never accepting
the responsibility for finishing the toilet roll, or the milk.
I miss coffee that's completely the wrong strength but

209

made with the best of intentions. I miss the ends of days when you're both too tired to talk and you sit in front of bad TV with your shoes off, and you just do nothing. Why? Why isn't it happening for me?

46

My palms sweat in the air-conditioning.

I'm going to fuck this up. I know I'm going to fuck this up.

She has the reasonable expectation that we will buy glasses because her old ones are broken, and I'm behaving as though my life depends on it. So I've fucked it up already. I needn't worry about it. I've already put Jeff's greatest fears about me into practice. I have already lived the fantasy of intimacy with Rachel Vilikovski a million times, and in the real world all I've done is injure her.

What a dickhead. I should live my life knowing that harm will come to me.

She's at Eyewear Now at one-thirty. She's wearing a short black dress and I'm fighting off the emergence of a speech impediment.

I say Hi.

Hi. She looks at me as though I might be kind of comical and she smiles, but only by lifting the right half of her upper lip.

Technically this may be no more than a quarter of a smile, but it kills me. I'm lucky she didn't use any more.

And she has a large irregular swelling between her eyes, and her broken glasses arranged so that she has good vision from the eye with the lens. Why is she wearing that short black dress? She looks far too good in it. The short black dress is a well-known weakener of weak men, and I'm as weak as they come. This is hardly fair. And she has such a shape under that black dress, such a cruel, slinky woman kind of shape. And still the quarter smile. I'm still copping the quarter smile.

I had to wear these glasses, she says. *My spare pair doesn't fit because of the swelling. So it's probably not a good day to be buying new frames, but I think I know what I want.*

I follow her in and I'm thinking the people in the store will be thinking we're together. That this is the way it works with us. I'm buying her glasses. And maybe she bought me this tie for my twenty-eighth. And that lint in the shirt pocket? Maybe it's one of her tissues. I never use tissues.

Black dress. *I think I know what I want.* She is a very powerful woman.

Vilikovski, Rachel, she's saying. *You'll have my prescription on file. I had an accident with the glasses.*

The next fifteen minutes are a joy as Rachel, who might know what she wants but clearly wants something very specific, tries on frame after frame, as best she can. And says things like, *So, does this go with my eyes? Is this right with my cheekbones? How does this make me look?* Before ending up with frames very like the ones I broke, but three times the price. And that doesn't bother her at all.

The glasses will take twenty minutes, so she says, *How about we go for coffee?* And the nearest place is the Koffies I usually frequent with Jeff, and that's where she walks.

And of course the girl who thinks I'm a hero is behind the counter again. I try not to make eye contact but she says to Rachel, *You must be very proud of him,* and looks at me, smiling.

Sure, Rachel says. *Who wouldn't be?* And she pays for the coffees, saying, *You only owe me glasses.*

We sit in a booth.

So why am I proud of you? Not that I'm not. Not that I'm sure there aren't a thousand reasons, but why?

Who knows? Because I just won some big dermatology award? She must have thought I was somebody else.

Really?

Yeah.

Maybe there's more to you than meets the eye, she says and shuts the eye on the lensless side of the frame to study me more closely.

And I'm sure it's all of the highest quality, I tell her.

She smiles and goes and gets herself a glass of water. She takes two Panadol when she sits down again.

Are you sure you should be taking that?

Hey, my Head Injury Card says paracetamol is fine.

Your head's still sore then.

Well, yeah. But with an egg like this what do you expect? I'm sure it'll go down in a day or two. This is not my normal look you know.

Yeah, I'm sorry. I'm really sorry about all that. Shit. I don't think I even apologised before. I think I knocked you out twenty-four hours ago and it didn't occur to me to apologise till just now. That's so bad. I'm sorry. Really. That's terrible. You had me worried yesterday, you know. I had these fears about you bleeding in your head and your brain getting crushed, and all that. I was sitting there last night thinking, if she goes to bed and her brain gets crushed I'll feel like shit.

She laughs. *Well, I thought about it, but I really didn't want to make you feel like shit, so I thought I'd live.*

Good choice.

The first ten minutes of the twenty minute wait has been the quickest of my life, but the conversation suddenly stalls and it becomes apparent that the only common ground we've established is based on the injury I have done her. That we've spent half an hour playing the roles of two people who know each other well, and now we realise we don't know each other at all. And the next ten minutes means a lot.

I'm going to fight this. This is when I can deteriorate into nervous smiles and long gazes out the window and a lot of coffee drinking, as though my coffee is of paramount importance. But not today.

So now that you've decided to live, I say to her, what are you going to do with the rest of your life? You and your fine new frames.

This is a bad line. A seriously crappy line. It's so bad it makes me sweat.

The rest of my life? And she thinks about this. *Bring about world peace. Bring an end to poverty.* And she's clearly despatching this with exactly the treatment it deserves. *Find a cure for all known diseases. And have my own incredibly low quality daytime TV show.*

Wow. That's great. Sort of Boutros Boutros-Ghali meets Oprah.

I'm thinking more like Boutros Boutros-Ghali meets Bert Newton.

That's a great show. That is a great show. So, at nine-thirty you restructure the World Bank, nine-forty you talk to Arthur from Bamix about some outstanding juicing device . . .

Nine-fifty and I've redrawn the map of the Balkans, and they all love what I've done with it, ten o'clock and I've got a segment on decoupage that really kicks arse.

This is a very good show. This is a show the world needs, or at the very least, deserves. You realise this could work on cable.

I'd never thought about cable.

Sure. It's the medium of the nineties. Well, that and CD-ROM and the Internet.

She nods, as though she's giving it a second's serious thought. *Lucky I didn't go ahead with the brain crushing then.*

We go back for the glasses and I have the pleasure of loading four hundred and fifty dollars onto my Visacard.

And we stand in the street, Rachel with the broken

glasses still fitted across her damaged face, twirling her new pair in her right hand.

They're nice, she says. *Thanks.*

That's okay.

And I'm thinking, thinking, thinking. Thinking, this is sorted out. I should let her go now, let her go and have a life. Thinking, no way.

You worry me with these headaches, I say to her, as though it's a considerate remark and not a tactical manoeuvre.

I'll be okay.

Yeah, well, you worry me. You will see someone if they get worse, won't you? If there might be any problem.

Sure.

Is it all right if I call you? To see if you're okay? You worry me, like I said.

It's fine. That'd be fine. You've got my numbers.

Yeah.

I look over my shoulder when I'm back at the edge of the mall, and she's walking away down Albert Street, her new glasses in her right hand, still twirling.

47

You wouldn't believe this woman, I say to Jeff. You just wouldn't believe her.

And I tell him about the last forty-five minutes. The short black dress. *I think I know what I want.* The quarter smile. The most expensive pair of glasses in the world, and not an eyelid batted. The TV show idea.

Shit, Boutros meets Bert, he says, almost in a whisper, his admiration more than apparent over the phone. *That's a great show.*

That's what I said.

I think she's a very powerful woman.

Yeah.

Rick, you're playing the big game now. Are you up to this?

I have no good answer. I have an obvious answer, which is No, but I have no good answer.

At home that night I think I shall invite her for dinner. I think I'll persuade her around to Zigzag Street and give her fine wine and a meal of several courses.

This plan is, of course, more comprehensively fucked than most. What would I cook? What could I do with even one course that could possibly impress Rachel Vilikovski? The pantry is now loaded with single-serve baked beans (in sauces of various flavours) and the fridge with Tim Tams. Jeff and Sal, aware of my needs, gave me a recipe book for Christmas called *Kid's Snacks and*

Lunches, and for about five seconds I actually browse through the table of contents quite seriously.

And I realise I'm planning to line the glorious Rachel Vilikovski up for a curried popcorn entree, baked beans on toast main and star-shaped Nutella sandwiches and Tim Tams for dessert. To look at this in the bluntest of terms, not even Brad Pitt would score after serving such a banquet. Besides, I have no idea which wines would go with each course.

So I'm thinking recipes, recipes, do I know any actual recipes? Years ago my mother taught me a few French things to do with chicken and I remember one occasion when I invited a young woman around, in anticipation of intercourse, and inadvertently used the wrong amount of the wrong flour and turned my sauce into something that looked much more like rabbit turds. But she wasn't averse to the intercourse, if I recall, so the night wasn't a complete waste.

But I'm sure I'm not like that now.

And no way would Rachel Vilikovski fall for a plate of warm rabbit turds around a chicken breast.

48

Perhaps it's all this contemplation of food that drives my grumbling bowel closer to crescendo. Or perhaps I am almost ready to take my seat for the unread acts of *The Spanish Tragedy*.

I show no mercy. I dine on baked beans on toast. Double beans.

I lie in bed, and the activity in my abdomen reaches seismic proportions.

In the morning the earth moves, all those peristaltic waves line up and push with a brutal purpose, finally fibre wins. And I'm a little dizzy when I stand afterwards, but much lighter, and my clothes move about me with great comfort.

I want to tell people how good beans are. I want to tell the people on the bus, Deb at work, but the right moment doesn't seem to arise.

Hillary arrives late morning, after visiting Barry in hospital.

He's really not bad, she says. *He's quite calm. Well, much calmer than he was. He said he had blinding headaches for a day and a half, but he's much better now without the chocolate-coated coffee beans. He has a theory that it was caffeine poisoning, and other than that he's fine. He's talking about coming back to work.*

Really?

I get the feeling his specialist is yet to be convinced.

She turned up while Barry was running the theory by me and she didn't say much. Oh, and he said he hoped you wouldn't feel bad about the hallucination thing.

He's clearly a sick man. These things happen.

He did say that he was sure the hallucination did you a disservice, and that in real life you were probably a lot better off.

Really? He said that?

Maybe. He also said that if he didn't come back here he might take up a lawn-mowing franchise.

She leaves me with this dubious suggestion. Barry struggling and sweating in a white towelling hat, huffing and puffing and lumbering up and down lawns, leaning on his rake and crapping on and on to his customers about this change of direction for him, this lifestyle choice. But the more I think about it, the more I think he'll be back. The chocolate-coated coffee bean theory gives him what he needs, a great bullshit story that says the breakdown was caused by some external force. Then it changes from a hint of personal vulnerability to another glorious episode in the near-glorious life of Barry the Great. And in a few years time it'll be, *More than enough caffeine to kill ten men, that's what the doctor said. They were amazed I pulled through, said they'd never seen anyone get back on top of things so quickly, having been so close to death.*

This is why I will never understand Barry. We are each composed of our own stories, but in mine the crap is preserved (in mine, the crap usually is the story), and in Barry's the crap is re-worked in the hope that it can be made to shine. In my stories I am the engaging fool. In Barry's he is the hero. And the stories could be identical, but this is what becomes of us in the telling. I fall short of greatness, but I survive the fall and the inelegant swan dive of my trajectory becomes a joke at my expense. Barry falls short of greatness, and wants to make it clear how close he got, that the margin was next to nothing, and it was only fate that turned it. I don't even know if he fools himself.

And in the end nobody likes him. Barry's no alchemist and crap doesn't shine. And I think he has some inkling of this and tries even harder, so they like him less. Maybe we should be sorry for him. Maybe now, while he's not here and I don't have to endure the bullshit I can be generous enough to be sorry for him.

Enough of Barry G., I have things to do.

I call the work number of Rachel Vilikovski.

It's a nursing home. But then, I don't know what I was expecting. I ask for her and the person says, *I think she's down at bingo at the moment, could she call you back?* So I leave my name and number and I'm left thinking bingo? Bingo? How much don't I know?

The phone rings.

Hi, she says.

I thought you were at bingo.

Bingo's over. Some people here have no idea how long bingo takes.

What do you do?

In bingo? Well you have these cards. Someone calls out numbers.

Yeah, thanks.

You asked.

Yeah. So how are you today? How's the head?

Getting there. In a couple of days I think my very attractive new glasses might actually fit. In the meantime I'm getting used to seeing everything through one eye. It's very annoying you know, getting new glasses and going to the trouble of having a spare pair, which I do, and then swelling in a way that means you can only wear the ones that are extra bendy in the middle because they're held together by surgical tape. And you know what? Just about nobody notices here, as long as you keep the energy up. So how are you?

Relatively calm today. Hardly any inclination to hurl footwear at all.

I think I have to go. They keep me busy here.

So what's next? After bingo?

World news.

World news?

Sure. Me, the Courier-Mail *and an enthusiastic discussion group. The issues of the day. How a president might be elected in a republic, which is controversial since the republic is not widely in favour here. What will happen in China when Deng dies. Remaining obstacles to a lasting peace in Northern Ireland.*

So this, in the end, is all equipping you for your future career on both the world stage and the small screen.

Exactly. You're smarter than I thought.

And with that deliberate ambiguity she goes. I call Jeff and he makes me recount every detail of the conversation (not that I put up any kind of struggle). He says, *She is a very powerful woman,* and tells me we should talk.

We meet at one-thirty at the usual place.

This is where I came yesterday with Rachel Vilikovski, I tell him.

I could tell. There's something different about the place. I could tell she was here. We get coffee and he says, *What about lunch?*

I grabbed a double bean enchilada on the way over.

Hey, you took my advice.

Sure.

I don't think you ever actually took my advice before. I thought I just gave it. Obviously I've misunderstood the process. I thought I was merely contributing to an established discourse. I didn't realise that you might ever actually take my advice. I'm going to have to be much more careful now. Much more circumspect.

So what am I going to do about Rachel Vilikovski?

Are you kidding? I'm not sure I can handle this now. Suddenly you reveal to me that you might actually be paying attention. You put this load of pressure on me and you go for the bean enchilada, and now you think I'm going to give you advice about someone like Rachel Vilikovski?

Yeah. That's exactly what I think.

Someone who sounds cool talking about bingo? I can't give advice about a person like that.

But beans, you told me about beans and I'm shitting again. Just today, and you don't know how good it feels. I'm just so peaceful abdominally now. I think I'm ready. Maybe.

Hey, shitting is good, but one thing at a time, okay? But don't think I'm not proud of you with the shitting.

Later, back at work, I'm thinking about her. And I don't think I've done this much fantasising since I sat up the back of physics in grade twelve, during the almost fatally tedious module on the Propagation of Waves in Fluid.

And the fantasies are wide-ranging, from the recollection of the way she says my name, as though she might mean it, to the wild and physical all over number thirty-four Zigzag Street. I imagine us up against the loofa'd wardrobe, then on top of the loofa'd wardrobe. And then she stops and says, *I can't here, not on this trash.* So in the end, it's my loofa art that brings me undone, and who could have thought that it might have such consequences?

Jeff calls, just when I'm at a low point because of the loofa art. Just when I'm realising that it symbolises the deep truth in crap, that it's a long way back for me, and maybe Rachel Vilikovski is a symbol of danger, an agent of destruction.

I tell him I've got to change. I've got to stop being this emotional yo-yo. I've got to stop being defined in terms of my relationships. That this is the worst kind of weakness. I've got to exist as an individual.

And he says, *But this is Rachel Vilikovski.*

Exactly.

So what are you going to do?

I'm not going to call her. I'm going to sort myself out.

222

All this relationship stuff has to be crap. I have to be okay when it's just me.

Yeah, great theory, but for god's sake get over it, okay? When did that Just Me shit ever work for you? You think it's working now? Don't misunderstand me, it's fine if it does work, but right now I'm not easily convinced that you're enjoying a life of quality as the solo man.

So I think about this, the solo man. The solo man, but no kayak, no rapids, no biceps, no soft drink down the chin. The solo man, the man alone, the man comfortable within his own vacuum. Non-ogamous.

I think I've got to take the time to sort myself out, I tell him, but we both know I hate the idea. We both know I'm wavering.

Sure. Sure. It's a good theory. You know I endorse it. If it's working out that way. But sometimes, maybe that time is a luxury you don't have. How sorted out do you need to be? How sorted out are you going to be? What ghosts are you trying to lay to rest here? This'll always be a risk. It'll never be totally safe. You will never be invulnerable, cause if you ever are this all means nothing anyway. I'm not saying call her or don't call her. That's not what I'm saying, okay? But some day, I think, you're going to be calling someone, or they're going to be calling you. And just because Anna left, doesn't mean that's what happens every time. Trust me. Whatever happened with Anna doesn't mean it'll never work out.

But what if it's me? What if there's something about me? Something about me that means it doesn't work.

Something about you? Rick, there's nothing about you that isn't about everybody. Your biggest mistake at the moment is over-thinking this to buggery and convincing yourself it's anything but totally normal. The standard life involves quite a number of relationships, all but the last of which don't work out. That's what happens. Just do the maths. You have n relationships, and n minus one of them end, unless you're polygamous.

But right from that girl at uni. Remember that girl at

uni? Remember? I basically blew my university days in the pursuit of one girl, and I'm no better now.

Uni. The girl at uni. Rick, that's bullshit. Take it from me. The only thing in the world that hasn't changed since the Girl at Uni Fiasco is my hairstyle. As if we haven't all been losers. If I took some of my early luck as representative of my future, I'd be nowhere now. I wouldn't've called anyone, ever. In grade twelve, the first girl I went out with, she impressed me so much I got really tense and vomited on her. We didn't go out again. And you know what? I've moved on from that. And if I'd met Sal then, I'd have fucked it up. But I didn't. I met her years later, when I knew I could do things differently. You should be grateful. You should just be grateful you didn't blow it with Rachel Vilikovski years ago. That at the age of twenty-eight, when you can handle things a little better, that this is when you get your chance.

So are you telling me something here?

No.

Are you telling me to do something?

No. I just don't want you to rule out any possibilities today. What's the worst that can happen? You get trashed again? Maybe. But maybe the worst is working out in a couple of months time that you should have given it a go. And by then she's changed jobs, moved house, fallen wildly in love with some arsehole and the moment's passed. Don't get me wrong, if you get trashed again it's going to be really boring for the rest of us, but we can live with that.

But why is it like this?

Like what?

Like this. What about just dating? Why isn't it that simple for me?

Because it just isn't. You don't ever let it be that simple, and I don't think that's going to change.

What if I want to change?

Change, I think, is just another of your fantasies, as though there's some major problem at the moment and if

224

you can work out what it is, things'll be fine. If you can work out what you did wrong with Anna, maybe you'll have an answer. But maybe you did nothing wrong with Anna. Maybe it was just one of those things. Maybe you can even stop dwelling on it now, and trying to work it out. Maybe you don't need to change. And at heart, you're a ruminator, a fantasiser. It's part of you. In fact, you're so good at it you sometimes have fantasies that you aren't. That you're some hard-nosed pragmatist, or some cool Lothario. And Rick, I've got news for you, that's not you. And it doesn't need to be. If you want to change your commitment phobia, fine. If you want to change your complex and irrational notions of guilt and redemption, fine. But small changes, okay?

But other people just date people. Other people just have sex with people and no-one gets hurt.

Yeah, I'm sure that's true. And I'm sure that sometimes people get hurt anyway. And this is your biggest fantasy of all, this is the house with three nineteen-year-old babes. This is the fantasy that things can be casual for you. That somewhere out there is a life with an abundance of inconsequential sex. And there probably is. But it's not your life. Your life is an abundance of consequences. And that's fine.

49

Thursday morning Rachel calls. She says she and her housemates are having a few people over for dinner tomorrow night and do I want to come? She says she's sorry it's not much notice, but the idea just occurred to them. She says, *Seven would be fine. You know where I live.*

I should tell her that I have a well established dialogue with a close friend that relies on there being some validity to my struggle over whether or not to make The Call, and that if she keeps calling first and suggesting things the dialogue is wasted. Particularly when I'm probably going to say yes every time. What kind of a struggle is that? This could really get my hopes up.

It could really get my hopes up, and I'm not sure where I want them to be.

Jeff and Sal come round with Baan Thai takeaway. This is big. Tonight I need two opinions (as if Jeff hasn't given me several already, and all of them from the heart).

I think she wants you, he says. *If you want to know, I think she wants you.*

You'll get his hopes up.

His hopes are up. They're up, aren't they Rick?

Hey, this is Rachel Vilikovski.

Exactly.

What do you mean? Sal says. *What do you mean exactly? Do you know this woman?*

226

All I know is what I've been told. That and the high regard Rick has for her.

The high regard Rick has for her.

Yeah.

Yeah, why not?

Because, you know, you worry me with this. You two boys, getting together and spinning this into some fantasy. Some fantasy where only Rick gets hurt. And I'm also not sure about the way Rachel Vilikovski gets treated in all of this. I'm not sure about the regard business.

The regard is entirely respectable.

Oh really? How do you regard her breasts?

Her breasts? I suspect her breasts are very fine.

And your aspirations. Do they involve intercourse?

It's possible.

So tell me more about this regard.

Oh, so I do get a turn to tell you things. I feel like I'm being done over in the witness box. You don't know a fraction of what it is we regard highly about her, and mostly it's things that would impress you. She's cool, confident, powerful. She's a very powerful woman, and you know that's what we like. You know that if she was only breasts and pelvis she'd mean nothing to us. Well, not much. I've got all this gender thing covered. I've read Naomi Wolf. I've read *The Beauty Myth*.

Really? And what are your views on The Beauty Myth?

It's no myth. Naomi Wolf's a babe.

Do you think that Rachel Vilikovski would be impressed with that line?

Rachel Vilikovski's getting nowhere near that line. With Rachel Vilikovski I intend to conduct myself with unimaginable subtlety.

Unimaginable subtlety. I'm not sure that there's anything subtle about you. Or is that just what makes it unimaginable? And what makes you think she'd like subtlety anyway? She seems pretty up front to me.

Yeah, that worries me.

*Why? Because you aren't in control? Because this
whole thing can't be decided by the endless theorising of
two boys in a coffee shop? Sometimes I wonder if it's only
the process that matters to you and the women are almost
incidental. All the women do is make you think you're
straight, when you're actually in love with each other, and
just dressing it up as mutual intellectual masturbation.*

But Sal, Jeff says, *what about Rachel Vilikovski? If
Rick and I worked out we loved each other it'd be a tragic
waste of a babe.*

*I'm sure she'd get over it. And she'd probably never
realise how lucky she was, not having to spend who knows
how long around the peripheries of the crap you two go
on with. I don't know why you don't just flop them out,
compare sizes and be done with it. And then we could all
get on with things.*

Look, Sal, we can't even use the urinals in public
toilets. We're a way short of actually flopping anything
out. And I think we're both a bit scared for Jeff's sake.
We want this to remain an equal relationship, after all.
How many inches was it?

*I told you I don't know Imperial. It's as long as my
arm, okay? I have to use an extension ladder to give him
a blow job, okay? He's so big I can't go down on him, I
have to go up on him, okay? How big do you want his
dick to be, Rick? Word is yours isn't so special.*

What?

*This is all too easy really, isn't it? You think your dicks
are so important women would bother to talk about them?
You know Rick, I think I've had the opportunity to meet
half a dozen women who've acquainted themselves with
your penis, and not one of them's said a word about it.
And I bet you hate that idea.*

I don't know if I should hate it or be profoundly
relieved.

*And you know what? I never want to know the answer
to that. You boys, so much crap. Jeff had to stay at work*

late cause he spent the whole day talking crap to you yesterday. And some people think men don't talk.

I think you're being a bit harsh on crap Sal, Jeff says. *I think you're underestimating how useful this process is.*

Useful? Useful? You're such a pair of leisure-time philosophers. What about all your stupid theories? What about your cricket theories? I don't think any use has been found for them yet. It's the most boring game in the world, and the only thing more boring is talking about it, and the only thing more boring than that is the crap you two talk when you think you're talking about it. What about that time you decided every human achievement could be measured in units of milliBradmans? What about all those faxes you sent each other when you were trying to pick Australia's worst possible cricket team of the 1980s?

I don't think you're being entirely fair, Jeff says. *I think if you're trying to quantify human achievement the milliBradman is as good a unit as any. I'm sure most people would agree with that. And there was a lot of support for the cricket team idea. A lot of people wanted to see Bad Cricket, Bad Australia taking on Bad England.*

Listening to Jeff's defence I probably have to accept she has some kind of point. It may not have been the most useful thing two people have ever done. But what I don't understand is why this kind of fantasy is seen as both less credible and less acceptable than any form of sexual deviation (unless, of course, it is some form of sexual deviation). It's amazing how she can make some of our finest achievements seem like such disappointments.

So we drink the wine they've brought and eat the curries and Sal says, *Look, I just don't want you to come to any harm, okay? And I'm worried about this girl. I want you to be nice to her, and I want her to be nice to you. You're really a very fragile boy, even if you do go out of your way to appal me sometimes.*

Trust me Sal, I never have to go out of my way.

229

50

Of course, I realise that I know almost nothing about Rachel Vilikovski, and that in one way Sal's right. This has been talked up into a fantasy of some importance.

Two ways, she's right in two ways. Jeff can't get hurt, but it can trash me. So I tell myself to step back a little. I call Sal and tell her I'm okay, and that I'm stepping back a little.

In the cab on the way to Rachel's, I omit to put this into practice.

I gaze out at the slowly darkening twilight sky, I guard my carefully chosen bottle of chardonnay (seriously good, but not outstanding—three golds, no trophies) and I watch the streets and the traffic go by. And I think of Rachel at her rusty gate, her three concrete steps. Just Rachel even though I know it's a dinner party. Rachel in Tuesday's black dress and the dark frames of her new glasses. Quartering her smile and giving me my share.

The cab pulls up and the cabbie says, *Have a good one mate*, as he drives away.

I walk through the rusty gate, up the three concrete steps, along the path and up to the front door and the porthole window, and I knock. I hear footsteps, shoes on a polished floor. Rachel opens the door. I get the smile. Three days have passed and she's still a babe.

Hi, she says.

Hi.

And then I notice her new glasses are covering two black eyes.

It's a good look isn't it? she says. *Your doctor friend did say this could happen when the swelling went down, and he wasn't kidding. It hurts a lot less though. I thought about covering them up with make-up but this is really paper bag territory.*

I can't believe I did that.

What, you think I got hit twice in the same week?

No, I believe I did it. It looks like my work. I just can't believe it, you know? But you've got a great nose. Did anyone ever tell you that? It hasn't existed for me till now.

Thanks. It's always been one of my favourite parts of myself. Come on inside, she says. *No-one else is here right at the moment. The others just went down to the shops for a few ingredients.*

So who else is coming?

We've each invited someone, so there'll be six of us altogether. I don't know who the other two have invited. Their boyfriends are both away with work. But anyway, come in. Let's get a drink.

We go through the lounge room, past a dining table with a white linen tablecloth and a setting for six and into the kitchen. She takes my wine, says *Mmmm* graciously (or maybe honestly, since it's a good wine). *Shall we open this?*

Sure.

She pours us each a glass, gives me mine and raises hers, saying, *To well thrown shoes.*

I'm never going to live this down, am I?

So why should you live it down?

I ask her about the house and her housemates, mainly because I want to minimise the chance of awkward silences and the dumb things I tend to say to end them. She tells me the floors are uneven, the bathroom's bizarre, but she thinks the place has character. The best bedroom went to Melina who was there first, and the biggest went to Kathy who was there second.

And I was third, so even though I seem to be the only one who never goes away I have the third best room. Melina's involved with distance education and Kathy's a journalist, so they both travel round the state with work. Kathy's going out with a journalist too, and he's away on some story at the moment. Melina's man's an engineer in a gold mine in PNG. Hence their non-attendance tonight.

I don't think I ever found out exactly what work you do.

No, I don't think you did. I'm a recreation officer in a nursing home part-time, but that's only since late last year. The rest of the time I'm a visual artist, well, I paint mainly. And I think that's what I really want to do, but of course the nursing home has its moments. Bingo, world news, Christmas lights tours in the minibus.

You can do that in Brisbane?

Sure. Like most of us, you obviously thought this was a make your own fun kind of town, but I can assure you that at Bulimba Haven the Christmas lights tour is big. They all come along, even the ones who have no idea what Christmas is any more and point and shout enthusiastically at traffic lights. And I'm there going, Yes, good one Harry, it's Christmas at the intersections too. And we drive past all the shop windows and I talk us through it, standing up at the front with my microphone. And next, on Yvonne's side of the bus—Yvonne's the driver—and she uses her glass as a mike and points to the right, we can see the Christmas tree in King George Square. And now back on my side of the bus, bending, swapping hands and pointing to the left, you can see Santa and his elves in the window of David Jones. And what do you think they're making for the children? Then we try to name all the reindeer, which can become a little competitive. It doesn't really matter who said Blitzen first Gladys, does it? And on the way home, we sing carols. Did you know old people can't sing?

I think all of that's unfamiliar to me. I'm beginning to think my Christmases are pretty mundane.

I notice art work on the walls of the lounge room. Is any of this yours? I ask her.

Yeah. Most of it actually. It's got to go somewhere.

Do you mind if I look?

It's on a wall. It's for looking.

One of them looks exactly like Munch's *The Scream*, but when you get close you can see that along the bottom it says, 'The Terrible Moment When Anke Realises the Search for the Perfect Bagel Never Ends'. On another wall are three blocks of wood in a vertical column each with a burst blue balloon pinned to it under perspex.

This is great, I tell her. This is great stuff.

Really?

Sure. It's great.

I can't tell her it's the coolest thing I've ever seen, which is what I want to tell her. I can't tell her I want her right now. Here I am in her house, and for the moment it's just the two of us on the third time we've met and she's smart and funny and certainly a babe and I'm feeling better than I've felt for a long time. And I can't find the catch. Is she a lesbian, and we're just going to be good friends and I've missed the signals? Or maybe she thinks I'm something I'm not. Smarter, more interesting. Just because this all started when I knocked her out at medium range with another woman's shoe. And I think that's the most interesting thing I've done for years, and I can't live up to it, surely.

It's really good, I tell her. It's even funny. I just look at it and it makes me smile. I nearly laughed at the Munch joke. The search for the perfect bagel. Humour comes to post-modernism. It's great.

Are you kidding? Are you just having a go at me?

No. I mean it. I don't like much, but I really like this. I really do. The balloons. What a great idea. You know I once had an idea, and I always thought it might be a really bad idea so I kept it to myself, but what I thought was that you could make some powerful statement about the twentieth century outlook on everything as disposable by taking all the lint from a lot of clothes drier filters—you know the way it forms that sort of dirty pinky-grey mould in the filter—and by doing some big installation with them, piling up all these discs of filter lint. I thought that'd be good.

For a moment she says nothing. I am concerned that my idea might not be good. That it might indeed be very bad, and that I had been right to keep it to myself all this time. Wrong to bring it out now when it can do me most harm. I should have just told Jeff and given him a few minutes of laughing at me. Instead I told Rachel, Rachel Vilikovski, the fabulous Rachel Vilikovski before she's had the chance to learn there's more to me than just crap like this, and now she's looking at me as though I've made a big mistake. Maybe I should just tell her I loofa'd the fuck out of a wardrobe as well, and then take the rest of my bottle of wine from the fridge and walk back towards the West End shops till I find a taxi.

You are having a go at me, aren't you? she says.

What?

You're having a go at me. You don't like my work, and now you're having a go at me about it.

No.

So you're making up this thing about filter lint . . .

No, I mean it. I like your work. I really like it. And I really had the idea about filter lint. Not that it sounds like a very good idea right now, but I used to be . . . I used to share a flat with someone, until last year, and we had a drier, and I used to empty the drier and I couldn't be bothered throwing the lint out so it started piling up and then one day I thought, Hey, I know what I can do with this. And I never told anyone, and now I know why.

You mean it don't you? Either you mean it, or you're

234

still having a go at me. And if you mean it, then any doubt I have means I'm having a go at you about the filter lint idea. This is a tough one.

Oh, I know. Look, I've felt unwell ever since I mentioned post-modernism, in case that was stupid. And then I just plunged into the deeply personal lint filter story. I'm putting a lot on the line here.

I had a friend. He used to collect grass in jars. He also used to lie on the road to get a really close look at the stones. And he'd just lie there and go, Wow, and sometimes people would run out of buildings to save him. The number of times that boy got rolled on his side and had well-meaning fingers hooking into his mouth to clear any vomit . . .

Obviously there are a lot more people trained in CPR than you realise.

So maybe your lint filter idea is fine. And maybe I'm just a bit defensive about my stuff.

You shouldn't be. It's great. It's the people with lint filter ideas who should be defensive about their stuff.

Melina and Kathy arrive and, before I even know which is which, one of them says, *Hey, the dermatologist,* and I know tonight's not going to be easy. Their guests, also women, turn up closer to eight. I wonder if we were all told the same time. This has the danger of potentially leading to a lot of hopeful wondering.

I am introduced to everyone as *Richard Derrington, the guy who decked me,* and the shoe incident dominates early conversation.

Rachel tells me to put on some music and leans over close to me when I'm kneeling at the stereo cabinet making my choice. And the open door has the strange effect of separating us from everyone else.

You have great CDs, I tell her.

You expected crap maybe?

I didn't say there wasn't crap. It would be a brave person indeed who would try to defend the place of The Proclaimers' *Sunshine on Leith* among these fine albums.

235

It's a great album.
Don't do this.
I stand by my collection. So what are you going to play?
This one. The Triffids. *Calenture.* Did you know there's a theory that you can't actually have a successful dinner party unless this album is played?
Really? I've heard the same theory, but about Sunshine on Leith.
No-one ever said that about *Sunshine on Leith.*
So she lets me play The Triffids and she goes into the kitchen with Kathy to get on with dinner.
This leaves me with three women, all already on at least their second glass of wine, all thinking that maybe I set out to injure their friend (or friend's friend), that I am a man whose intentions are far from honourable. But really, what's an honourable intention any more? And as the conversation goes on it's only a matter of time before I am expected to accept personal responsibility for the subjugation of women, the invention of war and the phallocentrism of architecture.
And I tell them, sure, men have done a lot of bad things, but they weren't all done by me. I'm as unenthusiastic about the patriarchy as the next person. This only makes things worse.
Knowing I've got no chance on the subjugation issue, or on the matter of war, I take on the cause of the architects, from the Doric column to Harry Seidler. And argument seems to come at me from all corners, probably at least partly because I know nothing about architecture, even though I find myself raving about the little churches of Hawkesmoor, his fine pencilled spires, his neo-classical porticoes, his vestries just like home. And I tell them it's all about intimacy, not about genitals. Can't they understand that?
So what exactly, Melina says, *is your understanding of the neo-classical portico?*

I understand it to be the front bit, I tell her. Where
you go in.

And I know I'm gone.

The conversation starts to resemble what I think must
be Sal's fantasy about this evening rather than mine. I'm
half tempted to see if I can set up the Naomi Wolf joke.

And in the middle of it all, I wonder if I did some
awful subtle male thing that made Anna leave. Nothing
as obvious as starting a war, but something criminally
insensitive, and I can't work it out. But with the energy
of the discussion that all seems academic.

Dinner's ready, Rachel says, walking in with Kathy
behind her, each of them carrying a fragrant curry. She
sits next to me and says, *It sounded interesting in here.
I bet you're glad you came.*

Well, I will go committing acts of violence, however
inadvertent.

And the debate ranges across other topics, and on
occasions I am not required to be the enemy. But usually
I'm treated like I'm fair game.

When the table's clear Rachel says, *Come into the
kitchen and help me make dessert*, and she gives me fruit
to cut. *I'm sorry about that*, she says. *You were really
cannon fodder in there weren't you? In case you're wondering, that's not why I invited you.*

It was fine. I should take responsibility for my actions.
I just didn't realise they were so wide-ranging, or that
so many of them had occurred long before I was born.

So I cut. Bananas, strawberries, melon. Rachel leaves
the pan she is heating a sauce in to inspect my work.

*Could the banana pieces be a little thinner maybe?
And maybe the small strawberries only need to be halved.*

And the melon. You'd better let me know the problem with the melon now too, or I'll keep cutting it just
like this. And then everyone'll be sick, won't they?

*Oh, I'm sorry, I forgot to tell you. I'm impossible to
help in the kitchen. That's why Kathy and I did one curry
each. That's why no-one else is helping now. I'm aware*

*that my ways of cutting are very particular, and that my
requirements paralyse anyone's attempts to help me. But
don't let that put you off.*

And I expect you really believe the search for the
perfect bagel never ends.

*Oh, absolutely. Do you know how meticulous you have
to be just to make a bagel, just to meet the minimum
technical requirements, without even contemplating perfec-
tion? A bagel is a very specific thing. I had one today, I
bought one for lunch and it was a focaccia with a hole
in it. No way was it a bagel. It even had sesame seeds
on it. It's as though any bread product with a hole in the
middle, with the possible exception of the doughnut, can
be called a bagel.*

Maybe they were just concentrating on getting the
hole right and they'll work on the dough later.

Come on. It wasn't even a good hole.

She looks again at my chopping, my clumsy damaging
of fruit with a sharp instrument, wonders whether to say
anything.

So I tell her I'm actually working on the Chinese
theory that any fruit or vegetable will tell the cutter
which way it should be cut.

*Well I don't think you're listening, are you? Listen
closer. You can hear them. Can you hear them now?* And
our heads touch at the temples as we lean down towards
the chopping board. *Can you hear them saying, Do it
Rachel's way. Do it Rachel's way.* Said with the tiny voice
of a strawberry.

I tell her I think the bananas disagree.

Melina walks in the kitchen door, sees us leaning over
with our heads together, turns on her heel straight away,
says, *Whoops,* quite theatrically to the others at the table.
There is a flurry of whispered voices.

We're just cutting fruit, Rachel shouts to them. *For
god's sake.* She looks back at me and says, *You can't even
have a conversation with a strawberry round here.*

And she heats the fruit in the pan and we serve it into bowls.

Melina looks at hers and says, *Yes, it looks like fruit two people have been very close to.*

It was all a Chinese theory, Rachel says, *but it was a bit beyond me.*

After coffee I call a cab and it's there quicker than I'd like.

I'll show you out, Rachel says.

We walk down the wooden steps to the path, and outside there's the first hint of cool in the air with the beginning of autumn.

I'm glad you could come, she says.

Yeah, me too, thanks. It was nice. You have uncompromising friends.

She laughs. The cabbie is waiting.

I'll see you soon then, I say to her.

Yeah. Good. That'd be good.

And there is a strange frozen moment when neither of us moves. Neither of us makes the move. The cabbie taps his horn.

Okay, well I'll call you, if that's okay.

Yeah. That'd be good.

I get in the cab and as we drive away I can hardly see her in the dark, standing at the top of her concrete steps before turning to walk inside.

51

When I'm talking to Jeff after dinner on Saturday, I expect I'm sounding too excited about what is, after all, objectively next to nothing. There is no way I can stress to him the validity of eye contact or the bumping of heads.

I'm quite prepared, he says, to accept that Rachel Vilikovski is all we had hoped. And that her telling of the Christmas lights story was very special and her artwork indicative of a great talent, as well as a facility for comedy. And 'well-meaning fingers'? 'Well-meaning fingers' about that guy lying on the road. How bold is that? No-one uses the transferred epithet just in conversation any more. She's formidable. But I still think you should keep it in your pants. Just in case it's not happening the way you think it is. Don't get me wrong, I think she likes you. I think that's a very real possibility, but taking it all one step at a time would be fine.

Please. I'm so boned it's like I've got three femurs. I haven't been this barred up since the Propagation of Waves in Fluid. That must mean something.

What?

The Propagation of Waves in Fluid. Senior physics. You never did that?

I never did senior physics. And you know, if I had, I just don't think it would have given me a memorable boner.

You had to be there.

I'm kind of glad I wasn't.

Okay, what I'm saying is, I'm noticing the awakening of certain urges. These are compelling issues of biology that have been dormant for some time, other than one unfortunate recent though very intimate false alarm. And these urges are becoming difficult to resist, despite the recklessness inherent in answering their call.

What are you getting at?

Timing. This timing business. It's not easy. And anyway, what about the other day? What about time being a luxury I don't have?

Who said that shit?

You did.

I think you're taking it out of context.

I think it couldn't be more in context.

It must have sounded good at the time.

You give me advice because it sounds good?

Sure. I know you like the sounds of advice. You find them very reassuring. Anyway, that timing shit was all about the initial call. She's made the call now. You're onto the next level, and these are the sounds of advice for the next level, and they are the sounds of calm. And anyway I think we're both aware that, with the possible exception of the bean issue, you're just not content-oriented. Advice is really just a warm, safe squeeze of reassurance for you and the content exists only at an intellectual level and has no practical role at all.

Hey, I'm a very rational man.

That's a sweet idea, but don't get attached to it.

Sal comes back into the room, with a small box in one hand. *We've bought you this,* she says. *Because we know planning isn't your best thing. And you should know that it was Jeff's idea, and I only agreed because of my interest in the safety of Rachel Vilikovski.*

I undo the bow, unwrap the paper, lift the lid. And inside is a yellow fluoro rooster condom.

It's for your wallet, she says. *Since the days of Plum Bob may be over.*

You think this is worthy of Rachel Vilikovski?

Hey, you think what's in your pants is worthy of Rachel Vilikovski.

I laugh. And I imagine myself wiggling my roostered penis in the direction of a perplexed, though glorious, Rachel Vilikovski, and this seems like the ultimate crap downfall. So I laugh more. I laugh and my feet lift off the ground, which is fine, until a week of double bean enchiladas has its say, and I fart. A monosyllabic, fairly loud musical fart.

And it's strange. I've been close to Jeff and Sal for at least a couple of years, and it never occurred to me to think of which of the three of us might be the first to drop a musical fart in a social situation.

Jeff laughs so much that if he'd even gone near a bean recently he'd be farting right along with me.

Are you just glad to be here or is that a goose in your pants? he says, when he can finally manage speech.

It's a goose, I tell him. I have it wedged between my buttocks and I pass my flatus through it, up through its fundament and out its beak.

How very Rabelaisian of you.

Rabelais. What shit you come out with, Sal says. *A couple of boys laughing at a fart and you think you're Rabelais.*

Rabelais' entire career was based on laughing at farts. On taking old stories and putting the fart jokes back in. If Rabelais couldn't have laughed at a fart he would have been nothing. Just some doctor.

I expect Rachel Vilikovski laughs at farts. And if it's good enough for her and Rabelais, then I figure it's good enough for the rest of us.

So what's next with Rachel Vilikovski? Sal says. *Have you got a plan? I mean, I'm sure you've got a thousand plans, most of them dangerous, but is there one you think you might actually carry out, assuming willingness on her part?*

Movie? I think a movie. I think a movie, maybe Monday, maybe call and suggest any day next week, but lean towards Monday because of understandable biological urges. I figure neutral ground, date movie venue, so I'm thinking Metro, maybe Village Twin.

Village Twin is good, Sal says. *Cheaper, lots of appropriate coffee opportunities for before or after. This is a very sane plan so far.*

Thank you. So. Coffee. Before or after? I'm thinking, and you'll like this, I'm thinking before. I'm thinking a later session of the movie and coffee before. So not dinner, and not home to anyone's house. Okay? Coffee, movie, see you soon.

Good, very good, very calm.

Yes, very calm. And this is its essence. Its elegant slowness. I will not be bringing her home. I will not be taking to her with the rooster. The cock will not crow. Watch me. Elegant slowness. But, that being said, I shall not undertake to resist her advances.

52

Sunday morning I pace. I tell myself calm. I tell myself elegant slowness.

So why am I not calm? Why am I not elegant? Slow?

I should call her, call her and, well, just suggest a movie maybe. *Bullets over Broadway*, eight forty-five tomorrow, Village Twin, coffee first, New Farm Deli, eight.

I don't call. I pace. I unpack a box with inconsequential contents. I walk onto the front verandah with a can of paint and a brush. I walk up to the unfinished railing third from the far left. I walk back inside.

What's going on? I haven't been like this for years, not even with the girl at uni. It's like I'm back at school staring down at the mesmerising patterns of the wave tank, thinking, well, if I'm going to fail physics I might as well do it with an erection, and thinking about some girl I met at a dance. And since then? Half the time since then was the girl at uni (and that's appalling in itself, half of my adult life so far, such as it is, used up so pointlessly). The other half seems, now that I think about it, to have involved me falling into relationships with people I knew. Even Anna. I knew Anna through other people for a while before we started doing anything together. So this is my first good old-fashioned crush in ten years.

And it has all the parts of the crush. The excitement,

the fear, the ridiculous inability to get on with life (not that that's anything new), but also the tenuousness of association. And that's important. If you take an interest in the friend of a friend, someone you meet at a friend's party, something like that, there are channels available. Not the same urgency. Not that school dance thing, where any meeting might be your last. This is more like that, a force that pushes hard against elegant slowness.

So. Twenty-eight and a crush. Twenty-eight and a big fat crush. And like any crush, I'm making up the magical, powerful, clever, funny Rachel Vilikovski from the hints I'm given. And, a crush being based at least as much on what you don't know as what you do, I'm creating a hell of a Rachel Vilikovski, and I have no idea if it's like the real thing.

The phone rings. It's going to be Jeff, calling to see if I've called her yet. And I'll tell him I haven't got round to it. And I'll try to make it sound casual, and he'll recognise that for the crap it is. I get to it just before the answering machine cuts in.

Hi. It's Rachel. The magical, powerful, clever, funny Rachel Vilikovski even though I'm not ready for her yet. Rachel Vilikovski, the woman who comes with more adjectives than some languages, and she doesn't even know it.

Hi.

So how are you?

Good. Fine. Just doing some renovating.

Really? I didn't see you as much of a renovator.

No. It's a problem. As a renovator, perhaps like many other things, I'm a theorist rather than a practitioner.

Why does that not surprise me?

Hey, where would we be without theorists? We'd all just do things. We'd all just make things happen. And what sort of a place would this be then?

So do you ever do anything, or do you always just think about it?

But thinking's the best kind of doing, isn't it? Once

245

you carry anything through you really start to limit the possibilities. Anyway, I was just about to actually do some renovating and then I thought I'd call you instead.

That's easy for you to say now.

No, I was. I've got friends who'll back me up.

Friends? Friends who'll back you up? You have a support crew?

And you don't? Friday night you didn't have a support crew? They didn't seem like they were rushing to play on my team.

It's good for you. You need toughening up. So what do your friends think? Now that you've all got together and worked this through, somewhere down behind the tuck shop after school. What's the plan?

There's no plan. I just have friends. Friends who asked what I did on Friday night, etcetera. And I might have said to them that I might be going to call you today.

No plan?

No plan.

So what were you going to say when you called me?

Okay. Well, I'd had an idea . . .

As distinct to a plan.

Exactly. An idea. It involved a movie, possibly *Bullets over Broadway* some night this week. Of course, you might have already seen *Bullets over Broadway*, in which case, this being merely an idea, that's not a problem, and we could see something else. If you wanted to. And if you haven't seen *Bullets over Broadway*, and you want to, we could see it. Maybe early-ish this week, since I might have work things on later.

Okay, okay. So when-ish? When-ish is early-ish?

Maybe, you know, maybe even Monday. Ish.

That's tomorrow.

Well, some other time then.

Tomorrow's fine.

Fine? Good. Well, maybe eight forty-five. There's an eight forty-five session.

Have you got the paper open in front of you?

No. Yes. Well, not exactly in front of me, but I can see it from here. So I could see there was an eight forty-five session. I think it says eight forty-five. Let me just get closer and check.

Respectable pause. Sounds of movement.

Yeah, eight forty-five. I must have just left it open at that page, reading the reviews or something.

Yeah. Lucky.

Yeah. So, maybe we could meet for coffee beforehand. Maybe at the New Farm Deli.

Sure.

What? About eight o'clock?

Yeah. Good. Okay, well, I'll see you there.

So she leaves me to get back to my not renovating. And trying to convince myself that that was all fine, that she knows me to be a sophisticated man who happened to have a newspaper near him when he needed it. And I trust she has an appreciation for the elegance, the slowness of it all.

53

By eight-ten I have spent fifteen minutes pacing alone outside the New Farm Deli.

In the world of signs, this is not good.

Rachel Vilikovski is nowhere to be seen.

I go into the deli, I buy a coffee. Around me people sit in groups from two to ten in size, and I am the only group of one. And there is no way I look cool. No way I look like the sort of person who can sit in a coffee shop alone, reading a Veny Armanno book and attracting the attention of sixteen-year-old babes. Not tonight. Tonight I am sure it is visible that I am only half a night out.

At the counter the man says, *Is there a Richard Derrington here?*

This is bad. I knew it was bad. It's bad. I go to the counter.

Rachel called, he says. *She said to tell you she's running a bit late and she'll meet you at the movie.*

I sit and try to finish my coffee. Who can finish coffee at a time like this? I can just imagine it. Eight-thirty. Eight-forty. Eight forty-five. Standing outside *Bullets over Broadway*. Eight-fifty. Nine. Going home. Remembering it far from fondly, even though I never saw it. There is a precedent for this. *Educating Rita*, years ago. I arranged to meet a girl at *Educating Rita* and she didn't turn up. I was such a loser I hung around for two hours in case we'd arranged to meet at the next session. Months later I bumped into her, when she was mid-relationship with someone else, and she got really shitty with me for standing her up. Of course, when we talked it became apparent that she thought it was *Educating Rita* at the Forum, and I thought it was *Educating Rita* at the Wintergarden. So we'd been round the corner from each other. I'd been a block away from her. A block away from who knows what? The moment had passed.

So I wait at the Village Twin. Eight twenty-five. Outside the Village Twin trying not to look up and down Brunswick Street. Trying to gaze nonchalantly at the fluoro lights of the medical centre across the road. Eight-thirty. Telling myself not to look at my watch. Ten minutes pass. Eight thirty-two.

Richard Derrington, she says behind me. I turn around. *You were away somewhere then.*

Yeah. I'm back now. Hi.

Hi.

She gives me a smile, more than just a quarter now, but no explanation.

We go into the movie, and it's been years since I've been on a movie date. In fact, last time I went on a movie date, it was probably just organised as a parent-free pash venue and the movie was irrelevant. I assume that would be inappropriate now. I assume that as I am now a very sophisticated man, with a previously well-described multifaceted approach to my liaison with Rachel Vilikovski, that I should not attempt to jump her bones in *Bullets over Broadway*. I imagine she has some expectation that she will be watching the film. The cock will not crow, I tell myself, the cock will not crow.

This is fine. No-one jumps anyone. Totally like grown-ups, we watch the movie, despite my unseemly urges to go the pash at several points. And the only thing that isn't completely fine is my rumbling bowel gas and my urge to fart. That would not be good, I tell myself. There will be better times to fart than this.

In the street afterwards she says, *Hey, we didn't have the coffee.* I don't point out to her that one of us managed without any problem at all. *We should have coffee.*

Sure.

So, it's about eleven now. Where can we get coffee?

I don't know.

Okay. What about your place? It's not far from here.

Yeah. Good idea.

And I don't point out that this is looking like a Moccona ad backwards.

Well, let's go then.

Where's your car?

Kathy dropped me off. She's going to pick me up later.

Where?

Wherever. By midnight I told her. When all glass slippers turn back to old shoes again. Besides, it's a school day tomorrow, remember? We can't be up late, can we? I told her I'd call her, wherever I was at midnight.

So we go in my car. We go back to my house in my car. Rachel Vilikovski and me. And there are several possibilities here. I could be misunderstanding things, even now. Still a possibility. Or maybe I'm not having any say in the running of this show at all. Maybe Rachel Vilikovski has no respect for elegant slowness. And maybe I've been saving up my supply of erections for the past six months or more, just so I can use them all this week. Suddenly, from the libido of a dead man, to this. I expect I shall break out in acne any day, and start going to school dances, or at least dreaming of richly-patterned propagating waves.

We arrive at 34 Zigzag Street.

There's a message on the answering machine. I press the button. Jeff's voice says, *So have you flayed that poor woman to death with Bob yet?*

Fucking wrong numbers, I say, and push the rewind

button. Why do they leave messages? They must work out it's a wrong number.

Who's Bob?

Who knows?

So I actually get away with it. The Krapmeister fights back. I feel good. I feel good about tonight. I have all the explanations I need for any eventuality and I have the glorious Rachel Vilikovski in my house.

I show her round and she says, *So exactly which bits are you renovating?*

I started on the verandah. I haven't really done much inside yet.

I have friends who renovated. It took them ages and to stay sane they always kept one room for indoor soccer.

So that's where I went wrong.

She sees the piano. *Do you play?*

Well, I had lessons. Years ago.

Play this, she says, pulling the sheet music for 'Always on my Mind' from the top of the piano.

'Always on my Mind'?

Sure.

I've never played it before.

So why was it on top? Now you have to play it and sing.

Really?

Really.

So I think, why not? And I do 'Always on my Mind' for her, straight to start with, and then I get carried away and say, Okay, now as Elvis. And then I do Willie Nelson. And before I explain that I don't have the gear to do the Pet Shop Boys she says, *Do you ever get very bored here?*

I hear Greg at the door and I let him in, thinking, why didn't you come earlier? Why didn't you turn up before Elvis? Or at least before Willie?

Great cat, she says. *He's sort of quaintly dishevelled.*

Really? He's the together one of the two of us.

And Greg goes and fetches Purvis, Purvis the fucking Sock Friend, as though Rachel might be interested.

Oh, how sweet, she says, stroking Greg and looking Purvis in the eye. *He's got a little friend. And what's his friend's name?*

Why does his friend have to have a name?

Come on, what's his name? He's got a face. I bet he's got a name.

Purvis. Purvis the Sock Friend.

Purvis the Sock Friend? she says, and she's smiling. *Do you have any human contact at all?* And she's looking at Purvis, straight into his crazy dazed face. *This is your own little world here, isn't it?*

I told you I shouldn't live alone.

So all of a sudden the lid is lifted off this crap universe, this peculiar *little world* where I make up different versions of the one uninspiring song and turn socks into cat toys. We shouldn't have come back here. I should have stuck to the plan. I had no idea this house was filled with so many traps.

So why is she still behaving as though she likes me? Still standing close to me with her fatal grey eyes and her new glasses and her yellowing bruises.

We go out onto the verandah and sit on the old sofa with coffee and a packet of Tim Tams, and even with the lounge room lights shining out through the windows it's still quite dark. My biological urges are stirring again and I think I might be going to make a move. I tell myself to be calm. Timing is all. Be elegant and slow.

This is a great place, she says. *It's got a really nice feel about it.*

Yeah. Yeah, it has. I thought maybe I was the only person who thought that, since it was my grandparents' house.

No. It's a great place. It's very friendly. Some houses are cold and unwelcoming and just don't seem like places people could live in, but this has a really good feel.

Did you know that in Bolivia, when they build a new

252

house they burn a desiccated llama foetus and bury it under one corner? Just to give the place the right feel.

I'm regretting this round about the point where I say Bolivia, but once you've said Bolivia there's really no turning back. I'm clearly not as calm as I'd hoped.

Llama foetuses. Where did you get that from?

I must have read it somewhere. In-flight mag maybe. She laughs. *You are a very strange boy.*

Is that a problem? Not that I accept that I'm strange, but just supposing you're right, is it a problem?

No. No, I don't think it's a problem at all.

Good. And I think you've seen all the strange things anyway. I think after this I become really normal. Sophisticated in fact. That could be the word.

Don't hurry. Normal is terribly overrated. And I'm not at all sure how I feel about sophisticated.

I lean forward to pick up a Tim Tam, and I take the opportunity to sneak slightly closer towards her. I lean forward again, take a sip of coffee, sneak a little more. And I'm about to make my move when a silent but very nasty fart catches me unawares and dumps itself into the sofa. So I have to stay still. One move and the fart gets out.

She laughs, or at least seems to struggle not to, and turns it into a cough.

I think there's a problem. I decide to go for a pre-emptive strike.

Do you smell something? I say, as though I haven't just farted very nastily. I think it must be the sofa. It's pretty old and I think a dog used to sleep on it. I think it needs cleaning. It does have a few unexpected smells.

Yeah, and at first, I must admit, you aren't thinking dog.

And just when I'm telling her I remember the dog well, and I'm about to invent a name, I really let one go. A definitive, heroic, exuberant, far-from-silent fart. A fart that suggests I have sat on a bugler in the instant he blows charge. Right now it feels like the last post.

This fart has such momentum I'm sure it briefly separates me from the cushion. This fart could not be kept secret in a war zone, let alone the attractive quiet of a dimly lit verandah.

So you didn't fart, she says, laughing with a quite unnecessary loudness, *but I think that dog chased a duck into your sofa.* She laughs so much she nearly falls off. She starts calling the duck out of the cushion. *Here ducky ducky ducky. Here ducky ducky.*

With the panic-mediated increase in muscle tone, I fart again.

She squawks with laughter. Why do her ridiculous noises come out of her more respectable top end? I think tears are running down her cheeks now. I can't believe it. I get this girl back here and I'm about to make a move and I blow out enough methane to light the city.

And just when you were about to make a move too, she says.

What do you mean?

You were just about to make a move. That's the tragedy of it. Here we were sitting on the sofa on the dimly lit verandah and you were sneaking towards me and at the critical moment this is what happens. It's tragic timing.

No, it's not true.

You still say you didn't fart?

No. I might not have been making a move. Maybe.

Don't lie to me Richard Derrington. Trying to make a move with a few Tim Tams, an old sofa and a hundred litres of bowel gas. That might be what you sophisticated men try on a girl, but don't think I can't see through it. And do you know what the worst thing is?

What? I thought the fart was the worst thing. Well the farts, the three of them. There was no dog.

Really? No, the worst thing is, it's midnight, and I've finished my coffee and I have to go home. Remember? And now you're going to think it's all because of the fart, which it isn't.

What?

I have to go. Really. Look, it was a big finish. I don't think we can top it. Not tonight anyway.

Can I take you home?

Kathy said to call. She said I had to call and she'd get me, wherever I was. She's, well, she's just being a friend, you know. You know what they're like, full of advice, full of help. Well, I'd better call her. This sounds bad, doesn't it. Well, there's more to it. It's no big deal. We just had a few hassles early this evening, well, she did, and I said I'd call her by midnight. She doesn't like being home alone, that's not the hassle, but it's an issue too. She can't sleep when she's home alone, and Mel's away doing some quality assurance thing in the south-west region. So I'd better call.

I take her to the phone and while she's making the call I rinse the coffee cups, and I'm sure I have never felt a bigger loser in my whole life than I do at this moment. I can hear her talking to Kathy and saying, *No, no, it's been great, really*, and laughing and saying, *Nothing, nothing. I'll tell you later.*

She comes into the kitchen and says, *She'll be here in ten minutes*, and then she starts laughing again. *Stop looking like someone died. Leave the cups till later and sort out that look on your face.*

And the car's there soon enough, driving slowly down Zigzag Street and pulling up outside.

Better go, she says. *It's been a lovely evening.* And then she bursts out laughing again. *Sorry.*

Kathy honks the horn.

We have another pause when no-one moves, then Rachel leans forward, kisses me quickly on the mouth, smiles. Says, *I'll call you.* And she's gone.

54

So, I'm telling Jeff, the only time I ever take your fucking advice and I end up bathing some babe in toxic waste.

He drinks a mouthful of coffee.

I must admit I didn't think it was the most dangerous piece of advice I'd ever given you. Eat more beans. Who would have thought that eat more beans could be the thing that would bring you down. From Krapmeister to Fartmeister.

I can't believe it. I really like this girl and this is what I do. What a debacle. She doesn't turn up for coffee. We go back to my place, and I haven't hidden any of the things I'd like to, I get tense and make a fucked remark about desiccated llama since it actually seems appropriate, right up to the word Bolivia, but once you've said Bolivia you're history and you're committed to the desiccated llama remark, however completely obviously fucked it is. Then I fart all over her.

Hey, she farts too. This'll be fine. She's not such a babe she doesn't fart.

I bet she doesn't fart. She's such a babe I bet she has no waste products at all. Anyway, what's all this reassurance? What about that girl you vomited on in grade twelve? You didn't go out any more.

That was grade twelve.

Yeah, but . . .

Context. Context is everything. That was an example

of something completely different, whatever it was an example of. You're making this unnecessarily complicated. Anyway, she should never have gone out with me in the first place. I was a real dork in grade twelve.

So what do I do? I don't know if I'm crazy about her, or just fucking crazy.

They're not mutually exclusive states.

Why am I like this? Why am I flatulent and bewildered? Why is this not easy?

What's ever easy for you? What ever comes without the pain of deliberation? Look, it's a timing thing. Rachel Vilikovski happens to have come along at a time when you're going through a crazy patch. It's a shit, but that's when she came along. It would have been great if the two of you had been able to get down to diaries about it. If you'd been able to say, well, maybe late April I'll have my head together, and pencilled her in. But it's not like that. A couple of months early, you throw a shoe in her face, and it's hard to turn back from there. But everyone's life is like that. You've got to stop thinking this is unique.

The shoe isn't unique?

The shoe is very uncommon. The timing is typical. Years ago I had a friend who got trashed, pretty badly trashed. And I wasn't having a great run either. Have I told you this one? Hungry Jacks at Taringa?

I don't think so.

Okay, I remember driving out of Hungry Jack's at Taringa one night with this guy. We were each feeling pretty bad and we'd just got ourselves Bacon Double Cheeseburgers. And as we drove out, back onto Moggill Road, he said to me, Mate I think we're going to be doing this for a long time. And he didn't say it like a good thing or a bad thing, just a thing. Within a week of that he'd met a girl. And we all thought, fine, he's trashed, this is a rebound. Three months later they were engaged. In less than a year they were married. And Hungry Jack's at Taringa, the thing the two bachelor boys were going to be doing for a long time, we never did it again. Never

257

again was it just the two of us. And the night they
announced their engagement we drank a lot and I fell
asleep on the sofa and he woke me at about three am and
he said, I just wanted to say thanks for not calling me a
fucking hypocrite. And I would've, if he hadn't seemed so
cheery about everything. I thought it was crap. I thought
it was all bullshit. Not the two of them getting engaged,
but the idea that these sort of things can happen so
quickly. And then, a few years later, I met Sal. I was
involved with someone at the time. A very reasonable
person, and it was all fine. I got to know Sal as just
another friend, and then something clicked in my head so
loud I almost heard it. So I trashed Louisa, just like that.
My head was filled with Sal, and nothing had happened
between us. She was all I could think about. And at
Louisa's brother's engagement party, I trashed her, I
trashed Louisa, and I left. I trashed her in the kitchen,
and everyone thought it was the onions when they came
in and saw her crying. And I told her it wasn't her, but
she wouldn't believe it. She kept calling me saying, What
have I done? What have I done? Even weeks later. And
it took about three weeks for Sal and me to realise this
was it. Three weeks. We suddenly worked it out, that we
would be together, that we didn't want it to end. Of
course, we couldn't tell anyone. People think you're crazy
if you tell them that at three weeks. And Louisa was still
calling me, still saying, What have I done? Still wanting
to sort it out. And it seemed as though she was talking
about some other life, not about the month before.

So what are you getting at?

You're not very bright are you? Okay, one step at a
time. Me, not a known risk taker, not a known romantic,
okay? And it happened to me. That means it can happen
to anyone. It doesn't mean, necessarily, that it's happening
to you now. But just because the timing's fucked, and
you'd like to be a bit more ready, a bit more together, a
bit more cool, a bit less likely to fart on her, or play
thousands of versions of crap songs, or expose her to the

bizarre excesses of your home life, just because the timing's not the way you'd like it to be and you have almost no judgement at all doesn't mean it's not happening.
What?
Look, sometimes these things just happen, and that's the way it is. And you can't pick when they happen and the level of control you have is surprisingly little, even if you had any before. I'm not saying that's what this is. I can't know that. But if it is, or if there's even the possibility . . .
What? If there's even the possibility, what?
Just don't close your mind to it. That's all I'm saying.
So what do I do?
What do you think you should do?
I'm the last person I'd go to for advice.
That's probably a good start. Okay. I suspect that this is a lot less complicated than you believe. I suspect it may even be quite simple, and farts and sock friends and insights into indigenous Bolivian cultural practices may be far less meaningful than you think. If this is a chance worth taking, and I leave the 'if' issue up to you, it's you who's going to be taking it. And that's it. That's really all there is to it. If you think this might be a chance you don't want to miss, then it's a chance you've got to take.
Good advice. That's good advice.
Yeah. Sometimes the best advice says nothing at all. All this advice, and all you've ever done is eat beans. How do you think it makes me feel?
When I get back to work Deb says, *Your friend Rachel called again. She'd like you to call her at home.*
And there is much lifting of eyebrows, seeking knowledge.
Okay, I tell her. I'd better call her then. You'll excuse me if I shut the door, won't you? Confidential matters may be discussed.
Oh Ricky, they're my favourite. This isn't fair.
Life's not fair, babe.

259

55

Hi, she says. *So I take it you've managed to avoid naked flames since I last saw you?*

Yeah, thanks. But my real concern is for the ozone layer.

That's good. I like someone who's aware of their global responsibilities. You could be on my TV show.

Thanks.

Are you doing anything tonight?

Tonight?

Tonight's a problem? I'm sorry, is this a mistake? You need some space or something?

No. I hate space. I live in the inner city. Space scares me. Tonight is great. I'm very enthusiastic about tonight, and it just happens to be one of the seven available nights in my diary over the course of the next week.

What about work things? Those work things that might have been a problem later in the week?

I'm on top of them now. So what's tonight? Have you got any ideas? Or a plan even?

Ideas. No plan. Kathy's now gone up north doing some secret story on foxtail palm smuggling, so it's just me at home. So I thought maybe you could come over. We could have something to eat.

Good. That's a good plan.

It's not a plan. It's just an idea. A plan would be like, be here by seven and bring a bottle of that wine you brought on Friday and we'll get takeaway from Qan Heng's, pork balls followed by chicken with ginger and shallots and rice for two. Now that'd be a plan. But why don't you just come over after work?

Yeah. Good. I've got to get my stitches out, so I'll head home and do that and then I'll come over.

So for three hours I work hard. I focus and I deliver. Sure, my mind wanders, but only among pleasantries. I am forgiven all three farts, and I shall be with Rachel Vilikovski before the sun sets.

I tidy up several minor tasks that have needed tidying for some time. I go through three tapes dictating responses to things and when I give them to Deb I ask her if we shouldn't be taking more of an interest in Barry G, sending a card or something.

We did that last week babe, she says to me gently. *So that one's covered. But I think it's nice how you put in a couple of hours of actual work and you think you're really on top of everything again. Couldn't be your Rachel friend, could it?*

Now, Deb, you know me. I just love my work. And I don't need some Rachel friend in order to be able to function.

Sure babe. Whatever you say.

So, three hours of quality in the workplace and then I'm running to catch the bus. Even as I run I know it won't mean anything to the bus that I get there eight minutes before it leaves instead of three, but running is just what I do.

And when I get off I run from the bus stop, down Waterworks Road, down Zigzag Street. I give Greg an early dinner (otherwise I'll forget to feed him at all) and I dive into a room full of boxes and search till I find another bottle of chardonnay. I put it in the freezer and then I panic, thinking I might get caught up having my stitches out and the bottle might explode (I have no idea how long that takes), so I go and find another one and put it in the fridge. And I drive down the hill to the medical centre.

Just stitches, I say to the receptionist. Just two stitches to come out.

Do you have to see doctor?

He said no. He said to just drop in and someone would whip them out. He seemed to think it was no big deal.

She tells me to take a seat, and in about two minutes a nurse opens the door of the treatment room and calls me in. She looks at the wound, says, *That looks fine. I think we can just take those out.*

So in another five minutes I'm back at home, and the wine bottle in the freezer is barely cool.

It's still peak hour when I'm driving to West End, and I find this incredibly frustrating and I drive quite badly. It takes me nearly twenty minutes to get there, five whole songs and some talking on Triple J.

She's wearing jeans and a vaguely see-through white top when she comes to the door.

I think the wine should go in the freezer, I tell her. It's not cold at all.

She puts on her shoes and we walk down the road for coffee. And she doesn't say much on the way there and she's thinking hard as she cradles her cup and looks out at the traffic.

I'm sorry about last night.

You're sorry about last night. What have you got to be sorry about? You and your impressive sphincter tone.

I'm sorry about turning up late. Leaving like that.

Like what?

You know. Kathy at midnight.

Yeah, well she'd had some problem. You told me that.

Yeah. She did want me to be home. She doesn't sleep well when it's just her in the house.

Yeah. You said that.

Yeah. But earlier on. Not turning up.

It's no big deal. Is it?

I got a call. I haven't told you any of this, and I should have told you. I got a call from a guy I was going out with, well, when I say going out with, it was maybe more than that. About ten months ago we were going to move in together. I actually left the place I was living in and I moved my stuff to his place, and he just didn't cope. He said the commitment freaked him out. It was like he saw me putting my toothbrush next to his in the bathroom, and that was it. So we had a really bad weekend and, since it was his house, I had to leave. So that's how long I've been living in Drake Street. We tried to sort things out, and I'm still not totally sure what his problem was, but it never worked from there. Last night he called me to tell me he was getting married. To someone I'd never heard of before. And, don't get me wrong, I don't want anything like that with him, not any more, I'm pretty sure of that, but I wasn't totally ready for the news either. That was about seven. Seven o'clock that he called. So Kathy was concerned about my welfare. She wanted to make sure I got home. She said, this is not the night to do something with a man that you might regret later. So we agreed midnight.

Okay. I understand. That must have been tough.

It shouldn't be tough. You don't know how angry I was that it was even slightly tough. I was really annoyed that he could still get to me.

Yeah, but it's like that.

So that's okay? All of that?

Sure it's okay. And it's nice of Kathy to think of me as a man that you might regret later.

That's not what she meant. You know that's not what she meant.

Yeah, I know. This is all fine. I can't expect you not to have some kind of past.

We walk to Qan Heng's and by the time we get back to Drake Street, both the dinner and the wine are cold. I open the wine while Rachel microwaves the pork balls.

We sit on the small back deck looking over the untidy

grass of her garden and someone else's neat vegetables just beyond the fence. And we eat and drink and talk.

And I find that for some reason I'm telling her about Anna, about the trashing, and this is different to any other time I've told it. It's not as much like revisiting it, it's not like being trashed again just by telling it. So I tell her what it really felt like. The months of paralysing uncertainty, of wondering what I'd done. And I tell her there have been times when I've thought I might be going crazy, and it just shouldn't be like that. There should be some rational, linear process, where you progressively get over it. But it's not like that either. Some days you're okay, other days it's all back again. And you have no idea whether anything you're feeling is quite the same as it used to be. You're spinning out of control, and you wonder if you can possibly make a right decision any more.

You're such a theorist, aren't you? she says. *You have such a chaotic, busy brain.*

I do. I know. I'd like to think less. I'd like to be the kind of person who thinks less and just does things. Does crazy things on impulse and doesn't get hurt by them.

She laughs. *Why? Why do you want that and why do you think it's possible? And aren't you already the sort of person who picks up girls by throwing footwear in crowded places? Relax Richard Derrington. Relax if you can let yourself, but don't change all this. As if I haven't done more than enough thinking in the last ten months myself. I thought I knew what was happening with my life, and suddenly I didn't. I was depressed for quite a while. Hardly an entertaining housemate for Mel and Kathy. And they were worried for me when I told them I wanted to bring a boy round for dinner. We had big talks.*

I know big talks. I bore my friends stupid with big talks.

Hey, I'm not saying I bored mine. I'm just saying we had big talks.

So what did they say? What's the last thing Kathy said to you before she left town?

Be careful. She told me to be careful.

Yeah, I get that too.

They mean so well, don't they?

Yeah. And sometimes they don't have a clue.

At least mine have met you.

Yeah, but mine are really impressed with you. I'm sure they feel like they know you.

I can't imagine what you've been saying to them. I have no idea what you actually think I'm like. I bet it's nothing like me.

As if you're in any position to judge.

It's cooler now, and quite dark, so we go inside.

Just dump the plates by the sink, Rachel says. *I'll get to them some time.* And she piles up the plastic takeaway boxes and says, *Hey you could use these for your kind of art. You want to talk about the late twentieth century? You get a few thousand of these, used takeaway containers.*

Yeah, yeah I can see it. All kinds of arrangements, neatly geometric and haphazard, a whole room of them, built up like a decaying city. All kinds of residual stains and smells. And you could just call it *Eat Out.*

She laughs.

You were bullshitting me, weren't you?

Maybe.

Great. Completely suckered. Tricked into thinking I was a genius, just for a second. I thought I was going to get a government grant to eat a shitload of takeaway. I thought my life was about to have meaning.

Such a theorist. Looking for meaning. Some days you've just got to live, boy.

And she makes the move.

She puts her arms around me and kisses me, right there in the brightly lit kitchen next to the sink. And it seems infinitely more sophisticated than Tim Tams and a dark verandah and flatulence. But maybe that's just

265

her. And maybe I'm thinking too much right now, maybe this isn't a time for thinking at all.

She leads me into the lounge room and we sit on the sofa and she says, *No dog ever sat on this, just so you know,* and she kisses me again, before I have any chance to reply.

And she looks at me, biting the end of her lip and smiling at the same time.

I'm not sure I was planning this tonight, she says.

It's not a plan thing.

No. I'm just feeling vulnerable, that's all. Last night's call and things.

It's okay.

It's okay?

Sure it's okay. You think I don't feel vulnerable?

Okay. I just . . . maybe you can understand this. I hope you can understand this. I really like you. I want you to be here. And I want you to stay. But . . . And she takes off her glasses, wipes her eyes and starts to cry.

She leans against me and cries into my chest, and I can feel it moving right through her, every difficult breath. And I find myself stroking her hair and telling her it'll be all right, as though that's any use.

She stops, clears her throat, sits up and laughs at herself and leaves the room to find a tissue and blow her nose.

Okay, glad I've got that out of the way, she says. *I have no idea what happened then. I think I just let myself go and it suddenly felt a bit risky. You have this theory, well, I have this theory, and I expect that you, as a big fan of theories, have something quite like it, that if you take things slowly, you're not going to put as much on the line. You just edge along, one step at a time, and you can back out at any second and you've lost nothing.*

I have that theory, but at least I realise it's ridiculous. At least I know it's only a theory you believe in at really crazy times. The theory of elegant slowness, where you

266

have a plan, and it's one step at a time and no-one gets hurt.

Yeah, that's the one. So can we just take it easy, as much as we can? No plan, no one step at a time, no agreement to back off a bit, cause that only scares everybody and before you know it it's all messed up. I want you to stay tonight.

I think I can do that.

Good. I feel like a real mess now. Like that really took a lot out of me. I must have been tense. You know what I'd like? This is going to sound really dicky, but you know what I'd like you to do now?

What?

I'd like you to brush my hair. That'd be really nice. Does that sound weird? I'm not putting you off with that?

Not if you just mean, you know, regular, straightforward hairbrushing. I think I can do that. It's not a euphemism for some sexual practice I don't know about?

Not the way I want it. The way I want it it's incredibly innocent, but maybe really nice.

So she takes my hand and we go into her room and she picks up the hairbrush from the dressing table. She hands it to me, still with a slightly embarrassed smile, and she sits on the edge of her bed. I sit next to her and she says, *Okay, now you brush,* and she shows me just how she wants it. And she closes her eyes, and soon she's breathing as though she's asleep. I ask her how it is and she says, *Really nice.* And then she says, *Can we move round a bit so you can do more of my head?*

And she turns and sits cross-legged on the bed, and lifts her pillow up and holds it. There's a small box left lying where the pillow was and I ask her what it is.

Guatemalan worry dolls, she says, and picks it up to show me. She opens the frail wooden lid and inside are six tiny stick figures.

Hey, one of them looks just like Elvis.

Maybe a lot of people worry about Elvis. Do you know how these work?

No.

Well, you keep them under your pillow and every night before you go to sleep you can give each of them one of your worries, and then they do the worrying for you.

Wow, that's great.

And that's all I can say. Wow, that's great. When this makes me feel very strange and want her even more. I think I might be in far more danger than she is.

You sound like you meant that.

I did mean it. I think it's great. I love the idea that you have Guatemalan worry dolls under your pillow. I don't think you have any idea how desirable you are. You're an incredible combination of things, and I think you just don't have any idea how attractive it all is.

As opposed to you, Mr Insight. Correct me if I'm wrong, but if you had Guatemalan worry dolls you'd think they were crap, and if I'd made Purvis the Sock Friend, you'd think he was great. Doesn't this make you wonder? That it might be a lot of these little things, a lot of these things that you probably think are crap, that some people might actually find attractive about you. You and your scraggy cat and your shambles of a house and your loose association with reality. It's never occurred to you that people might like that, has it?

No. Why would people like it? It's the stuff I want to change.

Don't. Just brush my hair, okay?

So I brush. And in all my intimacy fantasies I never imagined this. Me brushing her hair and feeling like this. I feel her hair slip through the brush and through my fingers, stroke after stroke. I shape it over her ears and brush right out to its tips and watch it fall softly down to her shoulders. And I put the brush down and rub her neck when she wants me to, and she undoes buttons and I rub her shoulders. Then she's face down on the bed and I'm kissing her bare back, rubbing my hands over her back.

So it goes, until we're both wearing nothing and

holding each other, lying under a sheet in the dark with the moon coming in the window, over my shoulder, glinting in her eyes.

I can't see your face, she says. *I want to see your face.* So I roll onto my back and she lifts her head up and looks at me and says, *You will stay, won't you?*

Yes.

She leans over me and kisses me on the mouth, says, *Good*, and lies down again, and sleeps. I lie awake a while listening to the traffic, quite far away. I make myself think about other things, about Anna, as though I'm testing myself out. And I think right now I am where I want to be.

When it's light I wake on my side near the edge of the bed, as Rachel has already taken over the middle, and the sheet. Maybe it's good to get these things sorted out early.

I get up and shut the curtains so it's dark again, and we sleep till nearly nine.

I don't want to go to work today, she says, stretching. *I want to do other things today.*

So I call work and I tell them I had my stitches out last night, but there's a problem with the wound, so I may have to stay in bed for the next three days. Rachel takes the baton and calls her work and tells them it's to do with the head injury she suffered last week, and that it's quite possible she'll have to stay in bed for the next three days.

We make these calls in her lounge room, wrapped in the same sheet, and then we shuffle back to bed. I kiss her mouth and her breasts and things move quickly and her legs are round me and this is different to last night. And she's showing me where she wants to be touched and biting her lip again and breathing hard.

And she says, *Have you . . . have you got a condom?*

Then I have a bad feeling. I know we need a condom. I would almost give my life for a condom right now, a plain, lubricated Checkmate. But all I've got, and I know it's all I've got, is the rooster. This is an impossible bind. I can't get dressed now and drive down to the chemist and back and hope the mood won't be dead when I get here. The mood is now. The condom is the rooster.

Yeah, I say, and I reach for my wallet on the bedside table. I open the condom beneath the sheet, but there's that rooster head, lubricated in my hand. This is no regular colourless, flavourless plain Checkmate. Tell me if you have a problem with this, I say to her, and I guide her hand to it.

No.

So, I don the rooster. And I don't know what it does for her, but I'm already gone, completely lost in this as though there's nothing else. She closes her eyes and bites her lip again, grips hold of my back and we move against each other. I can feel her thigh under my hand, the muscles of her thigh contracting and relaxing, contracting and relaxing. We both start to sweat and there is sweat between us, sweat from our warm skins wrapped in this sheet, sweat prickling in my hair. And our breathing gets rough and her mouth's wide open now and I've got to hold back, I've got to hold back.

I do some counting, down from a thousand in threes and then thirteens, and this is just incredible. I square thirty-seven, and I can hear my own voice, just making senseless noise. I try to recall the names of all Australian batsmen who scored centuries on debut, in chronological order, and I've just reached Dirk Wellham when she says, *Yes, yes.*

Afterwards we lie wrapped in the sheet in our sweat for some time and our breathing slowly settles down. She smiles at me, laughs softly, flops her head flat back onto her pillow.

This is such a man thing, she says, *but I think I want to have another sleep.*

So sleep. You can owe me one.

And I unravel myself and go and attend to the rooster, now as limp as a chicken on a hook.

She is asleep when I get back, though I can't have been gone two minutes, so I move in beside her and she puts her arm over me and I sleep too.

I wake at about eleven and she's awake already and still there, which is a nice change. I want to tell her that usually when I have sex with someone they've got their head down a toilet screaming by now. But I don't.

It would be okay if you bought more of those, she says. I've never used anything like that before.

No, neither have I. I've only ever bought them for people as a joke.

I want to do it again.

You mean now?

Yeah. Now. There's a problem with now?

I only had one.

That's very disappointing. I really want to do it again now. Hey, maybe the girls have some stashed away. Let's check their rooms.

Is that okay?

Sure. They'd do the same. We share things. Girls do that. They'll probably just be regular ones though, but that's okay. Just stay here. She takes the sheet and goes. *Nothing in Mel's,* she calls out, and she goes into Kathy's. *Hey.*

What?

Wait and see.

And while she's out there she puts on a CD, The Triffids, *Calenture.* She comes back in with a yellow rooster condom from Kathy's bedside drawer and says, *I've just put 'Bury Me Deep in Love' on repeat if that's okay.* This time it takes at least as long, but I just go with it, no Australian batsmen, minimal maths. And we lie there quite a while after, on our sides, looking at each other, and we don't say much. I can't say much. If I say anything I think I'll say everything.

Eventually, when we've heard 'Bury Me Deep in Love' about a million times, I get up and I take the CD player off repeat and I fetch us glasses of water. On the way back I notice a guitar in Kathy's room. On impulse I go in and play a few chords, since it's been ages since I picked up a guitar.

Bring it in here, Rachel shouts. *Play something.*

The curtains are half open now and the room is almost glaringly bright. I give her the water and she tells me again to play something. So I sit in the old arm chair in the corner where the sun comes in and she drinks her water and I strum around a bit before working my way into a few things I think I'm borrowing from Bob Dylan, even though I'm making up the words.

She laughs and calls me a genius and insists on taking my photo and, since I'm stupidly happy, I let her. She says it'll look good with her mug shots from the medical centre.

You know what I should do? I say. You know what I should do at the next office Christmas party? I should take the mike and do Dan Hill's 'Sometimes When we Touch'. What do you think of that song?

I deliberately pick it because it's enduringly crappy and she, after a short pause, says, *I think it's one of the classic ballads*, and after a slightly longer pause she tells me to get fucked.

I laugh and she says, *You're a really funny guy. A really funny guy.*

We get dressed and we go out for burgers, and she says, *Let's go to your place. I want to help you paint.*

There are two messages on the answering machine when we get there. My mother saying, *Just calling to find out how the renovating's going*, and Hillary saying, *I guess you're not supposed to get up to answer the phone even. Well, I hope you're okay. I was just calling to tell you*, and for a moment I'm tense, suddenly thinking of things she might tell me, *that since the initial injury happened at work, technically, this should all be covered by worker's comp, so you'll have to make sure you get the paperwork sorted out when you come back.*

We walk through the rooms talking about various

things that might be done to improve them and she sees the loofa'd wardrobe.

Did you do this?

Yeah, maybe.

Pretty controversial. Pretty courageous. And she's nodding respectfully.

You like it?

She just smiles, the restrained smile of a small victory.

Are you bullshitting me?

And she looks at the wardrobe, looks back at me, says with a calm kind of cruelty, *It's a possibility.*

So I feed Greg, and she looks at my mother's paint scheme and she says, *Is this heritage? Is this really heritage, this place? What colour was this house when it was built?*

I go into my room and I get the silver cigarette case and I show her the letter from 1923. She reads it, a couple of times.

Then that's what it should be, I think. If you want to know what I think.

My mother wants heritage.

Then we'll talk to your mother, if you want. This house has heritage, small h heritage, its own thing. Maybe that's what you have to look after. It wasn't built in the 1880s. It was built in the 1920s, and it was built for a good reason. This is your grandparents' house. It's quite a letter, isn't it? It must be an interesting story, the two of them and what they went through.

Yeah. I don't know the story. I just found the letter a couple of weeks ago. I never knew any of it before then. My grandfather died when I was young and he never told me any of that. Neither did my grandmother and she only died a few months ago. I wish I'd found the letter before, or something else that might have made me ask something. It's like a space I want to fill in. Maybe I should talk to my mother.

My grandfather, the Vilikovski grandfather, I don't know much about him. He was a White Russian, an army

273

colonel, Anatole Vilikovski. He came from an aristocratic background. He was posted to the Ukraine very late in the war and he disappeared. The story is that this was deliberate, part of a Stalinist purge. I don't know the details. My grandmother had to get away, and she was pregnant with my father. So my father was born in Harbin, in China. They never heard anything about my grandfather again. We don't even have a photo. My grandmother said there was a portrait painted of him in uniform, when he was quite young, but it's hard to imagine that it survived. So, as far as I know she was the last person to die who knew his face. You're lucky with this letter.

Yeah.

So maybe I won't get all the answers, and maybe I won't need them. And maybe there are some questions I should just stop asking now. Some spaces that can be left as spaces if I can't fill them. Some things I don't need to know any more. Other things that I might know instead, that I might discover slowly.

We came here to paint, and we don't. I'm still stalled two and a half verandah railings into the renovation, but the story's very different now.

I go into the kitchen to make coffee.

Rachel says, *Hey, albums, vinyl. Can I put on some music?*

She sorts through the pile and plays *The Queen is Dead*. Leaves her fingerprints on some other part of my past. Turns it from a story and back into an album again. And one day maybe I won't recall who gave it to me, or if I do, I won't give it a second thought.

And I want to go into the lounge room now with her coffee and tell her. Tell her now. You remind me of no-one.

Acknowledgments

This is, of course, a work of fiction. There are, however, a number of people with a vested interest in some of its parts, I thank them for their generosity (and foolhardiness) in allowing me to borrow the things they've said, done and been that I've taken, given to fictional characters and put into this story.

Thank you Alison, Alison, Alison, Amanda, Anna, Dean, Dicka, Doug, Ermana, Fiona, Gerard, Greg, James, Jane, Jeff, John, Jon, Lydia, Matthew, Matthew, Michael, my parents and grandparents, Natasha (and her house), Nick, Paul, Purvis, Sarah, Simone, Stuart, Tara and Veny. The bits that aren't yours I made up.

Thanks also to Baan Thai for consistently excellent *panang nua*, to the staff and clientele of Le Chalet for their tolerance on the night of Jon's thirtieth, to everyone who was involved with the aforementioned videos, bands and world record attempts, and to Fiona, Laura and Bernadette for making this happen (and Nick for understanding the dilemmas surrounding the Swiss Army knife).

BELLA POLLEN

All About Men

£5.99

A Pan Paperback Original

'It's not so much that I'd like to rule the world, it's just that I'd like to keep it in the fridge and take a slice of it whenever I'm hungry.'

Having spent ten years on a blissful diet of self-obsession, co-dependency and American bacon, fashion designer Deli Madison's doomed personal life finally catches up with her. Too late she realises that marriage, motherhood and corporate madness are an uneasy recipe for a love triangle.

Deli is about to crash and burn.

From London to New York (and back again) Deli is forced to trawl the dustbin of her relationships looking for an omen. A sign. Or just one lousy clue that would allow her to discover something, if not all, about men . . .

MARTI LEIMBACH

Love and Houses

£5.99

By the author of *Dying Young*

A Pan Paperback Original

'Of all the people I know, men and women alike, I am the
only one whose spouse left them *not* for another lover. To
have driven away a man single-handedly, without rival, is a
very damning reflection on one's character and it puts me in
a special class of bad wife. However, for some reason, I also
feel rather proud. I can look at my marriage, my dead marriage, and say *I did this*. At least I have done *something*. And
I might be more upset about it than I already am, except
that I am hugely pregnant (seven months) and have two
mortgages on two different houses. The pregnancy part I'm
happy about, *happy* being a relative term in my case. What
I'm not so pleased about is being deeply in debt and with a
husband who has wandered off like a lost dog . . .'

Meg and Andy were a happy couple. They did couplish things.
But then Andy left. Meg would divorce Andy but her lawyer
has told her that she can't afford to. 'I'm sorry', he explained,
'I didn't want to tell you. It makes you sound so poor.' Meg
also thinks she might like to murder Andy, but it doesn't
seem appropriate as she is about to have his baby. Besides,
the worst part of it is . . . she still loves him.

BARBARA ELSE

The Warrior Queen

£6.99

A Pan Paperback Original

Kate Wildburn is in trouble. She's an extrovert, a lateral thinker and a talented pianist. She's also a good wife and mother, who has just one ambition: *to be the only faithful wife in the twentieth century.* She can't see the attraction of illicit sex. 'Getting used to new people's bits. I think it would be icky'.

Then she discovers that her balding surgeon husband, Richard, has not only got used to someone else's *bits*, it's the bits of someone she knows.

So Kate takes up her bow of gold, dons her 'breastplate of righteousness . . . and ruthless spurs of vengeance'. She won't give up until the battle's won. Richard's so-called Thursday games of squash must stop.

The Warrior Queen is a brilliantly subversive look at modern marriage. With her fine ear for male bluster and female bitchiness, and her subtle observations of chaotic family life, Barbara Else has created a true black comedy to entertain – and warn – readers from either of the warring camps.

ANNE BILLSON

Stiff Lips

Pan Books £5.99

'Sexy, sardonic and distinctly spooky . . . a tale to make you
shiver – if you don't die laughing first'
Cosmopolitan

Sophie, Clare's best friend has everything – the natural blonde
hair, the money, artistic talent, a deeply attractive, if currently
ex, boyfriend and most desirable of all, a beautiful new flat
in Notting Hill Gate. It couldn't be more different from
Clare's dreary existence on the wrong side of town. Clare's
had it up to here with not having it all.

But there's more to Sophie's fabulous new home than
meets the eye and if Sophie's got ghosts, then Clare wants
them too. If Sophie's got a new boyfriend, then Clare
wouldn't mind muscling in on him as well. Let's face it – she
wants Sophie's lifestyle. But how far is she prepared to go to
get it? Clare's going to make it to Notting Hill and live the
good life if it kills her. And it's starting to look as though it
might . . .

'*Stiff Lips* achieves an authentic and unsettling nastiness'
Sunday Times

'A vastly entertaining story . . . funny and spooky – an
excellent combination'
The Spectator

R. M. EVERSZ

Shooting Elvis

Pan Books £5.99

Confessions of an Accidental Terrorist

'Reads like *The Catcher in the Rye* with high explosives'
Daily Telegraph

Half an hour before the worst thing Mary Alice Baker expected was a parking ticket. But then she blew up LAX airport. By mistake.

Changing her name, her hair colour and her life, Nina Zero isn't admitting anything . . . even to the tabloids. Nina's no natural born killer, but an all-American girl has to stand up for her rights.

The first ever road movie to race across the page and a savagely wicked confession of an accidental terrorist who ends up Shooting Elvis – and more . . .

'A Generation X novel that skips the lifestyle accessories and goes to the heart of the malaise'
The Scotsman

'It's a groovy debut and no mistake'
Melody Maker

GAY LONGWORTH

Bimba

£6.99

A Pan Paperback Original

Blessed with good looks, great taste and bad judgement, Bimba is no ordinary babe. In the search for better sex and a brighter future, her life is suddenly taken out of control, away from her desk and into a far darker world.

From London to New York and then to Hong Kong, life is no longer a joke – and it's not just Bimba's sense of humour that's in jeopardy . . .

All Pan Books are available at your local bookshop or newsagent, or can be ordered direct from the publisher. Indicate the number of copies required and fill in the form below.

Send to: Macmillan General Books C.S.
              Book Service By Post
              PO Box 29, Douglas I-O-M
              IM99 1BQ

or phone: 01624 675137, quoting title, author and credit card number.

or fax: 01624 670923, quoting title, author, and credit card number.

or Internet: http://www.bookpost.co.uk

Please enclose a remittance* to the value of the cover price plus 75 pence per book for post and packing. Overseas customers please allow £1.00 per copy for post and packing.

*Payment may be made in sterling by UK personal cheque, Eurocheque, postal order, sterling draft or international money order, made payable to Book Service By Post.

Alternatively by Access/Visa/MasterCard

Card No.

Expiry Date

Signature   _____

Applicable only in the UK and BFPO addresses.

While every effort is made to keep prices low, it is sometimes necessary to increase prices at short notice. Pan Books reserve the right to show on covers and charge new retail prices which may differ from those advertised in the text or elsewhere.

NAME AND ADDRESS IN BLOCK CAPITAL LETTERS PLEASE

Name _____

Address _____

_____

_____

_____

Please allow 28 days for delivery.
Please tick box if you do not wish to receive any addi